SMP AS/A2 Mathematics

Core 2
for AQA

CAMBRIDGE
UNIVERSITY PRESS

The School Mathematics Project

SMP AS/A2 Mathematics writing team David Cassell, Spencer Instone, John Ling, Paul Scruton, Susan Shilton, Heather West

SMP design and administration Melanie Bull, Carol Cole, Pam Keetch, Nicky Lake, Jane Seaton, Cathy Syred, Ann White

The authors thank Sue Glover for the technical advice she gave when this AS/A2 project began and for her detailed editorial contribution to this book. The authors are also very grateful to those teachers who advised on the book at the planning stage and commented in detail on draft chapters.

PUBLISHED BY THE PRESS SYNDICATE OF THE UNIVERSITY OF CAMBRIDGE
The Pitt Building, Trumpington Street, Cambridge, United Kingdom

CAMBRIDGE UNIVERSITY PRESS
The Edinburgh Building, Cambridge CB2 2RU, UK
40 West 20th Street, New York NY 10011–4211, USA
477 Williamstown Road, Port Melbourne, VIC 3207, Australia
Ruiz de Alarcón 13, 28014 Madrid, Spain
Dock House, The Waterfront, Cape Town 8001, South Africa

http://www.cambridge.org/

© The School Mathematics Project 2004
First published 2004

Printed in the United Kingdom at the University Press, Cambridge

Typeface Minion *System* QuarkXPress®

A catalogue record for this book is available from the British Library

ISBN 0 521 60526 1 paperback

Typesetting and technical illustrations by The School Mathematics Project

The authors and publisher are grateful to the Assessment and Qualifications Alliance for permission to reproduce questions from past examination papers. Individual questions are marked AQA.

Using this book

Each chapter begins with a **summary** of what the student is expected to learn.

The chapter then has sections lettered A, B, C, ... (see the contents overleaf). In most cases a section consists of development material, worked examples and an exercise.

The **development material** interweaves explanation with questions that involve the student in making sense of ideas and techniques. Development questions are labelled according to their section letter (A1, A2, ..., B1, B2, ...) and answers to them are provided.

D Some development questions are particularly suitable for discussion – either by the whole class or by smaller groups – because they have the potential to bring out a key issue or clarify a technique. Such **discussion questions** are marked with a bar, as here.

K **Key points** established in the development material are marked with a bar as here, so the student may readily refer to them during later work or revision. Each chapter's key points are also gathered together in a panel after the last lettered section.

The **worked examples** have been chosen to clarify ideas and techniques, and as models for students to follow in setting out their own work. Guidance for the student is in italic.

The **exercise** at the end of each lettered section is designed to consolidate the skills and understanding acquired earlier in the section. Unlike those in the development material, questions in the exercise are denoted by a number only.

Starred questions are more demanding.

After the lettered sections and the key points panel there may be a set of **mixed questions**, combining ideas from several sections in the chapter; these may also involve topics from earlier chapters.

Every chapter ends with a selection of **questions for self-assessment** ('Test yourself').

Included in the mixed questions and 'Test yourself' are **past AQA exam questions**, to give the student an idea of the style and standard that may be expected, and to build confidence. Occasionally, exam questions are included in the exercises in the lettered sections.

Contents

1 Indices

In this chapter you will learn how to
- use the laws of indices to simplify expressions involving indices
- interpret positive, zero, negative and fractional indices
- solve equations that involve indices

A Positive and negative indices

A number such as 2^5 is called a power of 2 as it is of the form 2^n.
The 5 is called the index. (The plural is indices.)

The following examples demonstrate three basic rules for manipulating powers.
- $x^6 \times x^2 = (x \times x \times x \times x \times x \times x) \times (x \times x) = x^8$
- $x^6 \div x^2 = \dfrac{x \times x \times x \times x \times x \times x}{x \times x} = x^4$
- $(x^6)^2 = x^6 \times x^6 = x^{12}$

K The rules are
- $x^a \times x^b = x^{a+b}$ When multiplying powers, add the indices.
- $x^a \div x^b = x^{a-b}$ When dividing powers, subtract the indices.
- $(x^a)^b = x^{ab}$ When finding powers of powers, multiply the indices.

Using these rules, we can interpret expressions involving zero or negative indices.

The rule for multiplication gives $x^a \times x^0 = x^{a+0} = x^a$. It follows that

K $x^0 = 1$

The rule for multiplication gives $x^a \times x^{-a} = x^{a+-a} = x^0 = 1$. It follows that

K $x^{-a} = \dfrac{1}{x^a}$

Example 1	**Solution**
Evaluate $(-2)^3$.	$(-2)^3 = -2 \times -2 \times -2 = -8$

Example 2	**Solution**
Write 2^{-3} as a fraction.	$2^{-3} = \dfrac{1}{2^3} = \dfrac{1}{8}$

Example 3

Evaluate $\left(\frac{2}{5}\right)^{-2}$ as a fraction.

Solution

$\left(\frac{2}{5}\right)^{-2} = \dfrac{1}{\left(\frac{2}{5}\right)^2} = \dfrac{1}{\left(\frac{4}{25}\right)} = \dfrac{25}{4}$ *Generally* $\dfrac{1}{\left(\dfrac{a}{b}\right)} = \dfrac{b}{a}$

Example 4

Write $\dfrac{2^4 \times 2}{2^7}$ in the form 2^n.

Solution

$$\dfrac{2^4 \times 2}{2^7} = \dfrac{2^5}{2^7} = 2^{5-7} = 2^{-2}$$

Example 5

Write 9^4 as a power of 3.

Solution

$$9^4 = (3^2)^4 = 3^{2\times4} = 3^8$$

Example 6

Simplify $\dfrac{\left(a^4\right)^2}{a^3}$.

Solution

$$\dfrac{\left(a^4\right)^2}{a^3} = \dfrac{a^{4\times2}}{a^3} = \dfrac{a^8}{a^3} = a^{8-3} = a^5$$

Example 7

Simplify $\dfrac{3n^4 \times 2n^3}{15n^{10}}$.

Solution

$$\dfrac{3n^4 \times 2n^3}{15n^{10}}$$

$$= \dfrac{3 \times 2 \times n^4 \times n^3}{15n^{10}}$$

$$= \dfrac{6n^7}{15n^{10}}$$

$$= \dfrac{6}{15} \times \dfrac{n^7}{n^{10}}$$

$= \dfrac{2}{5} \times n^{7-10}$ *Any fractions should be simplified.*

$= \dfrac{2}{5}n^{-3}$ *This can also be written as $\dfrac{2}{5n^3}$.*

Example 8

Write $\dfrac{1-x}{x^3}$ as the sum of powers of x.

Solution

$$\dfrac{1-x}{x^3} = \dfrac{1}{x^3} - \dfrac{x}{x^3} = x^{-3} - x^{-2}$$

This is a sum as it could be written as $x^{-3} + -x^{-2}$.

Example 9

Solve the equation $3^x = \frac{1}{9}$.

Solution

$$3^x = \tfrac{1}{9} = \dfrac{1}{3^2}$$

$$\Rightarrow \quad 3^x = 3^{-2}$$

$$\Rightarrow \quad x = -2$$

Exercise A (answers p 126)

1 Evaluate the following as integers or fractions.

 (a) 3^5 (b) $(-2)^5$ (c) 2^{-5} (d) 5^0 (e) $(-10)^{-1}$

2 Evaluate the following as decimals.

(a) $\left(\frac{3}{10}\right)^2$ (b) 2^{-2} (c) 8^{-1} (d) 10^{-4} (e) 100^{-3}

3 Evaluate the following as fractions.

(a) $\left(\frac{1}{3}\right)^3$ (b) $\left(-\frac{4}{7}\right)^2$ (c) $\left(\frac{2}{3}\right)^{-1}$ (d) $\left(\frac{3}{4}\right)^{-2}$ (e) $\left(\frac{5}{2}\right)^{-3}$

4 Write each of these as a power of 2.

(a) 32 (b) $\frac{1}{8}$ (c) 0.5 (d) 1 (e) $\frac{1}{64}$

5 Write each of these in the form p^n, where p is a prime number.

(a) 256 (b) $\frac{1}{125}$ (c) $\frac{1}{16}$ (d) $\frac{1}{81}$ (e) 0.2

6 Write each of these as a power of 3.

(a) $\dfrac{3^2 \times 3^5}{3^4}$ (b) $\dfrac{3 \times 3^2}{3^5}$ (c) $\dfrac{1}{3^3 \times 3^4}$ (d) $(3^2)^5$ (e) $\dfrac{(3^3)^4}{3^2}$

7 Write each of these as a power of 2.

(a) 4^2 (b) 8^3 (c) 2×16^2 (d) 16^{-1} (e) 4×32^{-3}

8 (a) Write $\frac{1}{25}$ as a power of 5.

   (b) Hence show that $\left(\frac{1}{25}\right)^{-4}$ is equivalent to 5^8.

9 Write each of these as a power of 2.

(a) $\left(\frac{1}{4}\right)^5$ (b) $\left(\frac{1}{8}\right)^2$ (c) $\left(\frac{1}{16}\right)^{-1}$ (d) $\left(\frac{1}{2}\right)^{-3}$ (e) $\left(\frac{1}{32}\right)^{-2}$

10 Simplify each of these.

(a) $\dfrac{n^2 \times n^6}{n^9}$ (b) $\dfrac{2n^3 \times 6n}{4n^6}$ (c) $n^5 \div n^{-3}$ (d) $5n^3 \div \dfrac{1}{n^3}$ (e) $(n^3)^6 \div \dfrac{1}{n^2}$

(f) $6n^5 \div 3n^{-2}$ (g) $\dfrac{5n^4 \times n^3}{10n^6}$ (h) $3n \div 9n^{-4}$ (i) $\dfrac{4n^2 \times 5n^3}{12n^7}$ (j) $8n^2 \div \dfrac{6}{n^3}$

11 Write each of these as a sum of powers of 5.

(a) $5^3(5^2 + 5)$ (b) $\dfrac{5^2 + 5^3}{5}$ (c) $\dfrac{5^8 - 5^3}{5^2}$ (d) $\dfrac{5^2 + 5^4}{5^3}$ (e) $\dfrac{5^6 - 5^3 + 5^{-1}}{5^4}$

12 Write each of these as a sum of powers of x.

(a) $x^2(1 + x^3)$ (b) $x^3(x^4 - x^{-2})$ (c) $\dfrac{1 + x^2}{x^4}$ (d) $\dfrac{x^6 + x^2 - x}{x^5}$ (e) $x^2\left(\dfrac{1 - x^5}{x^6}\right)$

13 Solve each equation.

(a) $2^x = 512$ (b) $5^x = \frac{1}{25}$ (c) $2 \times 4^x = \frac{1}{8}$ (d) $\frac{1}{3}(2^x) = \frac{1}{96}$ (e) $6 \times 3^x = \frac{2}{27}$

14 Find the positive solution of each equation.

(a) $x^{-2} = \frac{4}{25}$ (b) $x^{-3} = \frac{8}{125}$ (c) $x^{-2} = 0.09$ (d) $4x^{-5} = \frac{1}{8}$ (e) $2x^{-2} = \frac{9}{8}$

B Roots and fractional indices

Square roots and cube roots occur often in solving area and volume problems.

For example, the cube root of 125 is 5 because 5 cubed $= 5^3 = 5 \times 5 \times 5 = 125$ and so, if a cube has a volume of $125\,\text{cm}^3$, then the length of each edge is the cube root of 125 which is 5.

We can also have fourth roots, fifth roots, sixth roots, and so on.

For example, the fifth root of 32 is 2 because $2^5 = 32$.

> **K** The symbol for the nth root of a is $\sqrt[n]{a}$.
> (When n is even, it stands for the **positive** nth root.)

For example, although 2^4 and $(-2)^4$ are both equivalent to 16, we choose the positive value for the fourth root, so $\sqrt[4]{16} = 2$.

We write the square root of x as just $\sqrt{x}$ rather than $\sqrt[2]{x}$.

The rules for manipulating powers enable us to interpret fractional indices.

The rule for multiplication gives $x^{\frac{1}{2}} \times x^{\frac{1}{2}} = x^{\frac{1}{2} + \frac{1}{2}} = x^1 = x$.

It follows that $x^{\frac{1}{2}} = \sqrt{x}$.

Similarly $x^{\frac{1}{3}} \times x^{\frac{1}{3}} \times x^{\frac{1}{3}} = x^{\frac{1}{3} + \frac{1}{3} + \frac{1}{3}} = x^1 = x$.

It follows that $x^{\frac{1}{3}} = \sqrt[3]{x}$.

> **K** In general, $x^{\frac{1}{n}} = \sqrt[n]{x}$ (the nth root of x).
> The rule for finding powers of powers gives
>
> - $x^{\frac{m}{n}} = \left(x^{\frac{1}{n}}\right)^m = \left(\sqrt[n]{x}\right)^m$ or
>
> - $x^{\frac{m}{n}} = \left(x^m\right)^{\frac{1}{n}} = \sqrt[n]{\left(x^m\right)}$

Example 10

Evaluate $64^{\frac{1}{3}}$.

Solution

$64^{\frac{1}{3}} = \sqrt[3]{64} = 4 \qquad (4^3 = 4 \times 4 \times 4 = 64)$

Example 11

Evaluate $16^{\frac{3}{2}}$.

Solution

$16^{\frac{3}{2}} = \left(16^{\frac{1}{2}}\right)^3 = \left(\sqrt{16}\right)^3 = 4^3 = 64$

Example 12

Evaluate $32^{-\frac{2}{5}}$.

Solution

$32^{-\frac{2}{5}} = \dfrac{1}{32^{\frac{2}{5}}} = \dfrac{1}{\left(\sqrt[5]{32}\right)^2} = \dfrac{1}{2^2} = \dfrac{1}{4}$

Example 13

Evaluate $\left(\frac{27}{64}\right)^{-\frac{2}{3}}$.

Solution

$\left(\tfrac{27}{64}\right)^{-\frac{2}{3}} = \dfrac{1}{\left(\frac{27}{64}\right)^{\frac{2}{3}}} = \dfrac{1}{\left(\sqrt[3]{\frac{27}{64}}\right)^2} = \dfrac{1}{\left(\frac{3}{4}\right)^2} = \dfrac{1}{\frac{9}{16}} = \dfrac{16}{9}$

Example 14

Write $8\sqrt{2}$ as a power of 2.

Solution

$8\sqrt{2} = 2^3 \times 2^{\frac{1}{2}} = 2^{3+\frac{1}{2}} = 2^{\frac{7}{2}}$

Example 15

Simplify $\dfrac{a^{\frac{1}{3}} \times a^{\frac{1}{2}}}{a^{\frac{2}{3}}}$.

Solution

$\dfrac{a^{\frac{1}{3}} \times a^{\frac{1}{2}}}{a^{\frac{2}{3}}} = \dfrac{a^{\frac{1}{3}+\frac{1}{2}}}{a^{\frac{2}{3}}} = \dfrac{a^{\frac{5}{6}}}{a^{\frac{2}{3}}} = a^{\frac{5}{6}-\frac{2}{3}} = a^{\frac{1}{6}}$

Example 16

Write $\dfrac{1+x}{\sqrt{x}}$ as the sum of powers of x.

Solution

$\dfrac{1+x}{\sqrt{x}} = \dfrac{1+x}{x^{\frac{1}{2}}} = \dfrac{1}{x^{\frac{1}{2}}} + \dfrac{x}{x^{\frac{1}{2}}} = x^{-\frac{1}{2}} + x^{\frac{1}{2}}$

Example 17

Solve $x^{\frac{2}{3}} = 25$.

Solution

$$x^{\frac{2}{3}} = 25$$
$$\Rightarrow \left(\sqrt[3]{x}\right)^2 = 25 \qquad or \ \left(x^{\frac{1}{3}}\right)^2 = 25$$
$$\Rightarrow \sqrt[3]{x} = 5 \qquad or \ x^{\frac{1}{3}} = 5$$
$$\Rightarrow \ x = 5^3 = 125$$

Exercise B (answers p 126)

1 Evaluate these.

(a) $36^{\frac{1}{2}}$ (b) $125^{\frac{1}{3}}$ (c) $16^{\frac{1}{4}}$ (d) $32^{\frac{1}{5}}$ (e) $1^{\frac{1}{6}}$

2 Evaluate these.

(a) $9^{\frac{3}{2}}$ (b) $64^{\frac{2}{3}}$ (c) $81^{\frac{5}{4}}$ (d) $243^{\frac{3}{5}}$ (e) $128^{\frac{2}{7}}$

3 Show that $125^{-\frac{2}{3}} = \frac{1}{25}$.

4 Evaluate these as fractions.

(a) $9^{-\frac{1}{2}}$ (b) $64^{-\frac{1}{3}}$ (c) $4^{-\frac{5}{2}}$ (d) $243^{-\frac{2}{5}}$ (e) $16^{-\frac{3}{4}}$

5 Show that $\left(\frac{1}{9}\right)^{\frac{3}{2}} = \frac{1}{27}$.

6 Show that $\left(\frac{4}{9}\right)^{-\frac{3}{2}} = \frac{27}{8}$.

7 Evaluate these as integers or fractions.

(a) $\left(\frac{1}{81}\right)^{\frac{1}{2}}$ (b) $\left(\frac{8}{27}\right)^{-\frac{1}{3}}$ (c) $\left(\frac{1}{4}\right)^{\frac{5}{2}}$ (d) $\left(\frac{8}{125}\right)^{\frac{2}{3}}$ (e) $\left(\frac{1}{8}\right)^{-\frac{4}{3}}$

8 Write each of these as a power of a.

(a) $a^{\frac{1}{2}} \times a^2$ (b) $\dfrac{a^3}{a^{\frac{1}{2}}}$ (c) $a^{\frac{1}{2}} \times a^{\frac{1}{4}}$ (d) $a^{-\frac{1}{2}} \times a^{\frac{3}{2}}$

(e) $\left(a^{\frac{1}{2}}\right)^3$ (f) $\left(a^{10}\right)^{-\frac{1}{5}}$ (g) $\dfrac{\left(a^{\frac{2}{3}}\right)^{\frac{1}{2}}}{a}$ (h) $\dfrac{a^{-\frac{1}{2}} \times a^{\frac{3}{4}}}{a^{\frac{3}{8}}}$

9 Write each of these as a power of 2.

(a) $\sqrt{2}$ (b) $\sqrt[5]{2}$ (c) $\dfrac{1}{\sqrt{2}}$ (d) $\dfrac{2}{\sqrt{2}}$ (e) $2\sqrt{2}$

(f) $16\sqrt{2}$ (g) $\dfrac{4}{\sqrt{2}}$ (h) $\dfrac{\sqrt{2}}{2}$ (i) $\dfrac{\sqrt{2}}{32}$ (j) $\dfrac{\sqrt{2}}{\sqrt[3]{2}}$

(k) $2\sqrt{2} \times 4\sqrt{2}$ (l) $\sqrt{8}$ (m) $\left(\sqrt{2}\right)^4$ (n) $\left(2\sqrt{2}\right)^2$ (o) $\left(4\sqrt{2}\right)^3$

10 Write $\left(x\sqrt{x}\right)^3$ as a power of x.

11 Write each of these as a sum of powers of x.

(a) $x^{\frac{1}{2}}\left(x^{\frac{1}{2}} + x^4\right)$ (b) $\dfrac{x^3 - x^5}{x^{\frac{3}{2}}}$ (c) $x\left(x\sqrt{x} - 1\right)$ (d) $\dfrac{1-x}{\sqrt{x}}$ (e) $x^2\sqrt{x}\left(\sqrt{x} + x^3\right)$

12 Write each of these in the form ax^m, where a and m are constants.

(a) $\left(2\sqrt{x}\right)^2$ (b) $5\left(\sqrt{x}\right)^3$ (c) $\dfrac{6x}{3\sqrt{x}}$ (d) $\dfrac{4x^2}{8\sqrt{x}}$ (e) $\dfrac{\left(4\sqrt{x}\right)^2}{12\left(\sqrt{x}\right)^3}$

13 Write each of these in the form $ax^m + bx^n$, where a, b, m and n are constants.

(a) $2\sqrt{x}\left(3\sqrt{x} - 4\right)$ (b) $x^2\sqrt{x}\left(5\sqrt{x} + \dfrac{2}{\sqrt{x}}\right)$ (c) $\dfrac{2x^2 + 3x^5}{x\sqrt{x}}$ (d) $\dfrac{x^2\sqrt{x} - 6\sqrt{x}}{9x}$

14 Solve each equation.

(a) $\sqrt[3]{x} = 3$ (b) $\sqrt{x} = \tfrac{1}{7}$ (c) $\sqrt[4]{x} = 1$ (d) $\sqrt[5]{x} = 2$ (e) $\sqrt[3]{x} = \tfrac{2}{5}$

15 Find a positive integer or fraction that satisfies each equation.

(a) $x^{\frac{1}{2}} = 5$ (b) $x^{-\frac{1}{2}} = \tfrac{1}{4}$ (c) $x^{\frac{1}{3}} = \tfrac{2}{3}$ (d) $x^{-\frac{1}{4}} = 1$ (e) $x^{\frac{2}{3}} = 9$

(f) $x^{\frac{4}{5}} = 16$ (g) $x^{-\frac{3}{4}} = \tfrac{1}{27}$ (h) $x^{-\frac{5}{2}} = \tfrac{1}{243}$ (i) $x^{\frac{2}{3}} = \tfrac{1}{9}$ (j) $x^{-\frac{3}{2}} = 8$

C Further problems

Sometimes there are different ways to solve an equation that involves indices. Each example below shows just one method of solution but you may be able to think of others.

Example 18

Solve $9^x = \tfrac{1}{27}$.

Solution

Write the expressions 9^x and $\tfrac{1}{27}$ as powers of 3.

$$9^x = (3^2)^x = 3^{2x} \quad \text{and}$$

$$\tfrac{1}{27} = \dfrac{1}{3^3} = 3^{-3}$$

$$\text{So } 9^x = \tfrac{1}{27} \quad \Rightarrow \quad 3^{2x} = 3^{-3}$$

$$\Rightarrow \quad 2x = -3$$

$$\Rightarrow \quad x = -\tfrac{3}{2}$$

Example 19

Solve $\dfrac{5^x}{\sqrt{5}} = \dfrac{1}{5}$.

Solution

Write the expressions $\dfrac{5^x}{\sqrt{5}}$ and $\dfrac{1}{5}$ as powers of 5.

$$\dfrac{5^x}{\sqrt{5}} = \dfrac{5^x}{5^{\frac{1}{2}}} = 5^{x-\frac{1}{2}} \text{ and}$$

$$\dfrac{1}{5} = 5^{-1}$$

$$\text{So } \dfrac{5^x}{\sqrt{5}} = \dfrac{1}{5} \quad \Rightarrow \quad 5^{x-\frac{1}{2}} = 5^{-1}$$

$$\Rightarrow \quad x - \dfrac{1}{2} = -1$$

$$\Rightarrow \quad x = -\dfrac{1}{2}$$

Example 20

Solve $16^x \times 2^{x-1} = 2\sqrt{2}$.

Solution

Work in powers of 2.

$$16^x \times 2^{x-1} = 2\sqrt{2}$$

$$(2^4)^x \times 2^{x-1} = 2 \times 2^{\frac{1}{2}}$$

$$\Rightarrow \quad 2^{4x} \times 2^{x-1} = 2^1 \times 2^{\frac{1}{2}}$$

$$\Rightarrow \quad 2^{5x-1} = 2^{\frac{3}{2}}$$

$$\Rightarrow \quad 5x - 1 = \dfrac{3}{2}$$

$$\Rightarrow \quad 5x = \dfrac{5}{2}$$

$$\Rightarrow \quad x = \dfrac{1}{2}$$

Example 21

Solve $3^{2x+1} - 10 \times 3^x + 3 = 0$.

Solution

Write 3^{2x+1} in terms of 3^x.

$$3^{2x+1} = 3^1 \times 3^{2x} = 3 \times (3^x)^2$$

Now write the equation $3^{2x+1} - 10 \times 3^x + 3 = 0$ in terms of 3^x.

$$3 \times (3^x)^2 - 10 \times 3^x + 3 = 0$$

Use the substitution $y = 3^x$ to rewrite the equation in terms of y.

$$3y^2 - 10y + 3 = 0$$

Solve the equation by factorising.

$$(3y - 1)(y - 3) = 0$$

$$\Rightarrow \quad y = \dfrac{1}{3} \text{ or } y = 3$$

$$y = \dfrac{1}{3} \text{ gives } 3^x = \dfrac{1}{3} \Rightarrow x = -1$$

$$\text{and} \quad y = 3 \text{ gives } 3^x = 3 \Rightarrow x = 1$$

Exercise C (answers p 126)

1 Solve each equation.

(a) $9^{x+1} = 81$ (b) $5^{3x} = 25$ (c) $3^{2x+1} = 1$ (d) $5^{x-3} = \frac{1}{5}$ (e) $2^{3x} = \frac{1}{64}$

2 Write each of these as a power of 3.

(a) $(3^x)^2$ (b) 3×3^x (c) 9×3^{3x} (d) $\dfrac{3^x}{3^2}$ (e) $\sqrt{3^x}$

3 Write each of these as a power of 2.

(a) 4^x (b) 8^x (c) $\left(\frac{1}{16}\right)^x$ (d) $\dfrac{32^x}{2}$ (e) $\dfrac{2^x}{\sqrt{2}}$

(f) $\dfrac{8^x}{4}$ (g) $\dfrac{4^5}{2^x}$ (h) $\left(\sqrt{2}\right)^x$ (i) $\dfrac{16^x}{2\sqrt{2}}$ (j) $\dfrac{8^x}{4^x}$

4 Solve each equation.

(a) $9^x = 3$ (b) $16^x = \frac{1}{4}$ (c) $8^x = \frac{1}{2}$ (d) $8^x = 4$ (e) $27^{2x} = 9$

(f) $243^x = \frac{1}{27}$ (g) $8^{2x} = 16$ (h) $25^{2x+1} = \frac{1}{5}$ (i) $125^{\frac{x}{3}} = \frac{1}{25}$ (j) $\left(\frac{1}{16}\right)^x = 8$

5 Solve each equation.

(a) $4^x \times 8^x = 2$ (b) $3^x \times 9^x = \sqrt{3}$ (c) $\sqrt{5} \times 5^x = 25$ (d) $7^x \times 49 = \sqrt{7}$

(e) $\dfrac{27^x}{9^x} = 9\sqrt{3}$ (f) $\dfrac{7^x}{\sqrt{7}} = \frac{1}{7}$ (g) $4^x \times 2^{3-x} = \frac{1}{8}$ (h) $9^x \times 3^{x-1} = \sqrt{3}$

(i) $8 \times 2^{3x} = 2\sqrt{2}$ (j) $\left(\sqrt{5}\right)^x = \dfrac{1}{\sqrt{125}}$

6 Solve each equation.

(a) $27^y = 3^{1+y}$ (b) $25^x = 5^{1-x}$ (c) $\left(\sqrt{3}\right)^p = 3^{p-3}$ (d) $\left(\frac{1}{4}\right)^n = 8^{n+1}$

7 Given that $y = 3^x$, show that $3^{2x} = y^2$.

8 Given that $u = 2^x$, show that $8^x = u^3$.

9 Given that $x = 5^n$, show that $5^{n+2} = 25x$.

10 (a) Using the substitution $y = 2^x$, show that the equation $2^{2x} - 5 \times 2^x + 4 = 0$ can be written in the form $y^2 - 5y + 4 = 0$.

(b) Hence solve the equation $2^{2x} - 5 \times 2^x + 4 = 0$.

11 (a) Using the substitution $n = 5^x$, show that the equation $25^x - 6 \times 5^x + 5 = 0$ can be written in the form $n^2 - 6n + 5 = 0$.

(b) Hence solve the equation $25^x - 6 \times 5^x + 5 = 0$.

12 (a) Using the substitution $u = 3^x$, show that the equation $9^x - 4 \times 3^{x+1} + 27 = 0$ can be written in the form $u^2 - 12u + 27 = 0$.

(b) Hence solve the equation $9^x - 4 \times 3^{x+1} + 27 = 0$.

13 (a) Using the substitution $y = 9^x$, write the equation $81^x - 4 \times 9^x + 3 = 0$ in terms of y.

(b) Hence solve the equation $81^x - 4 \times 9^x + 3 = 0$.

14 (a) Using the substitution $n = 5^x$, show that the equation $5^{2x+1} - 6 \times 5^x + 1 = 0$ can be written in the form $5n^2 - 6n + 1 = 0$.

(b) Hence solve the equation $5^{2x+1} - 6 \times 5^x + 1 = 0$.

15 (a) Using the substitution $u = 2^x$, show that the equation $4^{x+1} - 33 \times 2^x + 8 = 0$ can be written in the form $4u^2 - 33u + 8 = 0$.

(b) Hence solve the equation $4^{x+1} - 33 \times 2^x + 8 = 0$.

*16 (a) Using the substitution $y = 2^x$, show that the equation $4^{x-1} - 2^x + 1 = 0$ can be written in the form $y^2 - 4y + 4 = 0$.

(b) Hence solve the equation $4^{x-1} - 2^x + 1 = 0$.

*17 (a) Using the substitution $u = 4^x$, write the equation $2^{4x-1} - 4^{x+\frac{1}{2}} + 2 = 0$ in terms of u.

(b) Hence solve the equation $2^{4x-1} - 4^{x+\frac{1}{2}} + 2 = 0$.

Key points

- The rules for manipulating indices are $\quad$ (p 6)
  $$x^a \times x^b = x^{a+b}$$
  $$x^a \div x^b = x^{a-b}$$
  $$(x^a)^b = x^{ab}$$

- $x^0 = 1$ $\quad$ (p 6)

- $x^{-a} = \dfrac{1}{x^a}$ $\quad$ (p 6)

- $x^{\frac{1}{n}} = \sqrt[n]{x}$ (the nth root of x) $\quad$ (p 9)

- $x^{\frac{m}{n}} = \left(\sqrt[n]{x}\right)^m$ or $\sqrt[n]{(x^m)}$ $\quad$ (p 9)

Test yourself (answers p 127)

1 Evaluate the following as integers or fractions.

    (a) 2^{-4} **(b)** $49^{\frac{1}{2}}$ **(c)** $8^{-\frac{1}{3}}$ **(d)** $25^{\frac{3}{2}}$ **(e)** $16^{-\frac{3}{4}}$

2 Solve each equation.

    (a) $3^x = 1$ **(b)** $x^{-3} = \frac{1}{27}$ **(c)** $\left(\frac{1}{2}\right)^x = 4$ **(d)** $x^{\frac{1}{2}} = 5$ **(e)** $27^x = \frac{1}{9}$

3 Simplify $\dfrac{a^{\frac{1}{2}} \times a^{\frac{3}{4}}}{a^{\frac{1}{4}}}$.

4 Write $\dfrac{1 + x^2}{\sqrt{x}}$ as a sum of powers of x.

5 Show that $\dfrac{\sqrt{x}\left(5 - 6x^3\sqrt{x}\right)}{10x}$ is equivalent to $\frac{1}{2}x^{-\frac{1}{2}} - \frac{3}{5}x^3$.

6 Given that $5^x = 25^{y+2}$, show that $x = 2y + 4$.

7 Solve the equation $16^x = 2^{x+1}$.

8 (a) Express each of the following as a power of 3.

    (i) $\sqrt{3}$ **(ii)** $\dfrac{3^x}{\sqrt{3}}$

    (b) Hence, or otherwise, solve the equation $\dfrac{3^x}{\sqrt{3}} = \frac{1}{3}$. AQA 2003

9 (a) Write $\sqrt{2}$ as a power of 2.

    (b) Hence express $4\sqrt{2}$ as a power of 2.

    (c) Hence solve the equation $2^{3x+4} = 4\sqrt{2}$. AQA 2002

10 (a) Write each of the following as a power of 3.

    (i) $\frac{1}{27}$ **(ii)** 9^x

    (b) Hence solve the equation $9^x \times 3^{1-x} = \frac{1}{27}$. AQA 2002

11 Solve the equation $9^x = 27^{1-x}$.

12 (a) Using the substitution $u = 7^x$, show that the equation $7^{2x+1} - 8 \times 7^x + 1 = 0$ can be written in the form $7u^2 - 8u + 1 = 0$.

    (b) Hence solve the equation $7^{2x+1} - 8 \times 7^x + 1 = 0$.

2 Graphs and transformations

In this chapter you will learn how to
- sketch a range of graphs including $y = \frac{1}{x}$
- transform graphs by translating, reflecting and stretching, and determine their equations
- transform the graph of $y = f(x)$ to obtain graphs of the form $y = af(x)$, $y = f(ax)$, $y = f(x) + a$ and $y = f(x + a)$

A Further graphs (answers p 128)

You are already familiar with a range of graphs.
You have sketched linear, quadratic and cubic graphs, and circles.

The simplest examples of these are shown below.

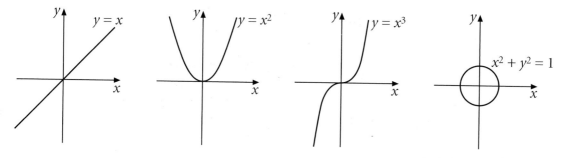

D **A1 (a)** Try to sketch a graph for each equation below.

Considering the following can help you decide on each shape.
- What happens when $x = 0$ or when $y = 0$?
- What happens as x gets very large and positive?
  Try thinking about $x = 100$ and other large positive values of x.
- What happens as x gets very large and negative?
  Try thinking about $x = -100$ and other large negative values of x.
- Are there any values for which y is not defined?
- Which values of x produce large values of y?
- Does the graph have any reflection symmetry?
- Does the graph have any rotation symmetry?

(i) $y = \dfrac{1}{x}$ (ii) $y = \dfrac{1}{x - 2}$ (iii) $y = \sqrt{x}$

(iv) $y = \sqrt[3]{x}$ (v) $y = \dfrac{1}{x^2}$ (vi) $y = \dfrac{1}{x^2 + 1}$

(b) Check your sketches on a graph plotter.

To draw the graph of an equation such as $y = \dfrac{1}{x}$, you need to consider what happens to y when x is very large or very small.

The graph of $y = \dfrac{1}{x}$ gets closer and closer to the x- and y-axes but never meets them.

Straight lines that are approached by a graph in this way are called **asymptotes**.

A sketch of the graph is

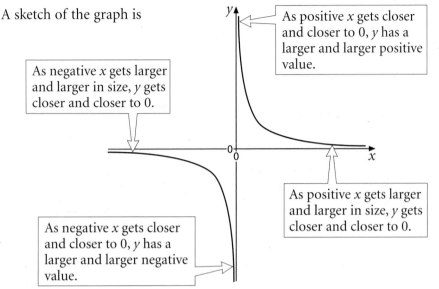

As positive x gets closer and closer to 0, y has a larger and larger positive value.

As negative x gets larger and larger in size, y gets closer and closer to 0.

As negative x gets closer and closer to 0, y has a larger and larger negative value.

As positive x gets larger and larger in size, y gets closer and closer to 0.

Exercise A (answers p 128)

1 Below is a sketch of the graph $y = \dfrac{1}{x-2} + 1$.
The dotted lines are asymptotes.

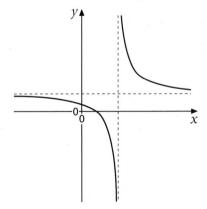

(a) (i) Look at the equation.
What happens to the value of y as positive x gets larger and larger?

 (ii) What is the equation of the horizontal asymptote?

(b) What is the equation of the vertical asymptote?

(c) What is the value of the y-intercept?

(d) What is the value of the x-intercept?

2 Each equation below belongs to one of the sketch graphs.

Match up the equations and graphs.

(a) $y = \dfrac{2}{x}$

(b) $y = \dfrac{1}{x} + 3$

(c) $y = \dfrac{1}{x+3}$

(d) $y = \dfrac{1}{x} - 1$

(e) $y = \dfrac{1}{x-1}$

(f) $y^2 = x$

(g) $y = \dfrac{1}{x^2} - 1$

(h) $y^2 = x^2 + 1$

(i) $\dfrac{x^2}{9} + y^2 = 1$

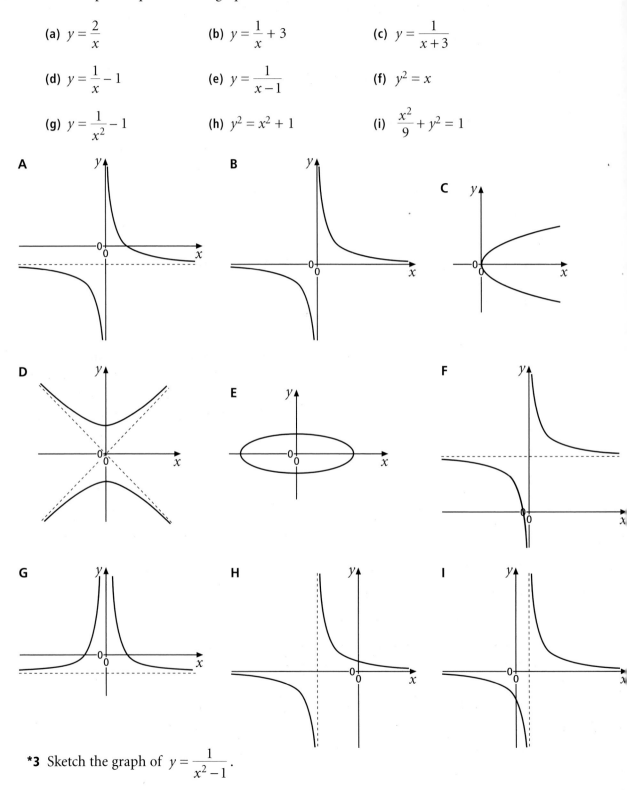

*3 Sketch the graph of $y = \dfrac{1}{x^2 - 1}$.

B Translating

K You have seen from earlier work that to find the equation of a graph after a translation of $\begin{bmatrix} a \\ b \end{bmatrix}$ you can replace x by $(x - a)$ and y by $(y - b)$.

For example, to find the equation of the graph of $y = x^2$ after a translation of $\begin{bmatrix} 3 \\ -2 \end{bmatrix}$, replace x by $(x - 3)$ and y by $(y + 2)$ to give $y + 2 = (x - 3)^2$.

This is usually written as $y = (x - 3)^2 - 2$.

Example 1

Find the equation of the graph of $y = \dfrac{1}{x}$ after a translation of $\begin{bmatrix} -4 \\ 1 \end{bmatrix}$ and sketch the transformed graph.

Solution

The translation is $\begin{bmatrix} -4 \\ 1 \end{bmatrix}$ so replace x by $x + 4$ and y by $y - 1$ to obtain $y - 1 = \dfrac{1}{x + 4}$.

This is equivalent to $y = \dfrac{1}{x + 4} + 1$.

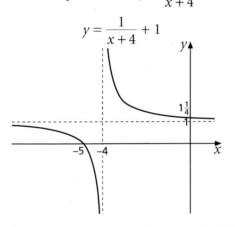

$y = \dfrac{1}{x + 4} + 1$

The asymptotes are drawn as dotted lines. The x- and y-intercepts of the asymptotes are shown.

The x- and y-intercepts of the graph itself are straightforward to calculate so they are shown too.

(When $x = 0$, $y = \dfrac{1}{0 + 4} + 1 = 1\frac{1}{4}$.

When $y = 0$, $\dfrac{1}{x + 4} + 1 = 0 \Rightarrow x = -5$.)

Exercise B (answers p 129)

1 The graph of $y = \dfrac{1}{x}$ is translated by $\begin{bmatrix} 5 \\ -1 \end{bmatrix}$.

(a) Find the equation of the new graph.

(b) Sketch the new graph, showing clearly any x- and y-intercepts.

(c) What are the equations of the asymptotes?

2 Describe the translation that maps $y = \dfrac{1}{x}$ on to $y = \dfrac{1}{x - 6}$.

3 Work out the equation of the image of

(a) $y = \sqrt{x}$ after a translation of $\begin{bmatrix} 5 \\ 0 \end{bmatrix}$

(b) $y^2 = x + 3$ after a translation of $\begin{bmatrix} 0 \\ 2 \end{bmatrix}$

(c) $y = x^2$ after a translation of $\begin{bmatrix} -1 \\ 0 \end{bmatrix}$

(d) $y = \dfrac{2}{x}$ after a translation of $\begin{bmatrix} 0 \\ -3 \end{bmatrix}$

(e) $xy = 3$ after a translation of $\begin{bmatrix} 2 \\ -3 \end{bmatrix}$

(f) $x^2 + 3y = 2$ after a translation of $\begin{bmatrix} -7 \\ -5 \end{bmatrix}$

4 Describe a translation that will transform

(a) the graph of $y = x^2$ to the graph of $y = (x + 5)^2$

(b) the graph of $y = 2\sqrt{x}$ to the graph of $y = 2\sqrt{x - 3}$

(c) the graph of $xy = 1$ to the graph of $x(y + 2) = 1$

5 The graph of $y = x$ is translated by $\begin{bmatrix} 3 \\ 3 \end{bmatrix}$.

(a) Find the equation of the image and write it in its simplest form.

(b) What do you notice? Can you explain this?

6 (a) Work out the equation of the image of $y = x$ after a translation of $\begin{bmatrix} 0 \\ 1 \end{bmatrix}$.
Write the equation in its simplest form.

(b) Work out the equation of the image of $y = x$ after a translation of $\begin{bmatrix} 3 \\ 4 \end{bmatrix}$.
Write the equation in its simplest form.

(c) What do you notice? Can you explain this?

C Reflecting (answers p 129)

C1 (a) For each equation below,
- sketch its graph
- sketch its image after a reflection in the x-axis
- write down the equation of the reflected graph

(i) $y = x + 1$ (ii) $y = x^2 + 1$ (iii) $y = x^3 + 1$

(b) What do you notice in each case about the equations of the graph and its image?

(c) What do you think will be the image of $y = x^4 + 1$ after a reflection in the x-axis?
Check on a graph plotter.

C2 Repeat question C1 but reflect each graph in the y-axis.

C3 (a) Sketch the graph of $y = (x - 1)^2$.

(b) What is the equation of this graph after reflection in the x-axis?

(c) What is the equation of this graph after reflection in the y-axis?

C4 (a) Sketch the graph of the circle $x^2 + (y - 1)^2 = 1$.

(b) What is the equation of this circle after reflection in the x-axis?

(c) What is the equation of this circle after reflection in the y-axis?

In the diagram below, the graph of $y = x + 2$ has been reflected in the x-axis.

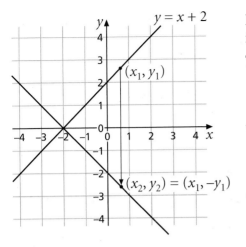

Let (x_1, y_1) be a point on $y = x + 2$ and let (x_2, y_2) be its image on the reflected line.

Then $(x_2, y_2) = (x_1, -y_1)$, giving

$$x_1 = x_2$$

and $\qquad y_1 = -y_2 \qquad$ *from rearranging* $y_2 = -y_1$.

We know that $y_1 = x_1 + 2$, so it must be true that

$$-y_2 = x_2 + 2$$

and so $-y = x + 2$ is the equation of the image.

This can be written as $y = -(x + 2)$
$$\text{or } y = -x - 2.$$

A similar argument can be produced for any equation and graph.

So, to find the equation of any graph after reflection in the x-axis, replace y by $-y$.

This may seem a complex way to analyse a simple process but it has the advantage that it can be applied to any equation.

For example, the image of $y^2 + x + y = 0$ after reflection in the x-axis is $\quad (-y)^2 + x + (-y) = 0$
$$\text{or} \qquad\qquad y^2 + x - y = 0.$$

If an equation can be written in the form $y = \ldots\ldots$ where the expression on the right-hand side does not involve y, the rule can be applied like this.

The reflected graph will have the equation $\quad -y = \ldots\ldots$
which is equivalent to $\qquad\qquad\qquad\qquad y = -(\ldots\ldots)$.

For example, the image of $y = x^2 - 5$ after reflection in the x-axis is $\quad y = -(x^2 - 5)$
$$\text{or} \quad y = -x^2 + 5.$$

C5 (a) What is the equation of the image of $y = x^2 + x$ after reflection in the x-axis?

(b) Check by using a graph plotter to draw both graphs.

C6 Show that the equation of any graph after reflection in the y-axis can be found by replacing x by $-x$.

C7 (a) What is the equation of the image of $y = x^2 + x$ after reflection in the y-axis?

(b) Check by using a graph plotter to draw both graphs.

*C8 (a) Find a rule that will give you the equation of a graph after reflection in the line $y = x$.

(b) Write down the image of each of the following after reflection in the line $y = x$.

(i) $y = x + 6$ (ii) $x + y = 10$ (iii) $x^2 + (y - 3)^2 = 9$

K To find the equation of a graph after reflection in the x-axis, replace y by $-y$.

To find the equation of a graph after reflection in the y-axis, replace x by $-x$.

Exercise C (answers p 130)

1 Find the image of each of the following after reflection in the x-axis.

(a) $y = x - 5$
(b) $y = \dfrac{1}{x} + 3$
(c) $y = x^3 + x$

(d) $x + y = 10$
(e) $xy = 10$
(f) $x^2 + y^2 = 5$

2 Find the image of each of the following after reflection in the y-axis.

(a) $y = x + 2$
(b) $y = \dfrac{1}{x} - 1$
(c) $y = x^2 + 2x$

(d) $y = 2x^2 - 5x$
(e) $x^2 - y^2 = 4$
(f) $y = x^2 - 3x + 5$

3 Show that the graph of $y = x^4 + x^2 - 9$ has the y-axis as a line of symmetry.

4 The circle $(x + 2)^2 + (y - 3)^2 = 1$ is reflected in the x-axis.

Show, by using the appropriate rule above, that the equation of the image can be written as $(x + 2)^2 + (y + 3)^2 = 1$.

D Stretching (answers p 130)

K A stretch from the origin in the x-direction by a scale factor k multiplies each x-coordinate by k.

In this diagram, a stretch by scale factor 3 in the x-direction maps the smaller triangle to the larger.

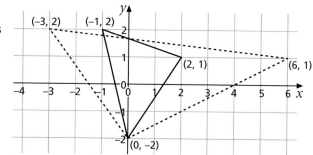

K A stretch from the origin in the y-direction by a scale factor k multiplies each y-coordinate by k.

In this diagram, a stretch by scale factor $\frac{1}{2}$ in the y-direction maps the larger triangle to the smaller.

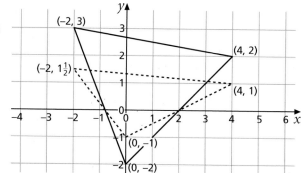

D1 (a) Plot the points $(2, 0)$, $(-1, -1)$, $(0, 1)$ and $(4, 3)$ and join them to make a quadrilateral.

(b) Draw the image of the quadrilateral after a stretch of scale factor 2 in the y-direction.

D2 (a) Plot and join the points $(8, 2)$, $(0, -1)$, $(-2, 0)$ and $(-4, 4)$ to make a quadrilateral.

(b) Draw the image of the quadrilateral after a stretch by scale factor $\frac{1}{4}$ in the x-direction.

D3 (a) For each equation below,
- sketch its graph and its image after a stretch by scale factor 2 in the x-direction
- find the equation of the image

(i) $y = x + 1$ **(ii)** $y = x^2$ **(iii)** $y = 2x - 3$

(b) Can you suggest a rule to work out the equation of a graph after a stretch by scale factor 2 in the x-direction?

D4 Repeat question D3 for a stretch by scale factor 3 in the y-direction.

In the diagram below, the graph of $y = x^2 + 1$ has been stretched by factor 3 in the x-direction.

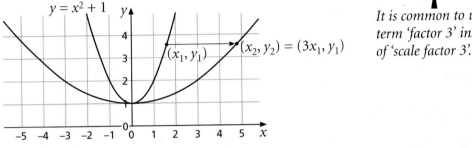

It is common to use the term 'factor 3' instead of 'scale factor 3'.

Let (x_1, y_1) be a point on $y = x^2 + 1$ and let (x_2, y_2) be its image on the stretched curve.
Then $(x_2, y_2) = (3x_1, y_1)$, giving

$$x_1 = \tfrac{1}{3}x_2 \qquad \text{from rearranging } x_2 = 3x_1$$

and $y_1 = y_2$.

We know that $y_1 = x_1^2 + 1$, so it must be true that

$$y_2 = (\tfrac{1}{3}x_2)^2 + 1$$
$$\Rightarrow \qquad y_2 = \tfrac{1}{9}x_2^2 + 1$$

and so $y = \tfrac{1}{9}x^2 + 1$ is the equation of the image.

A similar argument can be produced for any equation so, to find the equation of a graph after a stretch by factor 3 in the x-direction, replace x by $\tfrac{1}{3}x$.

This can be generalised.

K   To find the equation of a graph after a stretch by factor k in the x-direction, replace x by $\dfrac{1}{k}x$.

D5 Work out the equation of the image of
(a) $y = x$ after a stretch by factor 3 in the x-direction
(b) $y = x^2 - 4$ after a stretch by factor 2 in the x-direction
(c) $y^2 + x^2 = 7$ after a stretch by factor 5 in the x-direction
(d) $y = x + 6$ after a stretch by factor $\frac{1}{3}$ in the x-direction
(e) $y = x^2 + 3$ after a stretch by factor $\frac{1}{2}$ in the x-direction

Using an argument similar to the one on the previous page we can show the following.

Ⓚ   To find the equation of a graph after a stretch by factor k in the y-direction, replace y by $\frac{1}{k}y$.

For example, the image of $y^2 + x + y = 0$
after a stretch by factor 2 in the y-direction is $\left(\frac{1}{2}y\right)^2 + x + \left(\frac{1}{2}y\right) = 0$

$$\text{or} \quad \tfrac{1}{4}y^2 + x + \tfrac{1}{2}y = 0.$$

If an equation can be written in the form $y = \ldots\ldots$ where the expression on the right-hand side does not involve y, the rule can be applied like this.

The stretched graph will have the equation $\quad \frac{1}{k}y = \ldots\ldots$

which is equivalent to $\qquad\qquad\qquad y = k(\ldots\ldots).$

For example, the image of $y = x^2 + 1$
after a stretch of factor 2 in the y-direction is $\quad y = 2(x^2 + 1)$
$$\text{or} \quad y = 2x^2 + 2.$$

D6 Work out the equation of the image of

(a) $y + x = 4$ after a stretch by factor 3 in the y-direction

(b) $y = 4x^2 + 3$ after a stretch by factor $\frac{1}{4}$ in the y-direction

D7 Describe a stretch that will transform

(a) the graph of $y = x - 4$ to the graph of $y = 3x - 12$

(b) the graph of $y = x - 4$ to the graph of $y = 3x - 4$

(c) the graph of $y = x^2 + 1$ to the graph of $y = 9x^2 + 1$

Exercise D (answers p 131)

1 Find the image of each of the following after a stretch by factor 2 in the x-direction.

(a) $y = x + 3$ (b) $y = 4x - 1$ (c) $y = x^2 - 2$

(d) $y = x^2 + 2x + 1$ (e) $xy = 4$ (f) $x^2 + y^2 = 1$

2 Find the image of each of the following after a stretch by factor $\frac{1}{3}$ in the x-direction.

(a) $y = x - 1$ (b) $y = x^3 + 5$ (c) $y = \dfrac{1}{x}$

3 Find the image of each of the following after a stretch by factor 4 in the y-direction.

(a) $y = x + 6$ (b) $y = 3x - 2$ (c) $2y + x = 10$

4 Describe a stretch that will transform

(a) the graph of $y = x + 4$ to the graph of $y = 5x + 20$

(b) the graph of $y = x + 4$ to the graph of $y = 5x + 4$

(c) the graph of $y = x^2 - 3$ to the graph of $y = \frac{1}{25}x^2 - 3$

(d) the graph of $y = x^2 + x - 1$ to the graph of $y = 4x^2 + 2x - 1$

(e) the graph of $y = x^2 + x - 1$ to the graph of $y = 4x^2 + 4x - 4$

E Function notation

If an equation can be written in the form $y = \ldots\ldots$ where the expression on the right-hand side is in terms of x, we can use function notation.

For example, we can write $y = x^2$ as $y = f(x)$ where $f(x) = x^2$.

It gives us a useful way of describing transformed graphs.

Translating

For example, to find the image of a graph after a translation of $\begin{bmatrix} -4 \\ 2 \end{bmatrix}$ we can replace x by $x + 4$ and y by $y - 2$.

So the image of $y = f(x)$ can be written as $y - 2 = f(x + 4)$ or $y = f(x + 4) + 2$.

For $f(x) = x^2$, the image is $y - 2 = (x + 4)^2$, which can be written as $y = (x + 4)^2 + 2$.

In general, to find the image of a graph after a translation of $\begin{bmatrix} a \\ b \end{bmatrix}$ we can replace x by $x - a$ and y by $y - b$.

K So a translation of $\begin{bmatrix} a \\ b \end{bmatrix}$ transforms the graph of $y = f(x)$ to the graph of
$y - b = f(x - a)$ or $y = f(x - a) + b$.

Example 2

A function f is defined by $f(x) = \dfrac{1}{x}$.

State the geometrical transformation that maps the graph of $y = f(x)$ on to $y = f(x + 3)$ and hence sketch the graph of $y = f(x + 3)$.

Solution

x has been replaced by $x + 3$ so the transformation is a translation of $\begin{bmatrix} -3 \\ 0 \end{bmatrix}$.

A sketch of the graph of $y = f(x + 3)$ is shown below.

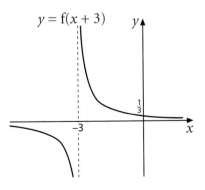

$y = f(x + 3)$

The vertical asymptote is drawn as a dotted line.

When $x = 0$, $y = f(0 + 3) = f(3) = \frac{1}{3}$.

Reflecting

To find the image of a graph after a reflection in the x-axis we can replace y by $-y$.

K So a reflection in the x-axis transforms the graph of $y = f(x)$ to
the graph of $-y = f(x)$ or $y = -f(x)$.

To find the image of a graph after a reflection in the y-axis we can replace x by $-x$.

K So a reflection in the y-axis transforms the graph of $y = f(x)$ to the graph of $y = f(-x)$.

Example 3

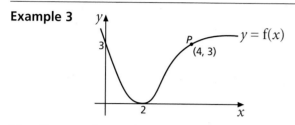

The diagram shows the graph of the curve $y = f(x)$. Point P (4, 3) lies on the curve.
Sketch the graph of $y = f(-x)$ and label clearly the image of point P.

Solution

x has been replaced by $-x$ so the transformation is a reflection in the y-axis.
A sketch of the graph of $y = f(-x)$ is shown below.

Even though you are not given an
expression for f(x) *you can use your*
knowledge of transformations to
draw the graph of y = f(-x).

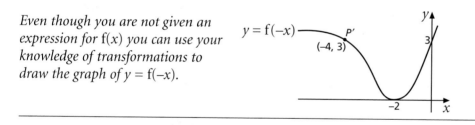

Stretching

To find the image of a graph after a stretch by factor k in the x-direction,
replace x by $\frac{1}{k}x$.

K So a stretch by factor k in the x-direction transforms the graph of $y = f(x)$ to
the graph of $y = f\left(\frac{1}{k}x\right)$.

To find the image of a graph after a stretch by factor k in the y-direction,
replace y by $\frac{1}{k}y$.

K So a stretch by factor k in the y-direction transforms the graph of $y = f(x)$ to
the graph of $\frac{1}{k}y = f(x)$ or $y = kf(x)$.

Example 4

The diagram shows the graph of the curve $y = f(x)$.
Point P (9, 4) lies on the curve.

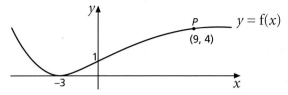

State the geometrical transformation that maps the graph of $y = f(x)$ on to $y = f(3x)$.
Hence sketch the graph of $y = f(3x)$ and label clearly the image of point P.

Solution

x has been replaced by $3x$ so the transformation is a stretch by factor $\frac{1}{3}$ in the x-direction.
A sketch of the graph of $y = f(3x)$ is shown below.

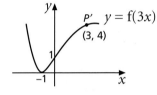

Example 5

State the geometrical transformation that maps the graph of $y = f(x)$ on to $y = 3f(x)$.

Solution

The equation $y = 3f(x)$ can be written as $\frac{1}{3}y = f(x)$.
y has been replaced by $\frac{1}{3}y$ so the transformation is a stretch by factor 3 in the y-direction.

An alternative method is to note that the equation $y = 3f(x)$ is written
in the form $y = kf(x)$ with $k = 3$.
So the transformation is a stretch by factor 3 in the y-direction.

Exercise E (answers p 132)

1 State the geometrical transformation that maps the graph of $y = f(x)$ on to
each of these.

(a) $y = f(x) + 6$ (b) $y = f(x + 6)$ (c) $y = f(x) - 1$ (d) $y = f(x - 1)$

(e) $y = 2f(x)$ (f) $y = f(2x)$ (g) $y = \frac{1}{3}f(x)$ (h) $y = f(\frac{1}{3}x)$

2 The diagram shows the graph of the curve $y = f(x)$.
X has coordinates $(1, 3)$.

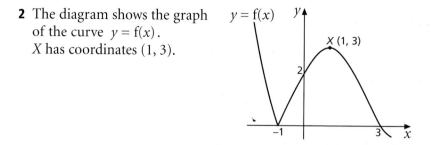

Sketch a graph for each function below, showing clearly the image of point X.

(a) $y = f(x) + 2$ **(b)** $y = f(x - 3)$ **(c)** $y = f(-x)$

(d) $y = -f(x)$ **(e)** $y = 3f(x)$ **(f)** $y = f(3x)$

3 The diagram shows the graph of the curve $y = g(x)$.
Q has coordinates $(-2, 3)$.

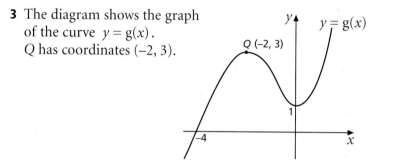

Sketch a graph for each function below, showing clearly the image of point Q.

(a) $y = g(x + 1)$ **(b)** $y = g(-x)$ **(c)** $y = g(2x)$

(d) $y = g(\frac{1}{2}x)$ **(e)** $y = \frac{1}{3}g(x)$ **(f)** $y = g(x - 2) + 3$

Key points

Transformation	For the equation of the image	Image of $y = f(x)$	
Translation of $\begin{bmatrix} a \\ b \end{bmatrix}$	replace x by $(x - a)$ and replace y by $(y - b)$	$y - b = f(x - a)$ or $\;\; y = f(x - a) + b$	(pp 19, 25)
Reflection in the x-axis	replace y by $-y$	$-y = f(x)$ or $\;\; y = -f(x)$	(pp 21, 26)
Reflection in the y-axis	replace x by $-x$	$y = f(-x)$	(pp 21, 26)
Stretch by factor k in the x-direction	replace x by $\frac{1}{k}x$	$y = f\left(\frac{1}{k}x\right)$	(pp 23–24, 26)
Stretch by factor k in the y-direction	replace y by $\frac{1}{k}y$	$\frac{1}{k}y = f(x)$ or $\;\; y = kf(x)$	(pp 23–24, 26)

Test yourself (answers p 133)

1 (a) Describe the translation that will map $y = \dfrac{1}{x}$ on to $y = \dfrac{1}{x+5}$.

(b) Hence sketch the graph of $y = \dfrac{1}{x+5}$.

(c) What is the equation of the vertical asymptote?

2 What is the equation of $y = x^2 + 2x$ after reflection in the y-axis?

3 Describe the transformation that maps the graph of $x + y = 5$ on to the graph of $x - y = 5$.

4 What is the image of $y = x^3$ after a stretch by factor $\frac{1}{2}$ in the x-direction?

5 (a) Sketch the graph of $y = 2\sqrt{x}$.

(b) The graph of $y = 2\sqrt{x}$ is stretched by a factor of 3 in the y-direction. What is the equation of the transformed graph?

(c) Describe the transformation that transforms the graph of $y = 2\sqrt{x}$ to the graph of $y = 2\sqrt{x} - 1$.

6 The diagram shows the graph of $y = f(x)$. Point P $(-3, -2)$ lies on the curve.

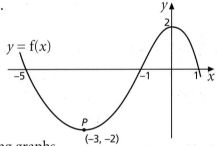

Sketch, on separate diagrams, the following graphs. On each graph label the image of point P, giving its coordinates.

(a) $y = f(-x)$ (b) $y = f(x + 3)$

7 The diagram shows the graph of $y = f(x)$. It has rotation symmetry about $(0, 0)$.

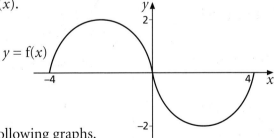

(a) Sketch, on separate diagrams, the following graphs.

  (i) $y = f(2x)$ (ii) $y = 2f(x)$

(b) Describe the transformation that maps the graph of $y = f(x)$ on to the graph of $y = f(2x)$.

8 Describe the transformation that maps the graph of $x^2 + y^2 = 9$ on to the graph of $x^2 + \frac{1}{4}y^2 = 9$.

3 Sequences and series 1

In this chapter you will
- use subscript notation when working with sequences
- generate a sequence using a rule for the nth term
- generate a sequence using an inductive definition (the first term and a rule to get from one term to the next)
- describe the behaviour of sequences, including those that converge to a limit
- learn what is meant by an arithmetic sequence
- find the sum of an arithmetic series
- use sigma notation when working with series

A Using a rule for the nth term (answers p 134)

A sequence is a list of numbers, arranged in a particular order.
The numbers in the list are called the **terms** of the sequence.

Sequences with a first and a last term are **finite**.
For example, the list of numbers

$$6, 7, 9, 8, 6, 8, 6$$

forms a finite sequence that has seven terms.

A sequence can be **infinite**. For example, the list of odd numbers

$$1, 3, 5, 7, 9, 11, \ldots$$

goes on for ever and forms an infinite sequence.

In mathematics, a sequence of numbers often follows a pattern that allows us to describe and understand its behaviour. For example, in the sequence of odd numbers each term is exactly 2 more than the previous one.

Notation

We usually represent the terms of a sequence by choosing a particular letter and using **subscript** notation (or **suffix** notation).
It is natural to use a subscript of **1** for the **1**st term.
Choosing a for the sequence of odd numbers above gives us

$$a_1 = 1, \quad a_2 = 3, \quad a_3 = 5, \quad a_4 = 7, \quad a_5 = 9, \quad a_6 = 11, \ldots$$

We can use a_n to represent the nth term of this sequence.

We often define a sequence by giving a rule for the nth term.
For example, a sequence defined by the rule $\quad b_n = 2n + 5$

$$\text{gives} \quad b_1 = (2 \times 1) + 5 = 7$$
$$b_2 = (2 \times 2) + 5 = 9$$
$$b_3 = (2 \times 3) + 5 = 11 \ldots$$

D **A1** For each of the sequences below,

(i) work out the the first six terms

(ii) work out the 10th, 25th and 100th terms

(iii) describe what happens to the terms of the sequence as n gets larger and larger

(a) $a_n = 6n - 1$ (b) $b_n = 5 - 3n$ (c) $c_n = 2n + 3$

(d) $d_n = n^2 + n - 3$ (e) $e_n = 5 + \dfrac{1}{10^n}$ (f) $f_n = \dfrac{n+3}{n}$

(g) $g_n = \dfrac{2n}{n+1}$ (h) $h_n = (-2)^n$ (i) $i_n = (-0.1)^n$

Sometimes the terms of a sequence get closer and closer to one particular value.

Consider the sequence defined by $u_n = 7 + \dfrac{1}{n}$.

As n gets larger and larger $\dfrac{1}{n}$ gets closer and closer to 0 so u_n gets closer and closer to 7.

We say that u_n **converges to a limit** of 7.

A graph helps to show the behaviour of this sequence: $8, 7\frac{1}{2}, 7\frac{1}{3}, 7\frac{1}{4}, 7\frac{1}{5}, 7\frac{1}{6}, \ldots$ getting closer to 7.

$$u_n = 7 + \frac{1}{n}$$

Exercise A (answers p 134)

1 A sequence of terms $u_1, u_2, u_3, \ldots$ is defined by $u_n = 4n + 1$.

(a) Find the values of u_1, u_2 and u_3.

(b) What is the value of u_{100}?

(c) Find the value of n for which $u_n = 81$.

(d) How many terms in this sequence are smaller than 100?

2 A sequence of terms $a_1, a_2, a_3, \ldots$ has nth term a_n where $a_n = 40 - 3n$.

(a) Find the values of a_1, a_2 and a_3.

(b) What is the value of a_{16}?

(c) How many terms in this sequence are positive?

3 The nth term of a sequence is p_n where $p_n = 2 \times 3^n$.

(a) Find the values of p_1, p_2, p_3 and p_{10}.

(b) What happens to the terms in this sequence as n gets larger and larger?

4 The nth term of a sequence is h_n where $h_n = \dfrac{2}{3^n}$.

(a) Find the value of h_{30} correct to two significant figures.

(b) What happens to the terms in this sequence as n gets larger and larger?

5 Match each sequence below to a description of its behaviour as n gets larger and larger.

(a) $u_n = 2^n + 5$

(b) $u_n = 50 - 2n$

(c) $u_n = \dfrac{4n - 1}{2n + 3}$

(d) $u_n = 2 + (0.1)^n$

(e) $u_n = 2 + (-0.1)^n$

A The terms decrease at a steady rate.

B The terms increase at a faster and faster rate.

C The terms go up and down but get closer and closer to a limit of 2.

D The terms increase but at a slower and slower rate, converging to a limit of 2.

E The terms decrease but converge to a limit of 2.

6 Match each sequence below to a graph that shows its behaviour.

(a) $u_n = 3n - 2$

(b) $u_n = \dfrac{3n - 1}{n + 1}$

(c) $u_n = 3 + (-0.7)^n$

7 Find an expression for u_n that fits each sequence.

(a) $u_1 = 1,\ u_2 = \frac{1}{2},\ u_3 = \frac{1}{3},\ u_4 = \frac{1}{4},\ \dots$

(b) $u_1 = 2,\ u_2 = \frac{3}{2},\ u_3 = \frac{4}{3},\ u_4 = \frac{5}{4},\ \dots$

8 The nth term of a sequence is $u_n = \dfrac{3n + 7}{n}$.

(a) Evaluate u_{1000}.

(b) Show that $\dfrac{3n + 7}{n} = 3 + \dfrac{7}{n}$.

(c) Hence show that, as n gets larger and larger, u_n converges to a limit of 3.

*9 Find an expression for the nth term of the sequence $\ -6,\ \frac{7}{2},\ -\frac{8}{3},\ \frac{9}{4},\ \dots$

B Inductive definition

The sequence defined by $u_n = 3n + 2$ has terms

$$u_1 = 5,\ u_2 = 8,\ u_3 = 11,\ u_4 = 14,\ u_5 = 17,\ u_6 = 20,\ \dots$$

Each term can be found by adding 3 to the previous term.

So we can write
$$u_2 = u_1 + 3$$
$$u_3 = u_2 + 3$$
$$u_4 = u_3 + 3 \ \dots$$

This can be summarised as $u_{n+1} = u_n + 3$.

A rule like this that takes you from one term to the next is called a **recurrence relation**.

If we know the first term and a recurrence relation for a sequence, then we can write down the sequence term by term.

For example, a sequence is defined by $u_1 = 5$ and the recurrence relation $u_{n+1} = 2u_n + 3$.

So $u_2 = 2u_1 + 3 = 2 \times 5 + 3 = 13$

$u_3 = 2u_2 + 3 = 2 \times 13 + 3 = 29$

$u_4 = 2u_3 + 3 = 2 \times 29 + 3 = 61 \ldots$

A definition of a sequence that states the first term and a recurrence relation is called an **inductive definition**.

Example 1

A sequence is defined by $v_1 = 16\,000$, $v_{n+1} = 0.85v_n$.

Work out enough terms of the sequence to find the smallest value of n for which $v_n < 10\,000$.

Solution

$v_1 = 16\,000$

$v_2 = 0.85 \times v_1 = 0.85 \times 16\,000 = 13\,600$

$v_3 = 0.85 \times v_2 = 0.85 \times 13\,600 = 11\,560$

$v_4 = 0.85 \times v_3 = 0.85 \times 11\,560 = 9826$ which is the first value that is less than $10\,000$

So the smallest value is $n = 4$.

Example 2

The sequence 5, 14, 36.5, 92.75, … is defined by a recurrence relation of the form $u_{n+1} = pu_n + q$ where p and q are constants.

Find the values of p and q and hence write down the recurrence relation.

Solution

$u_2 = pu_1 + q$ *gives the equation*　　　　　　　$14 = 5p + q$

$u_3 = pu_2 + q$ *gives the equation*　　　　　　$36.5 = 14p + q$

Subtract the first equation from the second.　　$22.5 = 9p$

$\Rightarrow \quad p = 2.5$

Substitute $p = 2.5$ in the first equation.　　　$14 = 12.5 + q$

$\Rightarrow \quad q = 1.5$

So the recurrence relation is $u_{n+1} = 2.5u_n + 1.5$.

Exercise B (answers p 134)

1 A sequence of terms $u_1, u_2, u_3, \ldots$ is defined by $u_1 = 2$, $u_{n+1} = 3u_n - 5$.

Write down the first six terms of this sequence.

2 Write down the first four terms of each sequence below.

(a) $u_1 = 6$, $u_{n+1} = 0.5u_n + 2$ (b) $u_1 = 10$, $u_{n+1} = 1.3u_n - 4$

3 A sequence is defined by $a_1 = 2$, $a_{n+1} = (a_n)^2$.

Work out enough terms of this sequence to find the smallest value of n for which a_n is larger than a million.

4 The sequence 2, 4, 7.2, 12.32, ... is defined by a recurrence relation of the form $u_{n+1} = pu_n + q$ where p and q are constants.

(a) Show that p and q satisfy the equations $4 = 2p + q$ and $7.2 = 4p + q$.

(b) Find the values of p and q and hence write down the recurrence relation.

5 The sequence 4, 3, 1, –3, ... is defined by a recurrence relation of the form $u_{n+1} = au_n + b$ where a and b are constants.

Find the values of a and b and hence write down the recurrence relation.

6 A sequence is defined by $u_1 = 9$, $u_{n+1} = ku_n + k$ where k is a constant.

In this sequence, $u_2 = 4$.

(a) Find the value of k and hence write down the recurrence relation.

(b) Find the value of u_4.

7 A sequence is defined by $u_1 = 5$, $u_{n+1} = u_n + p$ where p is a constant.

In this sequence, $u_4 = 17$.

Find the value of p.

8 A sequence is defined by $u_1 = 4$, $u_{n+1} = 2u_n + k$ where k is a constant.

In this sequence, $u_3 = 20.5$.

(a) (i) Write an expression for u_2 in terms of k.

    (ii) Hence write an expression for u_3 in terms of k.

(b) Form and solve an equation to find the value of k.

9 A sequence is defined by $u_1 = 2$, $u_{n+1} = pu_n + 1$ where p is a constant.

In this sequence, $u_3 = 11$.

(a) (i) Write an expression for u_2 in terms of p.

    (ii) Hence write an expression for u_3 in terms of p.

(b) Form and solve an equation to find the two possible values for p.

10 A sequence is defined by $u_1 = 4$, $u_{n+1} = pu_n + 7$ where p is a constant.

In this sequence, $u_3 = 9$.

(a) Show that one possible values for p is $\frac{1}{4}$ and find the other value of p.

(b) For each value of p, work out the first four terms of the sequence.

C Inductive definition and limits (answers p 135)

A spreadsheet is useful for a number of questions in this section.

C1 For each sequence below,

      (i) write down the first six terms, giving them to 4 d.p. where appropriate

      (ii) describe what happens to the terms of the sequence as n gets larger and larger

(a) $u_1 = 3, \ u_{n+1} = u_n + 5$

(b) $u_1 = 0, \ u_{n+1} = 4u_n$

(c) $u_1 = -2, \ u_{n+1} = 3u_n$

(d) $u_1 = 3, \ u_{n+1} = \frac{1}{3}u_n$

(e) $u_1 = 5, \ u_{n+1} = 2u_n - 1$

(f) $u_1 = 3, \ u_{n+1} = \frac{u_n}{2} + 1$

(g) $u_1 = 0.9, \ u_{n+1} = \sqrt{u_n}$

(h) $u_1 = 2, \ u_{n+1} = \frac{1}{u_n} + 5$

(i) $u_1 = 3, \ u_{n+1} = 2u_n - 3$

(j) $u_1 = -5, \ u_{n+1} = \frac{u_n}{5} - 4$

The sequence defined by $u_1 = 3, \ u_{n+1} = 2u_n - 3$ has terms 3, 3, 3, 3, 3, …
As all its terms are the same we call it a **constant sequence**.

C2 What value for u_1, with the relation $u_{n+1} = 2u_n - 1$, gives a constant sequence?

C3 $u_1 = c$ with the relation $u_{n+1} = 3u_n - 10$ gives a constant sequence.

(a) Explain why c must satisfy the equation $c = 3c - 10$.

(b) Solve the equation to find the value for c that gives a constant sequence.

C4 $u_1 = c$ with the relation $u_{n+1} = \frac{u_n}{3} + 6$ gives a constant sequence.

(a) Write down an equation that must be satisfied by c.

(b) Solve your equation to find the value for c that gives a constant sequence.

C5 For each of the following recurrence relations, find a value for u_1 that will give a constant sequence.

(a) $u_{n+1} = 3u_n - 8$

(b) $u_{n+1} = 4u_n + 9$

(c) $u_{n+1} = \frac{u_n}{2} - 1$

(d) $u_{n+1} = 6 - \frac{u_n}{5}$

C6 A sequence is defined by $u_1 = a, \ u_{n+1} = \frac{u_n}{3} + 4$.

Investigate the behaviour of this sequence for various values of a.
Do the sequences converge to a limit?
Comment on your results.

C7 A sequence is defined by $u_1 = b, \ u_{n+1} = \frac{u_n}{4} - 1$.

Investigate the behaviour of this sequence for various values of b.
Comment on your results.

The starting value $u_1 = 5$ with the recurrence relation $u_{n+1} = \dfrac{u_n}{2} + 1$ gives the sequence

$5, 3.5, 2.75, 2.375, 2.1875, 2.09375, \ldots$, which appears to converge to a limit of 2.

If the sequence does converge then u_{n+1} and u_n will get closer and closer to each other and must get closer and closer to the solution of the equation

$$c = \frac{c}{2} + 1$$

which is $c = 2$ as we expected.

K   If a recurrence relation gives a sequence that converges to a limit, then using the limit as a starting value must give a constant sequence.

However, finding a value that gives a constant sequence for a recurrence relation does not ensure that the relation will in fact give any other sequences that converge to it.

For example, $u_{n+1} = 2u_n + 1$ with $u_1 = -1$ gives the constant sequence $-1, -1, -1, \ldots$ but other values for u_1 give sequences that do not converge.

Example 3

The sequence defined by $u_1 = 3$, $u_{n+1} = 0.2u_n + 2$ converges to a limit l.
Write down and solve an equation to find l.

Solution

l must satisfy the equation

$$l = 0.2l + 2$$
$$\Rightarrow \quad 0.8l = 2$$
$$\Rightarrow \quad l = 2 \div 0.8$$
$$= 2.5 \qquad \textit{Working out some terms of the sequence confirms}$$
$$\textit{this: } 3, 2.6, 2.52, 2.504, 2.5008, 2.50016, \ldots$$

In the following example, a subscript of 0 is used for the first term.
This is often useful where time is involved.

Example 4

The population of slugs in a garden at time t days from the start of a survey is represented by p_t.
It is found that the numbers of slugs approximately fits the sequence defined by

$$p_0 = 10, \ p_{t+1} = 0.4p_t + 15$$

(a) Estimate the number of slugs in the garden after 3 days.

(b) The population of slugs converges to a limit. Determine the limit.

Solution

(a) $p_0 = 10$, $p_1 = 19$, $p_2 = 22.6$ and $p_3 = 24.04$ so the population is about 24 after three days.

(b) A limit l must satisfy the equation

$$l = 0.4l + 15$$
$$\Rightarrow \quad 0.6l = 15$$
$$\Rightarrow \quad l = 15 \div 0.6$$
$$= 25$$

Exercise C (answers p 135)

1 Each definition below defines a sequence that converges to a limit.
 Write down and solve an equation to find each limit, and work out enough
 terms to confirm your result.

 (a) $u_1 = 6, \ u_{n+1} = \dfrac{u_n}{3} + 5$ **(b)** $a_1 = -8, \ a_{n+1} = 0.5a_n - 1$

 (c) $p_0 = 0.6, \ p_{t+1} = \dfrac{p_t}{8} + 1$ **(d)** $b_0 = 10, \ b_{t+1} = 0.6b_t + 2$

2 The population of birds on a cliff face at time t days from the start of a
 survey is represented by p_t.

 It is found that the number of birds approximately fits the sequence defined by

$$p_0 = 15, \ p_{t+1} = 0.75p_t + 20$$

 (a) Estimate the number of birds on the cliff face after 2 days.

 (b) The population of birds converges to a limit. Determine the limit.

*3 Some sequences are defined by $u_1 = a, \ u_{n+1} = \dfrac{6}{u_n} + 1$.

 (a) Show that there are two possible values for a that give a constant sequence.

 (b) Consider the sequence where $u_1 = 5$.

   (i) Show that $u_2 = 2.2$.

   (ii) Work out the values of u_3 to u_{10}, correct to 4 d.p.

   (iii) The sequence converges to a limit. Write down the value of the limit.

 (c) Consider the sequence where $u_1 = -1.9$.

   (i) Will this sequence converge to a limit? What do you think this limit will be?

   (ii) Work out the first 12 terms of this sequence. Were you right about its limit?

*4 Investigate sequences that are generated by $x_1 = 0.4, \ x_{n+1} = rx_n(1 - x_n)$
 for various values of r.

 Mathematicians who work on chaos theory investigate recurrence relations
 like this one.

D Arithmetic sequences (answers p 136)

A sequence is defined by $u_1 = 5, \ u_{n+1} = u_n + 4$

$$\text{giving} \quad u_2 = 5 + 4 = 9,$$
$$u_3 = 9 + 4 = 13$$
$$u_4 = 13 + 4 = 17 \ \dots \text{ and so on.}$$

The sequence has a simple structure – each term is found by adding a fixed number to the
previous one. The number added on each time is sometimes called the **common difference**.

Any sequence with a structure like this is called an **arithmetic sequence**.

It has an inductive definition of the form $u_1 = a, \ u_{n+1} = u_n + d$ where a and d are constants.

D **D1** An arithmetic sequence is defined by $u_1 = 10$, $u_{n+1} = u_n + 3$.

    (a) Write down the first five terms.

    (b) Find the values of u_{10}, u_{100} and u_{1000}.

    (c) Find an expression for the nth term u_n in terms of n.

D2 An arithmetic sequence is defined by $x_1 = 10$, $x_{n+1} = x_n - 3$.

    (a) Find the values of x_{10}, x_{100} and x_{1000}.

    (b) Find an expression for the nth term x_n in terms of n.

An arithmetic sequence is defined by $u_1 = 3$, $u_{n+1} = u_n + 4$.
The terms follow this pattern:

$$u_2 = 3 + 4 \qquad\qquad = 3 + 1 \times 4$$
$$u_3 = 3 + 4 + 4 \qquad\quad = 3 + 2 \times 4$$
$$u_4 = 3 + 4 + 4 + 4 \quad\; = 3 + 3 \times 4$$
$$u_5 = 3 + 4 + 4 + 4 + 4 = 3 + 4 \times 4 \dots$$

This gives us the nth term $u_n = 3 + (n-1) \times 4$, which simplifies to $u_n = 4n - 1$.

K In general the arithmetic sequence with first term a and common difference d can be written

$$a,\ a + d,\ a + 2d,\ a + 3d, \dots$$

and the nth term is $a + (n-1)d$.

D3 An arithmetic sequence is defined by $x_1 = 6$, $x_{n+1} = x_n + 7$.

    (a) Find an expression for the nth term x_n in terms of n.

    (b) Work out the value of x_{100}.

D4 The sequence $11, 14, 17, 20, 23, \dots$ is arithmetic.
    Find an expression for the nth term.

Example 5

How many terms are in the finite arithmetic sequence $-10, -7, -4, -1, \dots 137$?

Solution

Using a for the first term and d for the common difference we have $a = -10$ and $d = 3$.

So an expression for the nth term is $\quad -10 + 3(n-1) = -10 + 3n - 3$
$$= 3n - 13$$

For the last term 137 we have $\qquad 3n - 13 = 137$
$$\Rightarrow \qquad 3n = 150$$
$$\Rightarrow \qquad n = 50$$

So the sequence has 50 terms.

Example 6

The 4th term of an arithmetic sequence is –2 and the 20th term of the same sequence is 22. What is the nth term of the sequence?

Solution

$$\text{From the 4th term} \quad a + 3d = -2$$

$$\text{From the 20th term} \quad a + 19d = 22$$

Subtract the first equation from the second.

$$16d = 24$$

$$\Rightarrow \quad d = 1.5$$

Substitute $d = 1.5$ in the first equation.

$$a + 4.5 = -2$$

$$\Rightarrow \quad a = -6.5$$

$$\text{So the } n\text{th term is } -6.5 + 1.5(n - 1)$$

$$= -6.5 + 1.5n - 1.5$$

$$= 1.5n - 8$$

Exercise D (answers p 136)

1 A sequence is defined by $u_1 = 5$, $u_{n+1} = u_n + 9$.

(a) Write down the first four terms.

(b) Find an expression for u_n in terms of n.

(c) Find the value of u_{50}.

2 The sequence 90, 88.5, 87, 85.5, ... is arithmetic.

(a) Find the 20th term.

(b) Find an expression for the nth term.

(c) Find the value of n for which the nth term in the sequence is 42.

3 The common difference of an arithmetic sequence is 3 and the 10th term is 35. What is the first term?

4 Work out how many terms there are in each of these finite arithmetic sequences.

(a) 5, 7, 9, ..., 97

(b) 6, 7.2, 8.4, ..., 27.6

(c) 5, 3.5, 2, ..., –40

(d) $\frac{2}{5}$, $\frac{4}{5}$, $1\frac{1}{5}$, ..., 40

5 The first term of an arithmetic sequence is 6 and the 10th term is 42. What is the 100th term of this sequence?

6 The 5th term of an arithmetic sequence is 0 and the 19th term is 7. What is the nth term of this sequence?

7 The 20th term of an arithmetic sequence is –44 and the 3rd term is 7.

8 The 7th term of an arithmetic sequence is 22.
The 15th term is six times the first term.
Find the first term and the common difference.

9 The 12th term of an arithmetic sequence is 35.
The 7th term is four times the 2nd term.
Find the nth term of the sequence.

10 The first term of an arithmetic sequence is six times the 5th term.
The sum of the 2nd and 8th terms is 8.
Find the 20th term of this sequence.

E Arithmetic series (answers p 136)

D **E1** The diagram shows some cans arranged in a pyramid.

    (a) How many cans are in this pyramid?

    (b) What about a pyramid like this with 100 cans on the bottom row?

The word **series** can be used to mean the sum of the terms of a sequence.
So an **arithmetic series** is the sum of the terms of an arithmetic sequence.

Examples of arithmetic series are

$$4 + 5 + 6 + 7 + \ldots \qquad \text{(an infinite series)}$$
$$19 + 21 + 23 + \ldots + 59 \qquad \text{(a finite series)}$$

Many mathematical problems lead to series.
For example, the pyramid problem in E1 (b) above can be solved by finding the sum

$$1 + 2 + 3 + \ldots + 98 + 99 + 100$$

One way is to consider the sum written out with its 'reverse' below it.

$$1 \ + \ 2 \ + \ 3 \ + \ \ldots \ + 98 + 99 + 100$$
$$100 + 99 + 98 + \ \ldots \ + \ 3 \ + \ 2 \ + \ 1$$

This gives 100 pairs of numbers that each add up to 101.
This gives a total of $100 \times 101 = 10\,100$.

However, this is twice the required sum so $1 + 2 + 3 + \ldots + 98 + 99 + 100 = \frac{10\,100}{2} = 5050$.

We can use this method to find the sum of the first n positive integers which can be written

$$1 + \quad 2 \quad + \quad 3 \quad + \ldots + (n - 2) + (n - 1) + n$$

with its reverse $\quad n + (n - 1) + (n - 2) + \ \ldots \ + \quad 3 \quad + \quad 2 \quad + \ 1$

This gives us n pairs of numbers that each add up to $(n + 1)$.

This gives a total of $n(n + 1)$, which is twice the required sum.

K So $1 + 2 + 3 + \ldots + n = \frac{1}{2}n(n + 1)$.

E2 Work out the sum of the first 50 positive integers.

E3 **(a)** **(i)** Work out the sum $1 + 2 + 3 + \ldots + 200$.

  (ii) Work out the sum $1 + 2 + 3 + \ldots + 150$.

 (b) Hence find the sum of the integers from 151 to 200 inclusive.

E4 Work out the sum $60 + 61 + 62 + \ldots + 250$.

E5 **(a)** Work out the sum of the first 20 positive integers.

 (b) Hence work out the sum of the first 20 multiples of 7.

E6 Work out the following sums.

 (a) $4 + 7 + 10 + 13 + 16 + 19 + 22 + 25 + 28 + 31 + 34 + 37 + 40 + 43$

 (b) $4 + 7 + 10 + 13 + \ldots + 301$

Using l for the last term, any arithmetic series and its reverse can be written

$$a \ + \ (a + d) \ + \ (a + 2d) \ + \ \ldots \ + \ (l - 2d) \ + \ (l - d) \ + \ l$$
$$l \ + \ (l - d) \ + \ (l - 2d) \ + \ \ldots \ + \ (a + 2d) \ + \ (a + d) \ + \ a$$

This gives n pairs of numbers that each add up to $(a + l)$.

This gives a total of $n(a + l)$, which is twice the required sum.

K So the sum to n terms of an arithmetic series is $\frac{1}{2}n(a + l)$
where a is the first term and l is the last term of the arithmetic sequence.

The last term can be written as $(a + (n - 1)d)$ where n is the number of terms.

So $\frac{1}{2}n(a + l) = \frac{1}{2}n(a + a + (n - 1)d) = \frac{1}{2}n(2a + (n - 1)d)$.

K The sum to n terms of an arithmetic series is $\frac{1}{2}n(2a + (n - 1)d)$
where a is the first term and d is the common difference of the arithmetic sequence.

Example 7

Find the sum of the arithmetic series $2 + 8 + 14 + \ldots + 284$.

Solution

$a = 2$ and $d = 6$ so the last term is $2 + 6(n - 1)$ where n is the number of terms in the series.

$$\text{Hence} \qquad 2 + 6(n - 1) = 284$$
$$6(n - 1) = 282$$
$$n - 1 = 47$$
$$n = 48$$

So the sum is $\quad \frac{1}{2}n(a + l) = \frac{1}{2} \times 48 \times (2 + 284)$
$$= 24 \times 286$$
$$= 6864$$

Example 8

Find the sum of the arithmetic series $3 + 4.5 + 6 + 7.5 + \ldots$ as far as the 50th term.

Solution

$a = 3$, $d = 1.5$ and $n = 50$

So the sum is $\frac{1}{2}n(2a + (n - 1)d) = \frac{1}{2} \times 50 \times (2 \times 3 + (50 - 1) \times 1.5)$

$$= 25 \times (6 + 49 \times 1.5)$$
$$= 25 \times 79.5$$
$$= 1987.5$$

Exercise E (answers p 136)

1 Find the sum of the first 200 positive integers.

2 Find the sum of the integers from 37 to 152 inclusive.

3 Find the sum of the integers from 200 to 400 inclusive.

4 Find the sum of all the integers between 1 and 1000 that are divisible by 3.

5 Find the sum of the first 40 terms of the arithmetic series $9 + 16 + 23 + \ldots$

6 The first term of an arithmetic series is 10 and the common difference is $\frac{1}{2}$.
Show that the sum of the first 100 terms of the series is 3475.

7 The 5th term of an arithmetic series is 16 and the common difference is -2.
(a) Find the first term.
(b) Find the sum of the first 30 terms of the series.

8 The first term of an arithmetic series is 1 and the 10th term is 7.
Show that the sum of the first 40 terms of the series is 560.

9 Evaluate the sum of the arithmetic series $2 + 7 + 12 + \ldots + 222$.

10 The first term of an arithmetic series is 3.
The sum of the first 25 terms is 525.
Find the 2nd term.

11 The sum of the 5th and 10th terms of an arithmetic series is $11\frac{1}{2}$.
The sum of the first 20 terms is 85.
What is the first term?

12 A car is accelerating from rest. In the first second it moves 3 m, in the second second it moves 5 m, in the third second it moves 7 m, and so on.
(a) How far will it travel in 15 seconds?
(b) How long will it take to cover a kilometre?

13 Each year for 20 years, Sue will pay money into a savings scheme.
In the first year, she will pay in £400. In the second year she will pay in £425.
In the third year she will pay in £450.

Her payments will carry on increasing like this.

(a) How much will she pay in the 20th year?

(b) How much will she pay in total over the 20 years?

14 Find, in terms of n, the sum of the first n odd numbers.

15 The sum of the first 30 terms of an arithmetic series is 90.
The sum of the next 10 terms is also 90.
Find the first term and the common difference.

16 A set of steps for the end of a pier are built of stone.
A sketch of the cross-section of the steps is shown.

Each step has a rise of 0.2 m
and a tread of 0.6 m.

Form a series to calculate
the area of the cross-section.

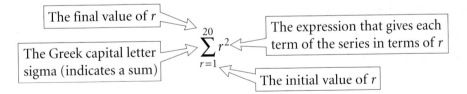

*17 The spool for a cassette tape has a circumference of 70 mm.
The thickness of the tape makes each turn is 0.075 mm longer than the previous one.

How many times will the spool turn playing a tape that is 54 metres long?

F Sigma notation

The sum of the first 20 square numbers can be written as $1^2 + 2^2 + 3^2 + 4^2 + \ldots + 20^2$.

We can use shorthand notation to write this sum as

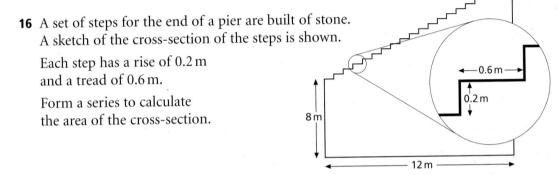

We can use any letter as the variable. For example,

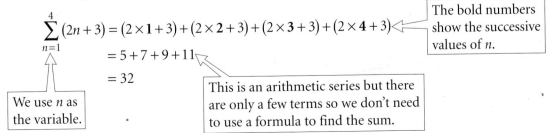

$$\sum_{n=1}^{4}(2n+3) = (2\times\mathbf{1}+3)+(2\times\mathbf{2}+3)+(2\times\mathbf{3}+3)+(2\times\mathbf{4}+3)$$

The bold numbers show the successive values of n.

$$= 5+7+9+11$$

$$= 32$$

We use n as the variable.

This is an arithmetic series but there are only a few terms so we don't need to use a formula to find the sum.

Example 9

Evaluate $\displaystyle\sum_{i=0}^{5} i^3$.

Solution

$$\sum_{i=0}^{5} i^3 = 0^3 + 1^3 + 2^3 + 3^3 + 4^3 + 5^3$$
$$= 0 + 1 + 8 + 27 + 64 + 125$$
$$= 225$$

Example 10

Evaluate $\displaystyle\sum_{r=1}^{40} (3r - 5)$.

Solution

$$\sum_{r=1}^{40} (3r - 5) = (3 \times 1 - 5) + (3 \times 2 - 5) + (3 \times 3 - 5) + \ldots + (3 \times 40 - 5)$$

$$= -2 + 1 + 4 + \ldots + 115 \qquad \textit{It's an arithmetic series with 40 terms so use a rule.}$$

$$= \tfrac{1}{2} \times 40 \times (-2 + 115) \qquad \textit{The rule that the sum is } \tfrac{1}{2}n(a + l) \textit{ is used here.}$$

$$= 2260$$

Example 11

The nth term of an arithmetic sequence is u_n where $u_n = 1 + 2.5n$.

Evaluate $\displaystyle\sum_{n=1}^{100} u_n$.

Solution

$$\sum_{n=1}^{100} u_n = u_1 + u_2 + u_3 + \ldots + u_{100}$$

$$= 3.5 + 6 + 8.5 + \ldots + 251$$

$$= \tfrac{1}{2} \times 100 \times (3.5 + 251) \qquad \textit{The rule that the sum is } \tfrac{1}{2}n(a + l) \textit{ is used here.}$$

$$= 12\,725$$

Exercise F (answers p 137)

1 Evaluate each of these.

(a) $\displaystyle\sum_{n=1}^{5} 2n$ 　　(b) $\displaystyle\sum_{i=0}^{7} (i + 1)$ 　　(c) $\displaystyle\sum_{r=1}^{3} r^3$ 　　(d) $\displaystyle\sum_{i=1}^{6} i$

(e) $\displaystyle\sum_{r=3}^{5} (3r - 1)$ 　　(f) $\displaystyle\sum_{n=4}^{7} n^2$ 　　(g) $\displaystyle\sum_{r=2}^{5} r(r + 1)$ 　　(h) $\displaystyle\sum_{i=2}^{4} \frac{1}{i}$

2 Evaluate each of these by using an appropriate rule.

(a) $\displaystyle\sum_{n=1}^{46} n$ 　　(b) $\displaystyle\sum_{i=1}^{40} 3i$ 　　(c) $\displaystyle\sum_{r=1}^{30} (r + 5)$ 　　(d) $\displaystyle\sum_{i=1}^{60} (2i + 7)$

(e) $\displaystyle\sum_{r=1}^{40} (0.5r - 3)$ 　　(f) $\displaystyle\sum_{n=1}^{25} (8 + 0.5n)$ 　　(g) $\displaystyle\sum_{r=1}^{50} (30 - 3r)$ 　　(h) $\displaystyle\sum_{i=1}^{100} (3 + 1.2i)$

3 (a) Evaluate **(i)** $\displaystyle\sum_{i=1}^{50} i$ **(ii)** $\displaystyle\sum_{i=1}^{30} i$ **(b)** Hence evaluate $\displaystyle\sum_{i=31}^{50} i$.

4 (a) How many terms are in the sum $\displaystyle\sum_{r=9}^{36}(2r+5)$?   **(b)** Show that $\displaystyle\sum_{r=9}^{36}(2r+5)=1400$.

5 Evaluate each of these.

   (a) $\displaystyle\sum_{n=10}^{20}(3n-2)$ **(b)** $\displaystyle\sum_{i=4}^{40}(1.4i+5)$ **(c)** $\displaystyle\sum_{r=25}^{70}(28-5r)$

6 (a) Show that $\displaystyle\sum_{r=1}^{20}(3r-1)=610$.   **(b)** Show that $\displaystyle\sum_{r=1}^{n}(3r-1)=\tfrac{1}{2}n(3n+1)$.

Key points

- Subscript notation can be used to label the terms of a sequence.
  For example: $u_1, u_2, u_3, u_4, \ldots$ (p 30)

- A sequence can be defined by a rule for the nth term such as $u_n = n^2 + 1$.   (p 30)

- An inductive definition defines a sequence by giving the first term and a rule
  such as $u_{n+1} = 4u_n + 1$ that gives each term in terms of the previous one.   (pp 32–33)

- Some sequences get closer and closer to a value called the limit.
  We say the sequence converges to a limit (or limiting value).

  The limit, l, of a converging sequence can be found from the inductive definition
  by replacing u_{n+1} and u_n by l to form an equation in l and then solving it.   (pp 31, 36)

- An arithmetic sequence is one where each term can be found by
  adding a fixed number (the common difference) to the previous one.   (p 37)

- An inductive definition of an arithmetic sequence is $u_1 = a$, $u_{n+1} = u_n + d$
  where a is the first term and d is the common difference.

  The sequence can be written $a, \ a+d, \ a+2d, \ a+3d, \ a+4d, \ \ldots$ (p 37–38)

- The nth term of an arithmetic sequence $u_1, u_2, u_3, \ldots$ is $u_n = a + (n-1)d$.   (p 38)

- When the terms of an arithmetic sequence are added together they form
  an arithmetic series. The sum of the first n terms of an arithmetic series is
  $$\tfrac{1}{2}n(2a + (n-1)d)$$
  or $\tfrac{1}{2}n(a + l)$ where l is the last term.   (p 41)

- The sum of the first n positive integers is $\tfrac{1}{2}n(n+1)$.   (p 40)

- Sigma notation can be used as a shorthand for series.
  For example, the sum of the first 20 multiples of 3 can be written as
  $$\sum_{i=1}^{20} 3i$$
      (p 43)

Mixed questions (answers p 137)

1 The 5th term of an arithmetic sequence is -1 and the 10th term of the sequence is 1.
Find an expression for the nth term of this sequence.

2 The sequence of terms $u_1, u_2, u_3, \ldots$ is defined by
$$u_1 = 8, \quad u_{n+1} = au_n + 1 \qquad \text{where } a \text{ is a negative constant.}$$
The third term of the sequence is $u_3 = 2.68$.
Find the value of a.

3 The sequence defined by $u_1 = 7, \quad u_{n+1} = 0.2u_n + 4$ converges to a limit k.
By forming and solving an equation, find the value of k.

4 Find the sum of the integers from 1 to 150 inclusive.

5 Find the sum of the 300 integers from 101 to 400 inclusive.   AQA 2001

6 Find the sum of the first 40 multiples of 5.

7 The 10th term of an arithmetic series is 20.
The common difference is 1.8.

(a) Find the first term.

(b) Find the sum of the first thirty terms of the series.

8 The sequence of terms $u_1, u_2, u_3, \ldots$ is defined by $u_n = 0.7n + 0.2$.

(a) Find the value of u_{10}.

(b) Evaluate $\displaystyle\sum_{n=1}^{200} u_n$.

9 The first term of an arithmetic series is -11 and the 9th term of the series is 1.

(a) Find the common difference and the sum of the first 20 terms of the series.

(b) Find the value of n for which the nth term of the series is 100.   AQA 2001

10 An arithmetic series has first term a and common difference d.
The sum of the first 19 terms is 266.

(a) Show that $a + 9d = 14$.

(b) The sum of the 5th and 8th terms is 7.
Find the values of a and d.   AQA 2003

Test yourself (answers p 137)

1 In a clinical trial, the concentration of a drug in the blood at time t hours from the start of the trial is denoted by p_t.

It is given that $p_{t+1} = a + bp_t$, where a and b are constants.

Measurements give $p_0 = 5.0$, $p_1 = 13.0$ and $p_2 = 14.6$.

(a) Find   (i) a and b

             (ii) the concentration of the drug in the blood after 3 hours

(b) The concentration converges to a limiting value w.
Write down and solve an equation for w.   AQA 2002

2 The nth term of an arithmetic sequence is u_n where $u_n = 10 + 0.5n$.

(a) Find the values of u_1 and u_2.

(b) Write down the common difference of the arithmetic sequence.

(c) Find the value of n for which $u_n = 25$.

(d) Evaluate $\displaystyle\sum_{n=1}^{30} u_n$.   AQA 2002

3 Find the sum of the integers from 1 to 300 inclusive.   AQA 2001

4 Find the sum of the 50 integers from 51 to 100 inclusive.   AQA 2003

5 (a) Find the sum of the 16 terms of the arithmetic series $2 + 5 + 8 + \ldots + 47$.

(b) An arithmetic sequence $u_1, u_2, u_3, \ldots$ has rth term u_r where $u_r = 50 - 3r$.

     (i) Write down the values of u_1, u_2, u_3 and u_4.

     (ii) Show that the sequence has exactly 16 positive terms.   AQA 2002

6 The first term of an arithmetic series is 6 and the common difference of the series is $1\frac{1}{3}$.

(a) Find the 10th term.

(b) Show that the sum of the first 400 terms of the series is 108 800.   AQA 2002

7 Find the sum of the first 50 terms of the arithmetic series $4 + 7 + 10 + \ldots$ AQA 2002

8 The 4th term of an arithmetic series is 25. The common difference is 3.

(a) Find the first term.

(b) Find the sum of the first 20 terms of the series.   AQA 2002

9 A pipeline is to be constructed under a lake. It is calculated that the first mile will take 15 days to construct. Each further mile will take 3 days longer that the one before, so the 1st, 2nd and 3rd miles will take 15, 18 and 21 days respectively, and so on.

(a) Find the nth term of the arithmetic sequence 15, 18, 21, $\ldots$

(b) Show that the total time taken to construct the first n miles of the pipeline is $\frac{3}{2}n(n + 9)$ days.

(c) Calculate the total length of pipeline that can be constructed in 600 days.   AQA 2002

4 Sequences and series 2

In this chapter you will learn
- what is meant by a geometric sequence
- how to find the sum of a finite geometric series
- how to find the sum of an infinite geometric series

A Geometric sequences (answers p 138)

A1 On Katy's first birthday, her uncle gives her 5p.
He promises to double the amount he gives her each birthday until she is 18.

(a) How much money has he promised to give her on her 18th birthday?

(b) Can you find an expression for the amount of money he gives on her nth birthday?

The amounts of money that Katy gets can be written as a sequence:

5, 10, 20, 40, 80, …

The sequence has a simple structure – each term is found by multiplying the previous one by a fixed number. The multiplier is sometimes called the **common ratio**.

A sequence with a structure like this is called a **geometric sequence**.

A2 Which of the sequences below are geometric sequences?
Find the value of the common ratio for each geometric sequence.

A   5, 15, 45, 135, …

B   2, 8, 32, 176, …

C   6, 2.4, 0.96, 0.384, …

D   3, 4, $5\frac{1}{3}$, $7\frac{1}{9}$, …

E   3, −6, 12, −24, …

F   4, −6, 8, −10, …

A3 Find the next two terms of the geometric sequence 8, 12, 18, 27, …

A4 What is the 8th term of the geometric sequence 15, 9, 5.4, 3.24, … ?

A5 Find the 6th term of the geometric sequence 3, $1\frac{1}{2}$, $\frac{3}{4}$, $\frac{3}{8}$, …

A6 What is the 20th term of the geometric sequence 3, 6, 12, 24, … ?

A7 Find the 2nd term of the geometric sequence 4, ___ , ___ , 108, 324.

A8 Each of these is a geometric sequence of positive numbers.
Find the missing terms in each one

(a) 16, ___ , 1, $\frac{1}{4}$, $\frac{1}{16}$

(b) 2, ___ , 50, ___ , ___

(c) ___ , 18, ___ , 72, ___

(d) 2, ___ , ___ , 128, ___

A9 The first term of a geometric sequence is 2.
The 4th term of the same sequence is −128.
What is the 2nd term in this sequence?

The geometric sequence 2, 6, 18, 54, 162, ... can be defined by $u_1 = 2$, $u_{n+1} = 3u_n$.

The terms follow this pattern:

$$u_1 = 2 \qquad\qquad = 2 \times 3^0 \qquad\qquad \text{(since } 2 \times 3^0 = 2 \times 1 = 2)$$
$$u_2 = 2 \times 3 \qquad\qquad = 2 \times 3^1$$
$$u_3 = 2 \times 3 \times 3 \qquad = 2 \times 3^2$$
$$u_4 = 2 \times 3 \times 3 \times 3 \qquad = 2 \times 3^3 \ \ldots \text{ and so on}$$

This gives us the nth term $u_n = 2 \times 3^{n-1}$.

K — In general, the geometric sequence with first term a and common ratio r can be written

$$a, \ ar, \ ar^2, \ ar^3, \ \ldots$$

and the nth term is ar^{n-1}.

Example 1

The sequence 7, 21, 63, 189, ... is geometric.
What is the 10th term?

Solution

Using a for the first term and r for the common ratio we have $a = 7$ and $r = \frac{21}{7} = 3$.

The 10th term is $\quad ar^9 = 7 \times 3^9$
$$= 7 \times 19\,683$$
$$= 137\,781$$

Example 2

The 3rd term of a geometric sequence is 10 and the 8th term is 320.
Find the common ratio and the first term.

Solution

Using a for the first term and r for the common ratio

The 3rd term is ar^2. $\qquad\qquad ar^2 = 10$

The 8th term is ar^7. $\qquad\qquad ar^7 = 320$

$$\text{Dividing gives} \qquad \frac{ar^7}{ar^2} = \frac{320}{10}$$

$$\Rightarrow \qquad r^5 = 32$$

$$\Rightarrow \qquad r = \sqrt[5]{32} = 2 \qquad \sqrt[5]{32} = 32^{\frac{1}{5}} \text{ and can be evaluated on a calculator.}$$

Now substitute $r = 2$ in $ar^2 = 10$ to give $\quad a \times 2^2 = 10$

$$\Rightarrow \qquad 4a = 10$$

$$\Rightarrow \qquad a = 2.5$$

So the first term is 2.5 and the common ratio is 2.

Example 3

What is the nth term of the geometric sequence 25, 10, 4, 1.6, ... ?

Solution

Using a for the first term and r for the common ratio we have $a = 25$ and $r = \frac{10}{25} = 0.4$.
So the nth term is $25 \times (0.4)^{n-1}$.

Exercise A (answers p 138)

1 The 2nd term of a geometric sequence is 7.
The 7th term is 224.

   (a) Find the 15th term.

   (b) Find an expression for the nth term of the sequence.

2 The nth term of a geometric sequence is $2 \times 5^{n-1}$.

   (a) Write down the first four terms of the sequence.

   (b) What is the common ratio?

3 A geometric sequence has first term 40 and common ratio 0.6.
Find the value of the 20th term, giving your answer to three significant figures.

4 The 3rd term of a geometric sequence is 5 and the 6th term is $\frac{5}{8}$.
Find the common ratio for this sequence.

5 The 2nd term of a geometric sequence is -12 and the 5th term is 324.

   (a) Show that the common ratio of the sequence is -3.

   (b) State the first term of the sequence.

6 The first term of a geometric sequence is 54 and the 4th term is 16.
Find the common ratio.

7 The first term of a geometric sequence is 1.5 and the 5th term is 24.
Find the two possible values for the common ratio.

8 In the year 2000, the hedgehog population on an island is 500.
The population is estimated to increase in a geometric sequence with common ratio 1.02.

   (a) Find the predicted hedgehog population in 2020.

   (b) By what percentage is the hedgehog population increasing each year?

9 On Ken's first birthday, his mother deposits £1000 in a savings account for him.
The annual rate of interest is 3%.
No more money is deposited in or withdrawn from this account.

   (a) Show that on Ken's 5th birthday, he has £1125.51 in his account.

   (b) How much does he have on his 10th birthday?

   (c) Find an expression for the amount of money in this account on his nth birthday.

10 A geometric sequence has a common ratio of 5.
The sum of the first three terms is 37.2.
Find the first term.

11 The first term of a geometric sequence is 3.
The sum of the first three terms is 129.
Find the possible values of the common ratio.

12 A geometric sequence has first term 81 and fourth term 3.
Show that the nth term of the sequence is 3^{5-n}.

B Geometric series (answers p 139)

D **B1** Imagine a board with 16 squares on it.
There is 1p on the first square, 2p on the second square,
4p on the third square, 8p on the fourth square, and so on.

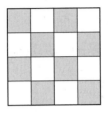

(a) Without doing any calculation, estimate
the total amount of money on the board.

(b) Work out how much money is on the last square.

(c) Can you work out how much money is on the whole board?

The money problem in B1 (b) above can be solved by finding the sum

$$S = 1 + 2 + 4 + 8 + \dots + 16\,384 + 32\,768$$

Writing the numbers as powers of 2 we have

$$S = 1 + 2 + 2^2 + 2^3 + \dots + 2^{14} + 2^{15}$$

Doubling this sum gives

$$2S = 2 + 2^2 + 2^3 + 2^4 + \dots + 2^{15} + 2^{16}$$

Now, subtracting gives

$$2S - S = (2 + 2^2 + 2^3 + 2^4 + \dots + 2^{15} + 2^{16}) - (1 + 2 + 2^2 + 2^3 + \dots\dots + 2^{15})$$

Most of the terms cancel, leaving

$$S = 2^{16} - 1$$

So $S = 65\,536 - 1 = 65\,535$, giving a total of £655.35 on the board.

D **B2** (a) Use a method similar to the one above to show that

$$1 + 3 + 3^2 + 3^3 + \dots + 3^{10} = \frac{3^{11} - 1}{2}.$$

(b) Hence evaluate $1 + 3 + 3^2 + 3^3 + \dots + 3^{10}$.

B3 Evaluate the sum $1 + 3 + 3^2 + 3^3 + \dots + 3^{12}$.

B4 How many terms are in the sum $1 + 5 + 5^2 + 5^3 + \dots + 5^8$?

B5 How many terms are in the sum $1 + 8 + 8^2 + 8^3 + \dots + 8^{n-1}$?

A **geometric series** is the sum of the terms of a geometric sequence.

The sum $1 + r + r^2 + r^3 + \ldots + r^{n-2} + r^{n-1}$ is a geometric series with n terms.

The first term is 1 and the common ratio is r.

Let

$$S = 1 + r + r^2 + r^3 + \ldots + r^{n-2} + r^{n-1}$$

Multiplying by r gives

$$rS = r + r^2 + r^3 + r^4 + \ldots + r^{n-1} + r^n$$

Now, subtracting gives

$$rS - S = (r + r^2 + r^3 + r^4 + \ldots + r^{n-1} + r^n) - (1 + r + r^2 + r^3 + \ldots + r^{n-1})$$

$$\Rightarrow \quad S(r-1) = r^n - 1$$

$$\Rightarrow \quad S = \frac{r^n - 1}{r-1}$$

The sum of the first n terms of a geometric series with first term a and common ratio r is

$$S = a + ar + ar^2 + ar^3 + \ldots + ar^{n-2} + ar^{n-1}$$

$$\Rightarrow \quad S = a(1 + r + r^2 + r^3 + \ldots + r^{n-2} + r^{n-1})$$

$$\Rightarrow \quad S = \frac{a(r^n - 1)}{r-1}$$

Using sigma notation we can write this as $\displaystyle\sum_{i=1}^{n} ar^{n-1} = \frac{a(r^n - 1)}{r-1}$.

Example 4

Find the sum of the first 10 terms of the geometric series $2 + 6 + 18 + \ldots$

Solution

The first term is $a = 2$ and the common ratio is $r = 3$.

The sum of the first 10 terms is $\dfrac{2 \times (3^{10} - 1)}{3-1} = 59\,048$.

Example 5

Evaluate $\displaystyle\sum_{i=1}^{15} 1.5 \times 2^{i-1}$.

Solution

$\displaystyle\sum_{i=1}^{15} 1.5 \times 2^{i-1} = 1.5 + 3 + 6 + \ldots + 1.5 \times 2^{14}$ is a geometric series with 15 terms.

The first term is $a = 1.5$ and the common ratio is $r = 2$.

The sum is $\dfrac{1.5 \times (2^{15} - 1)}{2-1} = 49\,150.5$

Exercise B (answers p 139)

1 Find the sum of the first 15 terms of the geometric series $1 + 4 + 16 + \ldots$

2 Add the first 12 terms of the geometric series $5 + 10 + 20 + \ldots$

3 Evaluate $\displaystyle\sum_{i=1}^{10} 6^{i-1}$.

4 Show that the first 10 terms of the geometric series $8 + 4 + 2 + 1 + \frac{1}{2} + \ldots$ add to give 15.98 (to two decimal places).

5 Show that the sum of the first 12 terms of the geometric series $1 - 3 + 9 - 27 + \ldots$ is $-132\,860$.

6 Calculate the sum of the first 15 terms of each of these geometric series. Where appropriate, give your answer correct to four decimal places.

   (a) $24 + 12 + 6 + 3 + \ldots$ **(b)** $3 - 6 + 12 - 24 + \ldots$

   (c) $6 + 4 + \frac{8}{3} + \frac{16}{9} + \ldots$ **(d)** $36 - 9 + \frac{9}{4} - \frac{9}{16} + \ldots$

7 Evaluate $\displaystyle\sum_{i=1}^{15} 1.6 \times (0.3)^{i-1}$ correct to four significant figures.

8 Evaluate the sum $1 + 3 + 3^2 + 3^3 + \ldots + 3^{14}$.

9 Legend tells that the Shah of Persia offered a reward to the citizen who introduced him to chess. The citizen asked merely for a number of grains of rice according to the rule:

   1 grain for the first square on the chessboard,
   2 grains for the second square,
   4 grains for the third square,
   8 grains for the fourth square and so on.

   (a) How many grains of rice did he request?

   (b) If a grain of rice weighs 0.02 g, what weight of rice did he request?

10 Evaluate the sum of the geometric series $3 + 6 + 12 + \ldots + 3072$.

11 A sequence is defined by $u_1 = 7$, $u_{n+1} = \dfrac{u_n}{4}$.

   Evaluate $\displaystyle\sum_{i=1}^{20} u_i$ correct to three decimal places.

12 An account pays 4% interest per annum.

   (a) A sum of £1 is invested in this account at the beginning of a year. No more money is invested and none is withdrawn. What is the total amount of money at the end of 20 years?

   (b) The sum of £200 is invested in the same way in the same account. What is the total amount of money at the end of 20 years?

13 The sum of the first x terms of the geometric series $2\frac{1}{4} + 4\frac{1}{2} + 9 + 18 + \ldots$ is $1149\frac{3}{4}$. Find the value of x.

C Sum to infinity (answers p 139)

You could use a spreadsheet for questions C1 to C4.

C1 Let S_n be the sum of the first n terms of the geometric series $1 + 2 + 4 + 8 \ldots$

(a) Evaluate S_{10}, S_{11} and S_{12}.

(b) Describe what happens to S_n as n gets larger and larger.

C2 Repeat question C1 for the geometric series $1 - 3 + 9 - 27 + \ldots$

C3 Let S_n be the sum of the first n terms of the geometric series $6 + 3 + 1\frac{1}{2} + \frac{3}{4} \ldots$

(a) Evaluate $S_{10}, S_{11}, S_{12}, S_{13}$ and S_{14}.

(b) What do you think happens to S_n as n gets larger and larger?

C4 Repeat question C3 for the geometric series $1 - \frac{2}{3} + \frac{4}{9} - \frac{6}{27} + \ldots$

Let S_n be the sum of the first n terms of the geometric series $5 + \frac{5}{3} + \frac{5}{9} + \frac{5}{27} + \ldots$

Can we predict what will happen to S_n as n gets larger and larger?

The series is geometric with first term 5 and common ratio $\frac{1}{3}$.

So $S_n = \dfrac{5 \times \left(\left(\frac{1}{3}\right)^n - 1\right)}{\frac{1}{3} - 1} = \dfrac{5 \times \left(\left(\frac{1}{3}\right)^n - 1\right)}{-\frac{2}{3}} = -\frac{15}{2} \times \left(\left(\frac{1}{3}\right)^n - 1\right)$.

Now, as n gets larger and larger $\left(\frac{1}{3}\right)^n$ gets closer and closer to 0.

So S_n gets closer and closer to $-\frac{15}{2} \times (0 - 1) = \frac{15}{2}$.

We say   'As n tends to infinity then S_n converges to a limit of $\frac{15}{2}$.'

or   'The sum to infinity of the series is $\frac{15}{2}$.'

As we have seen, not all geometric series have a 'sum to infinity'.
For example, the sum $1 + 2 + 4 + 8 + \ldots$ does not converge to a limit.

A geometric series has a sum to infinity if r^n converges to 0 and this happens only if $-1 < r < 1$.
We can write this as $|r| < 1$, which means the size of r (ignoring negative signs) is less than 1.

K   A geometric series has a sum to infinity only if $-1 < r < 1$ (that is, $|r| < 1$).

In general, the sum of the first n terms of a geometric series is $\dfrac{a(r^n - 1)}{r - 1}$.

Now if $-1 < r < 1$ then, as n tends to infinity, r^n converges to 0

and so $\dfrac{a(r^n - 1)}{r - 1}$ converges to $\dfrac{a(0 - 1)}{r - 1} = \dfrac{-a}{r - 1} = \dfrac{a}{1 - r}$.

K   If $-1 < r < 1$ then the sum to infinity of the geometric series $a + ar + ar^2 + \ldots$ is $\dfrac{a}{1 - r}$.

Sum to infinity is sometimes written S_∞.

Example 6

Find the sum to infinity of the geometric series $1 + \frac{2}{3} + \frac{4}{9} + \frac{8}{27} + \dots$

Solution

The first term is $a = 1$ and the common ratio is $r = \frac{2}{3}$.

So the sum to infinity is $\dfrac{1}{1 - \frac{2}{3}} = \dfrac{1}{\frac{1}{3}} = 3$.

Example 7

The 2nd term of a geometric series is –4 and the sum to infinity is 9.
Find the first term of this series.

Solution

The first term is a and the common ratio is r.

The 2nd term is –4.	$ar = -4$
The sum to infinity is 9.	$\dfrac{a}{1-r} = 9$
Multiply both sides by $1 - r$.	$a = 9(1-r)$
Multiply by r to obtain ar on the left.	$ar = 9r(1-r)$
Substitute $ar = -4$.	$-4 = 9r - 9r^2$

$$\Rightarrow \quad 9r^2 - 9r - 4 = 0$$
$$\Rightarrow (3r+1)(3r-4) = 0$$
$$\Rightarrow \quad r = -\tfrac{1}{3} \ \text{ or } \ r = \tfrac{4}{3}$$

Since there is a sum to infinity, $\frac{4}{3}$ is not a possible ratio as it is greater than 1.

So the common ratio is $-\frac{1}{3}$ and hence the first term is $-4 \div -\frac{1}{3} = 12$.

Exercise C (answers p 139)

1 For each geometric series below find the common ratio and, where possible, calculate the sum to infinity.

(a) $14 + 7 + \frac{7}{2} + \frac{7}{4} + \dots$

(b) $9 + \frac{9}{10} + \frac{9}{100} + \frac{9}{1000} + \dots$

(c) $1 - 2 + 4 - 8 + \dots$

(d) $4 - 3 + \frac{9}{4} - \frac{27}{16} + \dots$

2 The first term of geometric series is 5 and the 2nd term is 1. Find the sum to infinity.

3 The first term of a geometric series is 100 and the sum to infinity is 120. Find the common ratio.

4 Two consecutive terms in a geometric series are 12 and 8. The sum to infinity is 81. Find the first term.

5 The 2nd term of a geometric series is –6 and the sum to infinity is 8. What is the first term of the series?

*6 The terms of a geometric series are all positive.
The sum of the first two terms is 15 and the sum to infinity is 27.
What are the first two terms of the series?

Key points

- A geometric sequence is one where each term can be found by multiplying the previous term by a fixed number (the common ratio).   (pp 48–49)

- The nth term of a geometric sequence a, ar, ar^2, ar^3, ... is ar^{n-1} where a is the first term and r is the common ratio.   (p 49)

- When the terms of a geometric sequence are added together they form a geometric series $a + ar + ar^2 + ar^3 + ... + ar^{n-1}$.

  The sum of the first n terms of a geometric series is $\dfrac{a(r^n - 1)}{r - 1}$.   (p 52)

- If $-1 < r < 1$ the sum to infinity of a geometric series is $\dfrac{a}{1 - r}$.   (p 54)

Mixed questions (answers p 140)

A few of these questions involve arithmetic sequences and series.

An arithmetic series with n terms that has first term a and common difference d is

$$a + (a + d) + (a + 2d) + (a + 3d) + (a + 4d) + ... + (a + (n - 1)d).$$

The sum of this series is $\quad \frac{1}{2}n(2a + (n - 1)d)$

or $\quad \frac{1}{2}n(a + l) \qquad$ where l is the last term.

1 The 2nd term of a geometric series is 24 and the 5th term is 3.

(a) Show that the common ratio of the series is $\frac{1}{2}$.

(b) Find the first term of the series.

(c) Find the sum to infinity of the series.   AQA 2002

2 The 3rd term of a geometric sequence is 15 and the 4th term is 75.

(a) Find the first term.

(b) Write down an expression for the nth term.

(c) Find the value of the 8th term.

(d) What is the sum of the first 8 terms of the sequence?

3 Evaluate each of these.

(a) $\displaystyle\sum_{n=1}^{15} 10 \times \left(\tfrac{3}{2}\right)^{n-1}$

(b) $\displaystyle\sum_{i=1}^{30} (0.4i + 2)$

(c) $\displaystyle\sum_{p=1}^{10} 2 \times (-3)^{p-1}$

4 (a) The first three terms of a geometric sequence are a, b, c.
Each term represents an increase of p per cent on the preceding term.

(i) Show that the common ratio is $\left(1 + \dfrac{p}{100}\right)$.

(ii) It is given that $a = 2000$. Express b and c in terms of p.

(b) A deposit of £2000 is put into a bank account. After each year, the balance in the account is increased by p per cent. There are no other deposits or withdrawals. After two years the balance is £2332.80.

(i) Show that $p = 8$.

(ii) Given that after n years the balance is £u_n, write down an expression for u_n in terms of n.

(iii) Use your answer to part (b)(ii) to find the balance after 10 years. AQA 2003

5 A hospital offers Catherine a 30-day course of ultraviolet light therapy for her eczema. On day n of the course, she is to have t_n seconds of treatment, where

$$t_n = 69 \times 1.100\,21^{n-1}$$

(a) How long, to the nearest second, will Catherine's treatment be on

(i) day 10   **(ii)** day 30

(b) How much time will she spend in total having this treatment for her eczema?

6 The 3rd term of a geometric series is 81 and the 6th term is 24.

(a) Show that the common ratio of the series is $\frac{2}{3}$.

(b) Find the sum to infinity of the series. AQA 2003

7 A geometric series has first term 25 and 4th term $\frac{8}{5}$.

Find the common ratio and the sum to infinity of the series.

8 An infinite geometric series has common ratio r.
The 2nd term of the series is -12.
The sum to infinity of the series is 16.

(a) Show that r satisfies the equation $4r^2 - 4r - 3 = 0$.

(b) Hence find the value of r. AQA 2002

9 Evaluate the sum $\displaystyle\sum_{i=0}^{20} \frac{1}{4} \times 2^i$.

*10 The first term of a geometric series is 48.
The sum of the first, 3rd and 5th terms is 63.
The second term is negative. Find its value.

*11 Look carefully at the sequence of patterns $P_1, P_2, P_3, P_4, \ldots$.

(a) Show that there are 35 dots in P_5.

(b) Find a rule for the number of dots in P_n.

(c) Which pattern consists of 145 dots?

*12 A fractal is a pattern that can be divided into parts that are each a smaller copy of the whole pattern.

The 'box fractal' is shown below in its first few stages of development.

B_0 is a black square.
B_1 is derived by dividing B_0 into nine squares and removing four of them as shown.
B_2 is derived from B_1 by treating each black square in the same way.

Imagine this process continuing indefinitely.

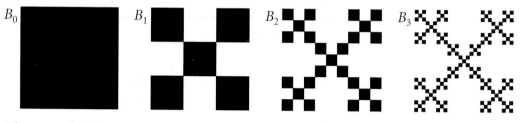

The area of B_0 is 1 square unit.

(a) Find the total area of the black squares in each of B_1, B_2, B_3, ...
Show that, as n tends to infinity, the area of the black squares in B_n converges to 0.

(b) (i) Show that the length of one side of B_0 is 1 unit.

(ii) If the perimeter of each of B_1, B_2, B_3, ... is the total perimeter of the black squares, show that, as n tends to infinity, the length of this perimeter tends towards infinity.

*13 Koch's fractal 'snowflake' curve is shown below in its first few stages of development. It was first described by Helge von Koch in 1904.

F_0 is an equilateral triangle.
F_1 is derived by trisecting each edge of F_0 and replacing the centre third of each edge by two sides of an equilateral triangle.
F_2 is derived from F_1 in the same way.

Imagine this process continuing indefinitely.

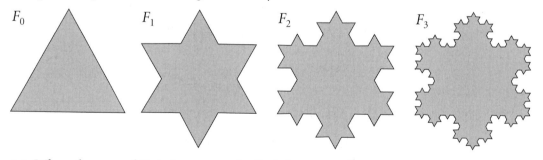

(a) When the area of F_0 is 1 square unit, find the areas of F_1, F_2, F_3, ...
Show that, as n tends to infinity, the area of F_n converges to a limit.
State the limiting value.

(b) Let the length of each side of F_0 be x units.
Does the perimeter of F_n converge to a limit too?

Test yourself (answers p 141)

1 The 3rd term of a geometric series is 54 and the 6th term is 1458.

   (a) Show that the common ratio of the series is 3.

   (b) Find the exact value for the sum of the first 15 terms of the series. AQA 2003

2 A geometric series has first term 81 and 6th term $\frac{32}{3}$.

   Find the common ratio and the value of S, the sum to infinity of the series. AQA 2001

3 The sequence of terms $u_1, u_2, u_3, \ldots$ is defined by
$$u_n = 5 \times 2^n$$

   (a) Show that the sequence is geometric and write down the common ratio.

   (b) Show that none of the terms in the sequence is a square number.

   (c) Work out the sum of the first 10 terms.

4 Find the sum of the geometric series $2 + 6 + 18 + \ldots + 2 \times 3^{n-1}$,
   giving your answer in the form $p^n - q$, where p and q are integers. AQA 2001

5 Evaluate each of these.

   (a) $\displaystyle\sum_{n=1}^{10} 4 \times 3^{n-1}$ **(b)** $\displaystyle\sum_{a=1}^{20} (2a+9)$ **(c)** $\displaystyle\sum_{r=1}^{15} \frac{1}{3} \times 2^{r-1}$

6 A geometric series has first term a and common ratio r, with $a > 0$ and $r > 0$.

   (a) The 2nd term of the series is 4 and the 8th term is $\frac{1}{2}$.

   Show that $r = \dfrac{1}{\sqrt{2}}$ and find the value of a in surd form.

   (b) Find the sum to infinity of the series in the form $k(\sqrt{2}+1)$, and
   state the value of the integer k. AQA 2001

7 **(a)** A geometric series has first term 1200 and common ratio r.
   Write down the 2nd and 3rd terms of the series in terms of r.

   (b) A total of £11 700 is to be shared amongst three people.
   The values of the three shares are the first three terms in a geometric series
   with common ratio r. The smallest share is to be £1200.

   (i) Show that r satisfies the equation $4r^2 + 4r - 35 = 0$.

   (ii) Hence, or otherwise, find the value of the largest share. AQA 2002

8 The first term of a geometric series is 20 and the sum to infinity is 50.
   Find the sum of the first 10 terms, correct to 2 d.p.

9 A sequence of terms $u_1, u_2, u_3, \ldots$ is defined by
$$u_n = 3n + 1$$

   (a) Find the sum of the first 20 terms of this sequence.

   (b) The terms u_1, u_9 and u_k are the first three terms of a geometric sequence.
   Find the value of k.

4 Sequences and series 2 | 59

5 Binomial expansion

In this chapter you will learn how to find any term in the expansion of $(1 + x)^n$.

A Pascal's triangle (answers p 142)

To multiply out or **expand** $(a + b)^2$, you can use a table:

$$\begin{array}{c|cc} & a & b \\ \hline a & a^2 & ab \\ b & ab & b^2 \end{array} \qquad (a + b)^2 = a^2 + 2ab + b^2$$

Similarly you can expand $(a + b)^3$ by multiplying $(a^2 + 2ab + b^2)$ by $(a + b)$:

$$\begin{array}{c|ccc} & a^2 & 2ab & b^2 \\ \hline a & a^3 & 2a^2b & ab^2 \\ b & a^2b & 2ab^2 & b^3 \end{array} \qquad (a + b)^3 = a^3 + 3a^2b + 3ab^2 + b^3$$

A1 (a) Expand $(a + b)^4$ by multiplying $(a^3 + 3a^2b + 3ab^2 + b^3)$ by $(a + b)$.

(b) Verify that $(a + b)^5 = a^5 + 5a^4b + 10a^3b^2 + 10a^2b^3 + 5ab^4 + b^5$.

Notice these things about the expansion of $(a + b)^5$:

- The terms start with a^5; in each following term the power of a goes down by 1 and the power of b goes up by 1, until b^5 is reached. The total power is always 5.
- The coefficients are 1, 5, 10, 10, 5, 1; they form a symmetrical pattern.

If you detach the coefficients from the expansions, you get an interesting pattern:

$$\begin{aligned} (a + b)^0 &= \mathbf{1} \\ (a + b)^1 &= \mathbf{1}a + \mathbf{1}b \\ (a + b)^2 &= \mathbf{1}a^2 + \mathbf{2}ab + \mathbf{1}b^2 \\ (a + b)^3 &= \mathbf{1}a^3 + \mathbf{3}a^2b + \mathbf{3}ab^2 + \mathbf{1}b^3 \\ (a + b)^4 &= \mathbf{1}a^4 + \mathbf{4}a^3b + \mathbf{6}a^2b^2 + \mathbf{4}ab^3 + \mathbf{1}b^4 \\ (a + b)^5 &= \mathbf{1}a^5 + \mathbf{5}a^4b + \mathbf{10}a^3b^2 + \mathbf{10}a^2b^3 + \mathbf{5}ab^4 + \mathbf{1}b^5 \end{aligned}$$

```
              1
            1   1
          1   2   1
        1   3   3   1
      1   4   6   4   1
    1   5  10  10   5   1
```

The triangular pattern of numbers is called **Pascal's triangle**, after the French mathematician Blaise Pascal (1623–63).

A2 (a) How are the numbers in each row of Pascal's triangle related to the numbers in the previous row?

(b) Write down the next row of the triangle and hence expand $(a + b)^6$.

(c) Can you explain the relationship between the rows of Pascal's triangle? (You might do so using the 'table' method of expansion above.)

Example 1

Expand $(1 + 2x)^4$.

Solution

This comes from the expansion of $(a + b)^4$, with a replaced by 1, and b by 2x.

The expansion starts with 1^4.
The next term includes 1^3 and $(2x)^1$.
After this comes a term with 1^2 and $(2x)^2$, and so on.
The coefficients, from Pascal's triangle, are 1, 4, 6, 4, 1.

The expansion is $(1 + 2x)^4 = 1^4 + 4\times1^3\times(2x)^1 + 6\times1^2\times(2x)^2 + 4\times1^1\times(2x)^3 + (2x)^4$

$$= 1 + 4\times2x + 6\times4x^2 + 4\times8x^3 + 16x^4$$
$$= 1 + 8x + 24x^2 + 32x^3 + 16x^4$$

Example 2

Expand $(1 - 3x)^3$.

Solution

This comes from the expansion of $(a + b)^3$, with a replaced by 1, and b by –3x.

The expansion is $(1 - 3x)^3 = 1^3 + 3\times1^2\times(-3x)^1 + 3\times1^1\times(-3x)^2 + (-3x)^3$

$$= 1 - 9x + 27x^2 - 27x^3$$

Exercise A (answers p 142)

Use Pascal's triangle (extended if necessary) to answer these questions.

1 Expand $(1 + x)^3$.

2 Expand each of these.

   (a) $(1 + 2x)^3$ **(b)** $(1 + 2x)^5$ **(c)** $(1 - x)^6$ **(d)** $(1 - 3x)^6$ **(e)** $\left(1 + \frac{1}{2}x\right)^7$

3 Expand   **(a)** $\left(1 - \frac{1}{2}x\right)^5$ **(b)** $(2 + x)^3$ **(c)** $(3 - 2x)^4$

4 (a) Expand $(1 + x)^8$ up to and including the term in x^3.

   (b) By substituting $x = 0.1$ in your result for (a), calculate an approximate value for $(1.1)^8$.

   (c) By means of a suitable substitution, use your result for (a) to calculate an approximate value for $(0.9)^8$.

If n is small, then the expansion of $(a + b)^n$ can be found by extending Pascal's triangle as far as is necessary.

However, for large values of n this method is cumbersome. What is needed is a way of calculating the coefficients for a given value of n. This is provided by the **binomial theorem**. In order to understand it, you need to know something about arrangements.

B Arrangements (answers p 142)

Suppose you have four letters: A, B, C, D. They can be arranged in order in different ways, for example ACDB, CBDA, DBAC, and so on. (Another word for an arrangement in order is 'permutation'.)

The first letter can be A, B, C or D. Each of these 4 choices can be followed by any of the 3 others, so these are the possible choices for the first two letters:

A then B, C or D: AB... AC... AD...
B then A, C or D: BA... BC... BD...
C then A, B or D: CA... CB... CD...
D then A, B or C: DA... DB... DC...

There are thus 12 choices for the first two letters. This is because there are 4 ways of choosing the first letter and each choice can be combined with 3 ways of choosing the second letter.

Each of these 12 possibilities can be followed by either of the remaining 2 letters. For example, AB can be followed by either C or D, giving ABC..., ABD... So altogether there are 24 choices for the first three letters.

Finally, for the fourth letter there is only one choice – the last remaining letter. For example, ABD must be followed by C, giving ABDC. So there are also 24 arrangements of all four letters.

B1 (a) How many arrangements are there of the five letters A, B, C, D, E?

(b) How can you work out the number of arrangements without having to list them all and count them?

Suppose you have seven letters to arrange in order. There are 7 choices for the first letter. Each of these can be combined with 6 choices for the second letter, and so on:

	1st		2nd		3rd		4th		5th		6th		7th	
Number of arrangements of 7 letters =	7	×	6	×	5	×	4	×	3	×	2	×	1	= 5040

The number $7 \times 6 \times 5 \times ... \times 2 \times 1$ is called **7 factorial** (written 7!).

In general,

$$n! = n(n-1)(n-2)(n-3) \times ... \times 3 \times 2 \times 1$$

B2 (a) Calculate the value of 6!.

(b) Given that $9! = 362\,880$, calculate 10!.

So far you have been looking at arrangements of a set of different letters. Now suppose that the letters are not all different, for example A, A, B, C.

Here are some of the arrangements: AACB, BAAC, CABA, ...

B3 (a) How many arrangements are there of the letters A, A, B, C?

(b) Why is the number half the number of arrangements of four different letters?

To see the effect of making some letters identical, first distinguish the identical letters. Think of the set A, A, B, C as A_1, A_2, B, C.

There are $4! = 24$ ways of arranging the four letters A_1, A_2, B, C. Here are some of them:

$$A_1A_2BC \quad A_2A_1BC \quad A_1BA_2C \quad A_2BA_1C \quad BCA_1A_2 \quad BCA_2A_1 \quad \ldots$$

Notice that these arrangements come in pairs, for example A_1A_2BC and A_2A_1BC. As the two letter As are really the same, both arrangements in this pair correspond to the same arrangement AABC.

So the number of arrangements when the two As are identical is $\dfrac{4!}{2} = 12$.

D **B4** Suppose you have the set A, A, A, B, C. First distinguish the As as A_1, A_2, A_3.

    (a) How many arrangements are there of the five different letters A_1, A_2, A_3, B, C?

    (b) Here is one of the arrangements: $A_1BA_3A_2C$.
    How many arrangements (including this one) correspond to the arrangement ABAAC?

    (c) How many arrangements are there of the set A, A, A, B, C?

Suppose three letters in a set of six are identical: A, A, A, B, C, D.
If the three As are distinguished, then the set becomes A_1, A_2, A_3, B, C, D and there are 6! arrangements.

These arrangements can be split up into groups
according to the positions occupied by the three As.
For example, one group is shown on the right.
This group corresponds to the arrangement AABDAC.

$$
\begin{array}{l}
A_1A_2BDA_3C \\
A_1A_3BDA_2C \\
A_2A_1BDA_3C \\
A_2A_3BDA_1C \\
A_3A_1BDA_2C \\
A_3A_2BDA_1C
\end{array}
$$

There are 3! arrangements in each group because there are 3! ways of arranging the 3 As within the group.

So when the As are identical, the number of arrangements is $\dfrac{6!}{3!} = 120$.

The general formula is this:

The number of arrangements of a set of n objects when r of them are identical is $\dfrac{n!}{r!}$.

Arrangements with objects of only two kinds

The special case that will be needed for the binomial theorem is where the set consists of n objects (letters) of which r are of one kind and the remaining $n - r$ are of another.

For example, suppose the set is A, A, A, A, B, B, B.

If all the As and all the Bs are distinguished, then there are 7! arrangements altogether.

Because the four As are identical, you have to divide by 4!. This gives $\dfrac{7!}{4!}$ arrangements in which the As are identical.
But because the three Bs are identical, you then have to divide this number by 3!.

Number of arrangements of A, A, A, A, B, B, B $= \dfrac{7!}{4! \times 3!} = \dfrac{7 \times 6 \times 5 \times 4 \times 3 \times 2 \times 1}{(4 \times 3 \times 2 \times 1) \times (3 \times 2 \times 1)}$

Notice that many of the factors in the numerator and denominator cancel out.

After cancelling out as many as possible, the result is $\dfrac{7 \times 6 \times 5}{3 \times 2 \times 1} = 35$.

The number of ways of arranging n objects of which r are of one type and $n - r$ of another is denoted by the symbol $\binom{n}{r}$. Its value is given by $\binom{n}{r} = \dfrac{n!}{r!(n-r)!}$.

In practice, many factors in the numerator and denominator cancel out.

For example, $\binom{8}{3} = \dfrac{8!}{3! \times 5!} = \dfrac{8 \times 7 \times 6 \times 5 \times 4 \times 3 \times 2 \times 1}{(3 \times 2 \times 1) \times (5 \times 4 \times 3 \times 2 \times 1)} = \dfrac{8 \times 7 \times 6}{3 \times 2 \times 1}$.

This leads to another formula:

$$\binom{n}{r} = \frac{n(n-1)(n-2)\dots}{r!}$$

Continue until you have r factors in the numerator.

So $\binom{n}{1} = n$ $\binom{n}{2} = \dfrac{n(n-1)}{2!}$ $\binom{n}{3} = \dfrac{n(n-1)(n-2)}{3!}$

Written in this way, the general formula is

$$\binom{n}{r} = \frac{n(n-1)(n-2)\dots(n-r+1)}{r!}$$

The rth factor here is $n - (r - 1)$ or $n - r + 1$.

Your calculator may use a different notation: ${}_nC_r$ or ${}^nC_r$. To calculate $\binom{7}{3}$, enter 7, press ${}_nC_r$ and then enter 3 = .

The letter 'C' in this notation stands for 'combination', which arises as follows. Suppose you have 7 people and you want to select a group of 3 from them, where the order of selection does not matter. Each 'combination' of 3 people corresponds to saying 'yes' (Y) to 3 people and 'no' (N) to the other 4 people. Here, for example, is one possible combination: Person: A B C D E F G

Decision: Y N N Y N Y N

Each combination corresponds to an arrangement of 3 Ys and 4 Ns.

So the number of combinations is $\binom{7}{3}$.

B5 Use one of the formulae above to calculate $\binom{9}{3}$. Then check using a calculator.

B6 Use a calculator to find the value of   (a) $\binom{6}{2}$ (b) $\binom{9}{4}$ (c) $\binom{20}{10}$

B7 (a) $\binom{7}{0}$ is the number of arrangements of 7 objects, of which none are of one type and 7 are of the other. So what is its value?

    (b) If you use the factorial formula to work out $\binom{7}{0}$, what value must you give to $0!$?

C The binomial theorem (answers p 142)

You should now be in a position to see how the work on arrangements relates to expanding expressions of the form $(a + b)^n$.

Consider $(a + b)^2 = (a + b)(a + b)$.

Normally when you expand this you get $a^2 + 2ab + b^2$.
However, for the time being distinguish between ab and ba.
ab arises from multiplying a in the first bracket by b in the second.
ba arises from multiplying b in the first bracket by a in the second.

$$ \overbrace{}^{ab} \atop (a + b)(a + b) \atop \underbrace{}_{ba} $$

Write a^2 as aa and b^2 as bb.

So $(a + b)^2$ is expanded as $aa + ab + ba + bb$.

C1 $(a + b)^3 = (aa + ab + ba + bb)(a + b)$.
Write out the expansion of $(a + b)^3$ in the form $aaa + aab + \ldots$
(In other words, don't simplify, combine terms or use indices.)

The expansion of $(a + b)^4$ is the result of multiplying out $(a + b)(a + b)(a + b)(a + b)$.
Each term arises from multiplying as from some brackets by bs from the others.

For example, this combination $(a + b)(a + b)(a + b)(a + b)$ gives the term $abba$.

The expansion of $(a + b)^4$, written without any simplification or index notation, is as follows:

$$
\begin{aligned}
(a + b)^4 = \quad & aaaa \\
& + aaab + aaba + abaa + baaa \\
& + aabb + abab + abba + baab + baba + bbaa \\
& + abbb + babb + bbab + bbba \\
& + bbbb
\end{aligned}
$$

The first term is of course a^4.

The second line contains all the terms that correspond to a^3b.
They consist of all the arrangements of 1 b and 3 as, so the coefficient of a^3b is $\binom{4}{1} = 4$.

The next line contains all the terms that correspond to a^2b^2.
They consist of all the arrangements of 2 bs and 2 as, so the coefficient of a^2b^2 is $\binom{4}{2} = 6$.

Similarly for the other two lines.

So $(a + b)^4 = a^4 + \binom{4}{1}a^3b + \binom{4}{2}a^2b^2 + \binom{4}{3}ab^3 + b^4$

This expansion of $(a + b)^4$ is an example of the **binomial theorem**:

$$ (a + b)^n = a^n + \binom{n}{1}a^{n-1}b + \binom{n}{2}a^{n-2}b^2 + \binom{n}{3}a^{n-3}b^3 + \ldots + b^n $$

An important special case arises by letting $a = 1$ and $b = x$:

K $$(1+x)^n = 1 + \binom{n}{1}x + \binom{n}{2}x^2 + \binom{n}{3}x^3 + \dots + x^n$$

which can also be written:

$$(1+x)^n = 1 + nx + \frac{n(n-1)}{2!}x^2 + \frac{n(n-1)(n-2)}{3!}x^3 + \dots + x^n$$

The values of the binomial coefficients can be found either from a calculator or by using one of the formulae. If the value of n is small, you could also find the coefficients by extending Pascal's triangle.

C2 (a) Write down the first four terms in the expansion of $(1 + x)^{10}$.

(b) By replacing x by $-x$, write down the first four terms in the expansion of $(1 - x)^{10}$.

Example 3

Find the coefficient of y^4 in the expansion of $(1 + 3y)^9$.

Solution

The term containing y^4 is $\binom{9}{4}(3y)^4 = 126 \times 81y^4 = 10\,206y^4$.

So the coefficient of y^4 is $10\,206$.

Example 4

Use the binomial theorem to find the value of $(1.02)^8$ correct to two decimal places.

Solution

Use the expansion of $(1 + x)^n$ with $x = 0.02$ and $n = 8$. Continue the expansion until the terms become so small that they do not affect the second decimal place.

$$(1.02)^8 = 1 + \binom{8}{1} \times (0.02) + \binom{8}{2} \times (0.02)^2 + \binom{8}{3} \times (0.02)^3 + \dots$$

$$= 1 + 8 \times 0.02 + 28 \times 0.0004 + 56 \times 0.000\,008 + \dots$$

$$= 1 + 0.16 + 0.0112 + 0.000\,448 + \dots = 1.17 \text{ (to 2 d.p.)}$$

Example 5

Find the coefficient of x^2 in the expansion of $(1 + 4x)^4(1 - 2x)^6$.

Solution

Expand each factor as far as the x^2 term. $(1 + 4x)^4 = 1 + 16x + 96x^2 + \dots$
$(1 - 2x)^6 = 1 - 12x + 60x^2 - \dots$

Pick out the terms that will give an x^2 when multiplied.

$(1 + 16x + 96x^2)(1 - 12x + 60x^2)$ Term in x^2 is $60x^2 - 192x^2 + 96x^2 = -36x^2$

So the coefficient of x^2 is -36.

Example 6

Find the term containing x^3 in the expansion of $(3 - 2x)^7$.

Solution

Use the binomial theorem for $(a + b)^n$ with $a = 3$, $b = -2x$ and $n = 7$.

The term containing x^3 is $\binom{7}{3} \times 3^4 \times (-2x)^3 = 35 \times 81 \times (-8x^3) = -22\,680x^3$.

Exercise C (answers p 142)

1 Write down the first four terms in the expansion of $(1 + x)^{12}$.

2 Find the coefficient of

(a) x^5 in the expansion of $(1 + x)^{10}$ (b) x^3 in the expansion of $(1 + x)^{20}$

3 Use the binomial theorem to find the value of $(1.03)^7$ correct to two decimal places.

4 Find the first four terms in the expansion of

(a) $(1 + 2x)^9$ (b) $(1 - 3x)^8$ (c) $\left(1 + \tfrac{1}{2}x\right)^{15}$ (d) $\left(1 - \tfrac{1}{5}x\right)^7$

5 (a) Expand $(1 - 2x)^5$ as far as the term in x^2.

(b) Hence find the coefficient of x^2 in the expansion of $(3 - 4x - x^2)(1 - 2x)^5$.

6 Find the coefficient of x^3 in the expansion of

(a) $(2 + x)^9$ (b) $(2 - x)^9$ (c) $(2 + 3x)^9$

7 In the expansion of $(1 + kx)^n$, where k and n are positive integers, the coefficient of x^3 is twice the coefficient of x^2.

(a) Prove that $n = 2 + \dfrac{6}{k}$.   (b) Find all the possible pairs of values of k and n.

Key points

- $n!$ (n factorial) is $n(n - 1)(n - 2)(n - 3) \times \ldots \times 3 \times 2 \times 1$ (p 62)

- $(1 + x)^n = 1 + \binom{n}{1}x + \binom{n}{2}x^2 + \binom{n}{3}x^3 + \ldots + x^n$

  The coefficient of x^r in this expansion is $\binom{n}{r} = \dfrac{n!}{r!(n-r)!} = \dfrac{n(n-1)(n-2)\ldots(n-r+1)}{r!}$

                                                      (pp 64, 66)

Test yourself (answers p 142)

1 Write down the first four terms in the expansion of $(1 + x)^{20}$.

2 Find the coefficient of x^3 in the expansion of   (a) $(1 + 4x)^7$ (b) $(1 - 2x)^{10}$

3 Expand $(1 + 2x)^5\left(1 - \tfrac{1}{2}x\right)^8$ as far as the term in x^2.

6 Trigonometry 1

In this chapter you will
- revise the sine and cosine ratios between 0° and 180°
- find lengths and angles in any triangle, using the sine and cosine rules
- calculate the area of any triangle
- learn about radian measure for angles
- calculate lengths of arcs and areas of sectors of circles

A Sine and cosine: revision (answers p 143)

The diagram shows a circle with radius 1 unit.
This is called the unit circle.

The angle $\theta°$ is measured in an anticlockwise direction
from the positive x-axis.

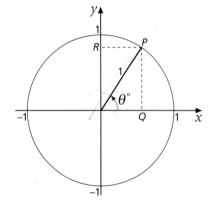

A1 Explain why the coordinates of P are $(\cos \theta°, \sin \theta°)$.

Cos $\theta°$ can be defined as the x-coordinate of P.
Sin $\theta°$ can be defined as the y-coordinate of P.

This allows us to define $\cos \theta°$ and $\sin \theta°$ for any angle $\theta°$.

A2 Without using a calculator, write down each of these.

    (a) $\cos 0°$ (b) $\sin 0°$ (c) $\sin 90°$ (d) $\cos 90°$

    (e) $\sin 180°$ (f) $\cos 270°$ (g) $\sin -90°$ (h) $\cos -90°$

A3 Without using a calculator, write down whether each of these is positive or negative.

    (a) $\cos 30°$ (b) $\sin 120°$ (c) $\cos 120°$ (d) $\cos 200°$

    (e) $\sin 330°$ (f) $\cos 330°$ (g) $\sin 220°$ (h) $\cos -120°$

A4 (a) When $90° < \theta° < 180°$, is the x-coordinate of P positive or negative?
       What does this tell you about $\cos \theta°$ when $90° < \theta° < 180°$?

    (b) What can you say about $\sin \theta°$ when $90° < \theta° < 180°$?

A5 Use the unit circle to show that $\sin 20° = \sin 160°$.

A6 Use the unit circle to show that $\sin (180° - \theta°) = \sin \theta°$ for all values
of $\theta°$ between 0° and 180°.

A7 Draw a sketch graph of $y = \sin \theta°$ for $0° < \theta° < 180°$.

A8 Use the unit circle to show that $\cos 20° = -\cos 160°$.

A9 Use the unit circle to show that $\cos(180° - \theta°) = -\cos\theta°$ for all values of $\theta°$ between 0° and 180°.

A10 Draw a sketch graph of $y = \cos\theta°$ for $0° < \theta° < 180°$.

A11 Use a calculator to find (to the nearest degree) the acute angle $\theta°$ such that $\sin\theta° = 0.63$. Use your previous results to find another angle (less than 360°) whose sine is 0.63.

A12 Use a calculator to find (to the nearest degree) the acute angle $\theta°$ such that $\cos\theta° = 0.63$. Use your previous results to find an obtuse angle whose cosine is –0.63.

Example 1

Find two angles (to the nearest degree) in the range $0° < \theta° < 180°$ such that $\sin\theta° = 0.8$.

Solution

Key in $\sin^{-1}0.8$

$\theta° = 53°$ is one angle.

To obtain the other angle think about the unit circle ...   *... or the graph of* $\sin\theta°$.

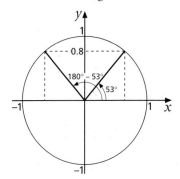   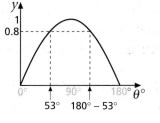

The other angle is $180° - 53° = 127°$.

Exercise A (answers p 143)

1 State whether each of these is positive or negative.
   (a) $\sin 95°$ (b) $\cos 95°$ (c) $\sin 170°$ (d) $\cos 170°$

2 (a) Use your calculator to find (to the nearest degree) the angle between 0° and 90° whose sine is 0.34.
   (b) Hence find the two solutions to $\sin\theta° = 0.34$ $(0° < \theta° < 180°)$.

3 Solve each of these equations, giving solutions between 0° and 180° to the nearest degree.
   (a) $\sin\theta° = 0.9$ (b) $\cos\theta° = 0.9$ (c) $\sin\theta° = 0.45$ (d) $\cos\theta° = -0.45$
   (e) $\sin\theta° = 0.53$ (f) $\cos\theta° = 0.53$ (g) $\sin\theta° = 0.07$ (h) $\cos\theta° = -0.07$

*4 Explain why, if $0° < \theta° < 180°$ and $-1 < k < 1$, $\sin\theta° = k$ has either no solution or two solutions for $\theta°$, but $\cos\theta° = k$ always has one solution.

B Cosine rule (answers p 143)

It is easy to 'solve' a right-angled triangle (find its unknown angles and sides)
by using Pythagoras's theorem and the sine, cosine and tangent ratios.
But if a triangle is not right-angled, we need other methods.

B1 Consider triangle ABC.

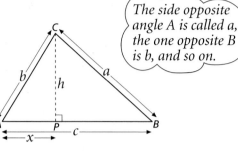

The side opposite angle A is called a, the one opposite B is b, and so on.

(a) Write PB in terms of c and x.

(b) Use Pythagoras in triangle CPB to write an
   expression for h^2 in terms of a, x and c.

(c) Use Pythagoras in triangle CPA to write an
   expression for h^2 in terms of b and x.

(d) Put your two expressions for h^2 equal
   to each other, and make a^2 the subject.

(e) Expand brackets and simplify this formula for a^2.

(f) In triangle CPA, write an expression for x in terms of b and angle A.

(g) Substitute the expression for x in the formula you obtained in part (e).
   Check that you have obtained $a^2 = b^2 + c^2 - 2bc\cos A$.

B2 Prove that the rule you obtained in B1
is still true when angle A is obtuse.

(Hint: you will need to use the fact
that $\cos(180° - \theta°) = -\cos\theta°$.)

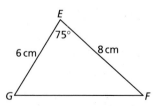

K The **cosine rule** states that $a^2 = b^2 + c^2 - 2bc\cos A$.

Similarly, $b^2 = a^2 + c^2 - 2ac\cos B$ and $c^2 = a^2 + b^2 - 2ab\cos C$.

Example 2

Find the length of side GF in triangle EFG.

Solution

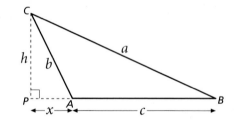

*The triangle is not right-angled. You know two sides
and the enclosed angle, so use the cosine rule.*

In triangle EFG, $e^2 = f^2 + g^2 - 2fg\cos E$

$$e^2 = 6^2 + 8^2 - 2\times6\times8\times\cos75°$$
$$e^2 = 75.153\ldots$$
$$e = 8.67 \text{ (to 2 d.p.)}$$

So the length of GF is 8.67 cm (to 2 d.p.).

Example 3

Find angle R in triangle PQR.

Solution

You know all three sides of the triangle, so use the cosine rule.

In triangle PQR, $\qquad r^2 = p^2 + q^2 - 2pq \cos R$

$$13.5^2 = 8.8^2 + 7.1^2 - 2 \times 8.8 \times 7.1 \times \cos R$$

$$\Rightarrow \quad 2 \times 8.8 \times 7.1 \times \cos R = 8.8^2 + 7.1^2 - 13.5^2$$

$$\Rightarrow \qquad \cos R = \frac{8.8^2 + 7.1^2 - 13.5^2}{2 \times 8.8 \times 7.1}$$

so $\quad \cos R = -0.4353\ldots$

$$R = 115.8\ldots°$$

$$= 116° \text{ to the nearest degree}$$

The cosine is negative, so the angle is obtuse.

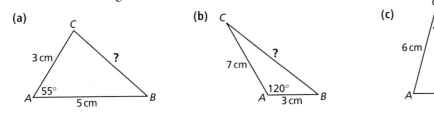

Exercise B (answers p 143)

1 Work out the length marked **?** in each of these triangles.

(a)   (b)   (c)

2 Work out the angle marked **?** in each of these triangles.

(a)   (b)   (c)

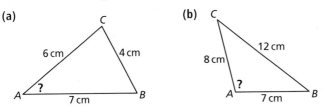
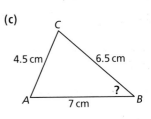

3 The hands of a clock are 10 cm and 7 cm long.
Calculate the distance between their tips when it is exactly 2 o'clock.

4 A triangle has sides 4 cm, 5 cm and 7 cm.
Calculate all its angles.

5 A is 2.1 km due north of B.
C is 3.7 km from B on a bearing of 136°.
Find the distance from C to A.

*6 In the triangle shown, $BC = 8$, $CA = 6$, $AB = 7$
and M is the mid-point of BC. Angle $AMC = \theta°$.

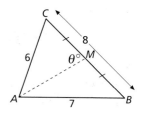

(a) Use the cosine rule to write down an expression
for AC^2 in terms of $\cos\theta°$, CM and AM.

(b) Write an expression for AB^2 in terms of $\cos\theta°$, BM and AM.

(c) Add the expressions you obtained in (a) and (b),
and hence calculate the length of AM.

C Sine rule (answers p 144)

The cosine rule enables you to find a side when you know two sides and the
angle they enclose, or an angle when you know all three sides.

You can solve other triangles using the **sine rule**.

C1 (a) In triangle APC, write h in terms of b and angle A.

(b) In triangle BPC, write h in terms of a and angle B.

(c) Put these two expressions for h equal to each other.

(d) Divide both sides of your equation in (c),
first by $\sin A$, and then by $\sin B$.

(e) Check that your result is $\dfrac{a}{\sin A} = \dfrac{b}{\sin B}$

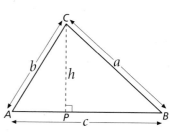

If we start with sides b and c and angles B and C, we can prove that $\dfrac{b}{\sin B} = \dfrac{c}{\sin C}$.

Combining these two results we have the **sine rule**:
$$\frac{a}{\sin A} = \frac{b}{\sin B} = \frac{c}{\sin C}$$

C2 In triangle ABC, angle A is obtuse.

(a) In triangle PAC, express h in
terms of b and angle PAC.

(b) Express angle PAC in terms of
angle A (i.e. angle CAB).
Rewrite the expression for h you
obtained in (a) in terms of angle A.

(c) Use the fact that $\sin(180° - \theta°) = \sin\theta°$ to simplify your expression.

(d) Now write an expression for h in terms of side a and angle B.

(e) Hence show that in this triangle $\dfrac{a}{\sin A} = \dfrac{b}{\sin B}$.

Since angles B and C are acute, $\dfrac{b}{\sin B} = \dfrac{c}{\sin C}$, as before. So $\dfrac{a}{\sin A} = \dfrac{b}{\sin B} = \dfrac{c}{\sin C}$.

Example 4

Find the length of side ST in triangle RST.

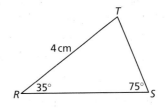

Solution

You know side RT and the angle opposite it.
You know the angle opposite side ST, so use the sine rule.

In triangle RST, $\dfrac{r}{\sin R} = \dfrac{s}{\sin S} = \dfrac{t}{\sin T}$ *You don't need the $\dfrac{t}{\sin T}$ part and could omit it.*

$$\dfrac{r}{\sin 35°} = \dfrac{4}{\sin 75°}$$

$$\Rightarrow \quad r = \dfrac{4 \times \sin 35°}{\sin 75°} = 2.375\ldots$$

so $ST = 2.4\,\text{cm}$ (to 1 d.p.)

Example 5

Find angle D in triangle DEF.

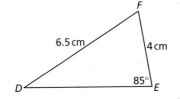

Solution

You know side e and angle E.
You know side d, so use the sine rule.

In triangle DEF, $\dfrac{d}{\sin D} = \dfrac{e}{\sin E}$

$$\dfrac{4}{\sin D} = \dfrac{6.5}{\sin 85°}$$

$$\Rightarrow \quad 4 \times \sin 85° = 6.5 \times \sin D$$

$$\Rightarrow \quad \sin D = \dfrac{4 \times \sin 85°}{6.5} = 0.613\ldots$$

Use your calculator. $D = 38°$ (to the nearest degree)   *$\sin \theta°$ and $\sin(180° - \theta°)$*
Another answer is therefore $D = 180° - 38° = 142°$ *both have the same value.*

But if $D = 142°$, then the angle sum of triangle DEF
is clearly greater than $180°$.

Hence the only possible solution here is
$D = 38°$ (to the nearest degree).

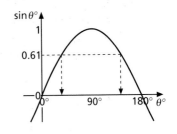

Example 6

Find angle R in triangle PQR.

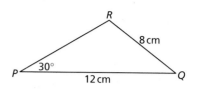

Solution

In triangle PQR, $\dfrac{p}{\sin P} = \dfrac{r}{\sin R}$

$$\frac{8}{\sin 30°} = \frac{12}{\sin R}$$

$$\Rightarrow \quad 8\sin R = 12\sin 30°$$

$$\Rightarrow \quad \sin R = \frac{12\sin 30°}{8} = 0.75$$

Use your calculator. $R = 49°$ (to the nearest degree)
Another answer is therefore $R = 180° - 49° = 131°$

Check whether both answers are possible.

If $R = 49°$, then $Q = 180° - 30° - 49° = 101°$
If $R = 131°$, then $Q = 180° - 30° - 131° = 19°$

Both answers are possible.

So $R = 49°$ or $131°$ (to the nearest degree).

$\sin \theta°$ and $\sin(180° - \theta°)$ both have the same value.

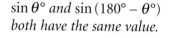
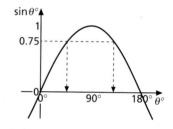

It may be helpful to sketch the two solutions as a further check.

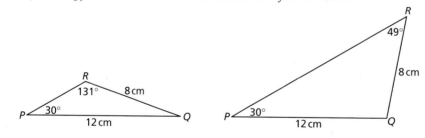

Exercise C (answers p 144)

1 Find the length marked **?** in each of these triangles.

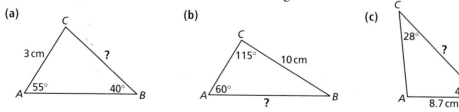

2 In triangle ABC, $c = 11$ cm, $a = 12$ cm and angle $A = 68°$.

(a) Draw a sketch of triangle ABC.

(b) Use the sine rule to calculate the value of $\sin C$.

(c) Your result in (b) can lead to two different values for angle C.
What are these (to the nearest degree)?

(d) For each of your possible values of angle C, find the value of angle B.

(e) Write down the value or values of angle C that are possible.
For each possible value of C draw a rough sketch of the triangle.

3 Find the angle marked **?** in each of these triangles.
Where there is more than one solution, give both.

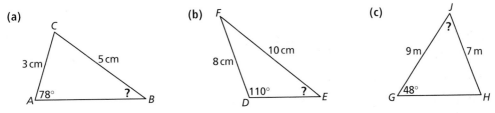

(a)   (b)   (c)

D Both rules

To solve many triangles you will need to use a rule twice, or use the sine rule and the cosine rule.

Example 7

Solve triangle DEF.

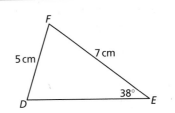

Solution

'Solve' means find all the unknown angles and sides.

Decide which rule to use first.
In this case, the sine rule is possible.

In triangle DEF, $\quad \dfrac{d}{\sin D} = \dfrac{e}{\sin E} = \dfrac{f}{\sin F}$

$\qquad \dfrac{7}{\sin D} = \dfrac{5}{\sin 38°} \qquad\qquad \dfrac{f}{\sin F}$ *is not needed.*

$\qquad \Rightarrow 7 \sin 38° = 5 \sin D$

$\qquad \Rightarrow \quad \sin D = \dfrac{7 \sin 38°}{5} = 0.8619\ldots$

Use the calculator. $\qquad\qquad D = 59.53\ldots° = 59.5°$ (to 1 d.p.)
Another answer is therefore $\quad D = 180° - 59.5° = 120.5°$

Check whether both answers are possible.

$\qquad\qquad$ If $D = 59.5°$ then $F = 180° - 38° - 59.5° = 82.5°$
$\qquad\qquad$ If $D = 120.5°$ then $F = 180° - 38° - 120.5° = 21.5°$

Both answers are possible. So $D = 59.5°$ or $120.5°$ (to 1 d.p.) $\qquad$ *(Solution continues over.)*

Deal with each possible value of D separately.
For each value, draw a sketch showing what you know so far.

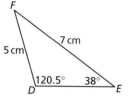

Use the result you obtained before rounding.

If $D = 59.53...°$

then $F = 180° - 38° - 59.53...° = 82.46...°$

Now use the sine rule again.

$$\frac{f}{\sin 82.46...°} = \frac{5}{\sin 38°}$$

$$\Rightarrow \qquad f = \frac{5\sin 82.46...°}{\sin 38°} = 8.05... = 8.1 \text{ (1 d.p.)}$$

So the first solution is $D = 59.5°$, $F = 82.5°$ and $DE = 8.1$ cm
(each answer to 1 d.p.).

Alternatively, if $D = 180° - 59.53...° = 120.46...°$
then $F = 180° - 38° - 120.46...° = 21.53...°$

and $\qquad \dfrac{f}{\sin 21.53...°} = \dfrac{5}{\sin 38°}$

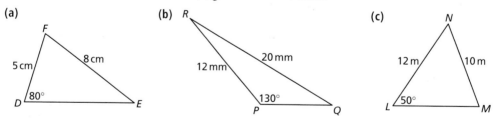

$$\Rightarrow \qquad f = \frac{5\sin 21.53...°}{\sin 38°} = 2.98... = 3.0 \text{ (1 d.p.)}$$

So the second solution is $D = 120.5°$, $F = 21.5°$ and $DE = 3.0$ cm (answers to 1 d.p.).

Exercise D (answers p 144)

1 Use the sine rule to solve (find all the unknown angles and sides in)
each of these triangles.
If there is more than one solution, give both solutions.

(a) (b) (c)

2 Use the cosine rule and then the sine rule to solve these triangles.

(a) (b)

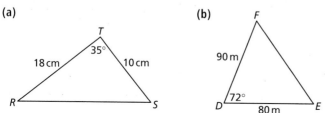

3 Solve these triangles.

(a)

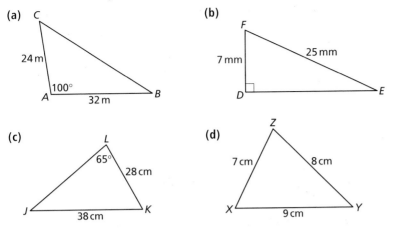

(b)

(c)

(d)

E Area of a triangle

There is a simple formula for the area of a triangle, when you know two sides and the angle between them.

In triangle PBC, $h = a \sin B$.

The area of triangle $ABC = \frac{1}{2}$ base$\times$height

$$= \frac{1}{2}c \times h = \frac{1}{2}c \times a \sin B$$

$$= \frac{1}{2}ac \sin B$$

By drawing perpendiculars to the other two sides we can show that:

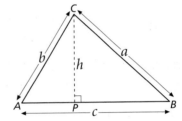

Area of triangle ABC
$= \frac{1}{2}ab \sin C = \frac{1}{2}bc \sin A = \frac{1}{2}ac \sin B$

This result also holds true for an obtuse-angled triangle.

Example 8

Find the area of triangle RST.

Solution

Area of triangle RST

$$= \frac{1}{2}rt \sin S$$

$$= \frac{1}{2} \times 6 \times 7 \times \sin 40°$$

$$= 13.498...$$

You know S, so the lengths in the formula are r and t.

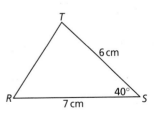

The area of triangle RST is $13.5 \, \text{cm}^2$ (to 1 d.p.).

Example 9

Find the area of triangle *PQR*.

Solution

To find the area you need two sides and the included angle.
So first find an angle, using the cosine rule.
Any angle will do; here angle P is found.

$$p^2 = q^2 + r^2 - 2qr\cos P$$
$$8^2 = 9^2 + 12^2 - 2\times9\times12\times\cos P$$

$$\cos P = \frac{9^2 + 12^2 - 8^2}{2\times9\times12} = 0.745\ldots$$

$$P = 41.8\ldots°$$ *Don't lose any accuracy at this stage.*

So area of triangle $PQR = \frac{1}{2}qr\sin P$

$$= \frac{1}{2}\times9\times12\times\sin41.8\ldots°$$
$$= 35.9991\ldots$$

So the area is $36\,\text{cm}^2$ (to the nearest cm^2).

Exercise E (answers p 144)

1 Find the area of each triangle.

(a)   (b)   (c)

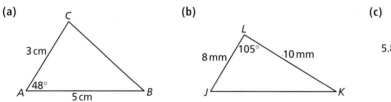
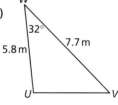

2 Triangle *RST* has *RS* = 8 cm, *ST* = 10 cm and *TR* = 11 cm.

(a) Use the cosine rule to find one angle of the triangle.

(b) Use your result to find the area of the triangle.

3 Find the area of each of these triangles.

(a)   (b)   (c)

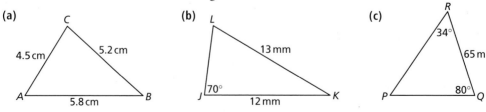

F Radians and arcs (answers p 144)

We measure angles in degrees for historical reasons:
the ancient Babylonians divided their day into 360 units
of time, and their circle into 360 units too.

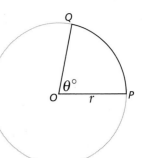

But using the degree as the unit of angle measurement
leads to complicated formulas.

For example, the distance all round the circle shown is $2\pi r$.

The arc PQ, which subtends an angle of θ degrees at the centre,
is therefore $\dfrac{\theta}{360}$ of the whole circle, or $\dfrac{\theta}{360} \times 2\pi r = \dfrac{\pi r\theta}{180}$.

To simplify this formula we use a different measure of angle
in more advanced mathematics.

This measure is called the **radian**.

One radian is defined as the angle subtended at the centre
of a circle radius r by an arc of length r (i.e. equal to the radius).

As an arc of length r subtends an angle of one radian, so the
whole circumference of the circle ($2\pi r$) subtends 2π radians.

So $360° = 2\pi$ radians.

F1 Write the following angles in radians, giving answers in terms of π.

(a) 180°   (b) 90°   (c) 60°   (d) 30°   (e) 270°   (f) 1°

F2 Work out the size of one radian in degrees.

F3 In a circle of radius r, an angle of one radian is subtended by an arc of length r.

(a) What length arc subtends an angle of 2 radians?

(b) What length arc subtends an angle of $\frac{1}{2}$ radian?

(c) What length arc subtends an angle of θ radians?

F4 A circle has a radius of 8 cm.
An arc subtends an angle of 0.25 radians at the centre of the circle.
How long is the arc, in centimetres?

Angles can be measured in radians, where 2π radians $= 360°$.
We can write 2π radians as $2\pi^c$ or 2π rad, but the ^{c} or rad is normally omitted.

Other important equivalents that you should remember are
$$180° = \pi \text{ rad} \quad 90° = \frac{\pi}{2} \text{ rad} \quad 60° = \frac{\pi}{3} \text{ rad} \quad 45° = \frac{\pi}{4} \text{ rad} \quad 30° = \frac{\pi}{6} \text{ rad}$$

If an arc subtends an angle of θ radians at the centre of a circle radius r,
the length of the arc is $r\theta$.

Example 10

A sector with angle 45° is cut from a circle of radius 8 metres.

Find

(a) the arc length RS (b) the perimeter of the sector

Solution

To use the formula for arc length, you must work in radians.

(a) The arc length $RS = r\theta = 8 \times \dfrac{\pi}{4} = 6.283\ldots$

Arc $RS = 6.3\,\text{m}$ (to 1 d.p.)

(b) Perimeter of sector $= OR + OS + \text{arc } RS = 8 + 8 + 6.283\ldots = 22.283\ldots$

Perimeter $= 22.3\,\text{m}$ (to 1 d.p.)

Some values of sine, cos and tan can be found easily using Pythagoras and symmetry.

A 45° right-angled triangle whose shorter sides are of length 1 unit has (by Pythagoras) a hypotenuse of length $\sqrt{2}$.

Hence $\sin 45° = \cos 45° = \dfrac{1}{\sqrt{2}}$ and $\tan 45° = 1$.

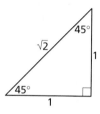

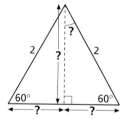

F5 The diagram shows an equilateral triangle with a perpendicular from the apex to the base.

(a) Copy the diagram and fill in the lengths and angle marked with **?**.

(b) Hence write down the sine, cos and tan of both 30° and 60°, giving them in surd form.

K You should know or be able to quickly work out that

$$\sin \frac{\pi}{4} = \sin 45° = \frac{1}{\sqrt{2}} \qquad \cos \frac{\pi}{4} = \cos 45° = \frac{1}{\sqrt{2}} \qquad \tan \frac{\pi}{4} = \tan 45° = 1$$

$$\sin \frac{\pi}{6} = \sin 30° = \tfrac{1}{2} \qquad \cos \frac{\pi}{6} = \cos 30° = \frac{\sqrt{3}}{2} \qquad \tan \frac{\pi}{6} = \tan 30° = \frac{1}{\sqrt{3}}$$

$$\sin \frac{\pi}{3} = \sin 60° = \frac{\sqrt{3}}{2} \qquad \cos \frac{\pi}{3} = \cos 60° = \tfrac{1}{2} \qquad \tan \frac{\pi}{3} = \tan 60° = \sqrt{3}$$

Exercise F (answers p 145)

1 Change the following angles into radians, giving answers in terms of π.

(a) 210°   (b) 135°   (c) 120°   (d) 330°   (e) 300°

2 Change the following angles into degrees.

(a) $\dfrac{\pi}{8}$ (b) $\dfrac{\pi}{10}$ (c) $\dfrac{\pi}{180}$ (d) $\dfrac{\pi}{4}$ (e) $\dfrac{5\pi}{6}$

(f) $\dfrac{5\pi}{4}$ (g) $\dfrac{5\pi}{12}$ (h) $\dfrac{7\pi}{4}$ (i) $\dfrac{2\pi}{9}$ (j) $\dfrac{4\pi}{3}$

3 Copy this table and complete it, giving exact values for sine, cos and tan.
All angles are between 0 and π radians.

Radians	Degrees	$\sin\theta$	$\cos\theta$	$\tan\theta$
$\dfrac{\pi}{6}$		$\dfrac{1}{2}$		$\dfrac{1}{\sqrt{3}}$
$\dfrac{2\pi}{3}$				
	135°			
$\dfrac{5\pi}{6}$				

4 The sector *OAB* is cut from a circle of radius 2 m.

(a) What is the length of arc *AB*?

(b) What is the perimeter of the sector?

5 The curved edge of the pendant shown shaded in the diagram
is an arc of a circle, radius 6 cm, which subtends
an angle of 110° at the centre of the circle.

(a) Calculate the length of the arc.

(b) Calculate the length of the straight line *PQ*.

(c) Hence work out, to 3 s.f., the perimeter of the pendant.

6 A circle has radius 7 cm.
An arc of the circle has length 10 cm.
What angle, in degrees, does the arc subtend at the centre of the circle?

7 A sector of a circle has an angle at the centre of $\dfrac{\pi}{4}$ and a perimeter of 12 cm.
Work out the radius of the circle.

G Area of a sector

The area of a complete circle of radius r is πr^2.

The sector POQ occupies $\dfrac{\theta}{2\pi}$ of the whole circle.

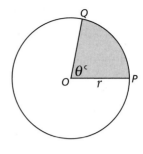

Hence the area of sector POQ is $\dfrac{\theta^c}{2\pi} \times \pi r^2$ or $\frac{1}{2}r^2\theta$.

> **K** The area of a sector of a circle, radius r, that subtends an angle θ at the centre is $\frac{1}{2}r^2\theta$.

Example 11

A sector with angle 55° is cut from a circle of radius 8 metres. Find the area of the sector.

Solution

To use the formula above, work in radians.

$55° = \dfrac{\pi}{180} \times 55$ radians, so the area of the sector is $\frac{1}{2}r^2\theta = \frac{1}{2} \times 8^2 \times \dfrac{\pi}{180} \times 55$

$$= 30.71\ldots$$

The area is $30.7\,\text{m}^2$ (to 1 d.p.).

Example 12

A circle, centre O, has radius 25 mm. A sector OAB of the circle subtends an angle at O of 40°.

Find the area of the segment bounded by the arc AB and the chord AB.

Solution

Draw a sketch.
Area of segment (shaded) = area of sector OAB – area of triangle OAB

To find the area of the sector OAB, work in radians.
$40° = \dfrac{\pi}{180} \times 40$ radians

So area of sector $OAB = \frac{1}{2} \times 25^2 \times \dfrac{\pi}{180} \times 40\ \text{mm}^2 = 218.16\ldots\,\text{mm}^2$ *Do not approximate yet.*

Area of triangle $OAB = \frac{1}{2} \times 25 \times 25 \times \sin 40° = 200.87\ldots\,\text{mm}^2$ *You can use radians or degrees here, as long as your calculator is in the corresponding mode.*

Area of segment $= 218.16\ldots\,\text{mm}^2 - 200.87\ldots\,\text{mm}^2$

$$= 17.29\ldots\,\text{mm}^2 = 17.3\,\text{mm}^2 \text{ (to 1 d.p.)}$$

Exercise G (answers p 145)

1 Find the areas to 1 d.p. of sectors with

   (a) angle 115° and radius 9 cm   **(b)** angle 20° and radius 20 m

   (c) angle 200° and radius 5.5 cm   **(d)** angle 19° and radius 45 mm

2 Find the areas of these sectors in terms of π.

   (a) angle $\frac{\pi}{4}$, radius 8   **(b)** angle 120°, radius 10

3 A sector has an area of 20 cm² and radius 8 cm.
   What angle, in degrees, does it subtend at the centre?

4 A sector has radius r cm and angle at the centre of θ radians.
   The perimeter of the sector is 18 cm.

   (a) Find an expression for θ in terms of r.

   (b) Find an expression for the area of the sector in terms of r.

5 An area in the shape of a sector is to be fenced off
   for a crowd at a concert. The sector has radius 400 m,
   and angle at the centre of 2^c.

   (a) Calculate the length of fence needed for the perimeter.

   (b) Health and Safety inspectors decide that the crowd
   density should not exceed 1 person per 2 m².
   Calculate the maximum crowd.

6 *OAB* is a sector of a circle, centre *O*, radius *r*.
   Find these in terms of r and θ.

   (a) The length *BC*

   (b) The area of triangle *OAB*

   (c) The area of the sector *OAB*

   (d) The area of the shaded segment

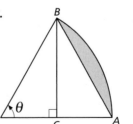

7 A circular cake of diameter 20 cm is cut along *AB*,
   halfway from the centre to the rim.

   (a) Show that the angle θ is 120°.

   (b) Calculate the area of the sector *OAB*, to 1 d.p.

   (c) Work out the area of triangle *OAB*, to 1 d.p.

   (d) Hence find the area of cake cut off, to 1 d.p.

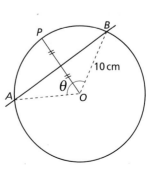

8 (a) The diagram shows an equilateral triangle *ABC* with sides of length 6 cm and an arc *BC* of a circle with centre *A*.

   (i) Write down, in radians, the value of the angle α.

   (ii) Find the length of the arc *BC*.

   (iii) Show that the area of the triangle *ABC* is $9\sqrt{3}$ cm².

   (iv) Show that the area of the sector *ABC* is 6π cm².

  (b) The diagram shows an ornament made from a flat sheet of metal. Its boundary consists of three arcs of circles. The straight lines *AB*, *AC* and *BC* are each of length 6 cm. The arcs *BC*, *AC* and *AB* have centres *A*, *B* and *C* respectively.

   (i) The boundary of the ornament is decorated with gilt edging. Find the total length of the boundary, giving your answer to the nearest centimetre.

   (ii) Find the area of one side of the ornament, giving your answer to the nearest square centimetre.

AQA 2002

Key points

- When solving a triangle *ABC* you can use

    the cosine rule:
$$a^2 = b^2 + c^2 - 2bc\cos A$$
$$b^2 = a^2 + c^2 - 2ac\cos B$$
$$c^2 = a^2 + b^2 - 2ab\cos C$$

    the sine rule:
$$\frac{a}{\sin A} = \frac{b}{\sin B} = \frac{c}{\sin C}$$
    (p 70, 72)

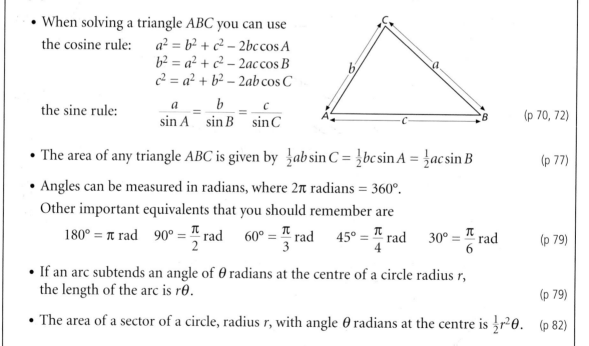

- The area of any triangle *ABC* is given by $\frac{1}{2}ab\sin C = \frac{1}{2}bc\sin A = \frac{1}{2}ac\sin B$ (p 77)

- Angles can be measured in radians, where 2π radians = 360°.

  Other important equivalents that you should remember are

$$180° = \pi \text{ rad} \quad 90° = \frac{\pi}{2} \text{ rad} \quad 60° = \frac{\pi}{3} \text{ rad} \quad 45° = \frac{\pi}{4} \text{ rad} \quad 30° = \frac{\pi}{6} \text{ rad} \quad \text{(p 79)}$$

- If an arc subtends an angle of θ radians at the centre of a circle radius *r*, the length of the arc is $r\theta$.   (p 79)

- The area of a sector of a circle, radius *r*, with angle θ radians at the centre is $\frac{1}{2}r^2\theta$.   (p 82)

Test yourself (answers p 145)

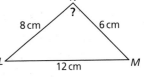

$$p^2 = 3^2 + 4^2 - 2 \times 3 \times 4 \times \cos P$$
$$p^2 = 9 + 16 - 24 \times \cos 52$$
$$p^2 = 25 - 14.775875410$$
$$p^2 = 10.22$$
$$p = \sqrt{10}$$

1 Work out the value of **?** in each triangle below.
Where there is more than one value, give both.

(a)

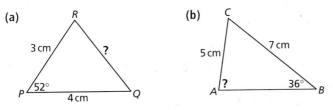

(b)

(c)

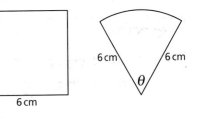

2 Find the area of each triangle in question 1.
Give both answers if there are two.

3 A sector of a circle, radius 5 cm, subtends 78° at the centre.
Calculate the sector's

   (a) arc length   **(b)** perimeter   **(c)** area

4 The area of a sector of a circle of radius 10 cm is 75 cm².
Find the arc length of this sector.

AQA 2003

5 The diagrams show a square of side 6 cm and a
sector of a circle of radius 6 cm and angle θ radians.

The area of the square is three times the area
of the sector.

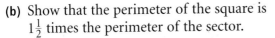

   (a) Show that $\theta = \frac{2}{3}$.

   (b) Show that the perimeter of the square is
       $1\frac{1}{2}$ times the perimeter of the sector.

AQA 2002

6 The diagram shows a sector of a circle, with centre O and radius 6 cm.

The mid-point of the chord PQ is M, and angle POM is $\dfrac{\pi}{6}$ radians.

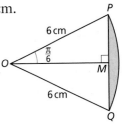

   (a) Write down the exact values of:

       (i) the lengths of PM and OM

       (ii) the length of the arc PQ

       (iii) the area of the sector POQ

   (b) Use the appropriate answers from part (a) to show that the area of
       the region shaded in the diagram is

$$m(2\pi - 3\sqrt{3})\,\text{cm}^2$$

   for some integer m whose value is to be determined.

AQA 2001

6 Trigonometry 1 | **85**

7 Trigonometry 2

In this chapter you will learn
- about the graphs of the sine, cosine and tangent functions (the 'circular functions')
- about relationships between the circular functions
- how to solve equations involving the circular functions

A Sines and cosines (answers p 146)

In chapter 6 you saw how to define the sine and cosine of an angle using the unit circle.

$\cos \theta°$ is defined to be the x-coordinate of P.
$\sin \theta°$ is defined to be the y-coordinate of P.

These definitions apply for all values of $\theta°$, both positive (anticlockwise) and negative (clockwise).

D **A1** Use the unit circle to decide which of these are the same as $\sin 50°$.

(a) $\sin 130°$ (b) $\sin 230°$ (c) $\sin -50°$ (d) $\sin 310°$

(e) $\sin 410°$ (f) $\sin 490°$ (g) $\sin -310°$ (h) $\sin -230°$

A2 Use the unit circle to explain why $\sin (-\theta)° = -\sin \theta°$ for all values of $\theta°$.

You saw in chapter 6 that $\sin (180 - \theta)° = \sin \theta°$.
You can also see from the unit circle that the angle $\theta°$ is equivalent to $360° + \theta°$, so

K $\sin (360 + \theta)° = \sin \theta°$.

The graph of $y = \sin \theta°$ also shows these equivalences.

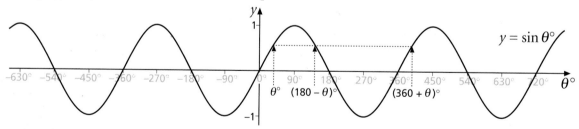

K $\sin (-\theta)° = -\sin \theta°$, so the curve has rotation symmetry about $(0, 0)$.
The curve repeats every $360°$, so $y = \sin \theta°$ has a **period** of $360°$.

A3 The sine of each of these angles is equal to either $\sin 20°$ or $-\sin 20°$.
Decide which in each case.

(a) $160°$ (b) $340°$ (c) $200°$ (d) $-20°$ (e) $-160°$

(f) $380°$ (g) $520°$ (h) $560°$ (i) $700°$ (j) $-700°$

D **A4** Use the unit circle to decide which of these are the same as $\cos 50°$.

(a) $\cos 130°$ (b) $\cos 230°$ (c) $\cos -50°$ (d) $\cos 310°$

(e) $\cos 410°$ (f) $\cos 490°$ (g) $\cos -310°$ (h) $\cos -230°$

A5 Use the unit circle to explain why $\cos(-\theta)° = \cos\theta°$ for all values of $\theta°$.

K You can see from the unit circle that $\cos(180 - \theta)° = -\cos\theta°$.
Also $\cos(360 + \theta)° = \cos\theta°$.

You can also see these from the graph of $y = \cos\theta°$.

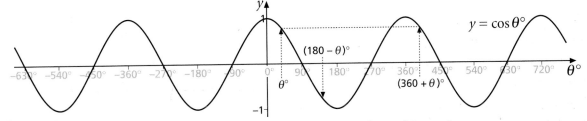

K $\cos -\theta° = \cos\theta°$, so the curve has reflection symmetry about the y-axis.
Like $\sin\theta°$, $\cos\theta°$ has period $360°$.

A6 Given that $\cos 20° = 0.94$ (to 2 s.f.), find each angle $\theta°$ such that

(a) $\cos\theta° = 0.94 \ (-90° \le \theta° \le 0°)$ (b) $\cos\theta° = -0.94 \ (90° \le \theta° \le 180°)$

(c) $\cos\theta° = 0.94 \ (270° \le \theta° \le 360°)$ (d) $\cos\theta° = -0.94 \ (-270° \le \theta° \le -180°)$

A7 (a) If $0° \le \theta° < 360°$, then one solution to $\cos\theta° = 0.73$ is $\theta° = 43°$.
What is the other solution?

(b) If $0° \le \theta° < 360°$, one solution to $\cos\theta° = -0.17$ is $\theta° = 100°$.
What is the other solution?

(c) If $0° \le \theta° < 360°$, and you know one solution to $\cos\theta° = k$,
explain how you find another solution.

K When you solve an equation like $\sin\theta° = k$ or $\cos\theta° = k$ (where $-1 < k < 1$),
there are two solutions for $\theta°$ between $0°$ and $360°$.
Further solutions for $\theta°$ can be found by taking each of these two solutions and
adding or subtracting multiples of $360°$.

Example 1

Find all the angles $\theta°$ (to the nearest degree), where $-360° < \theta° < 360°$, such that $\sin\theta° = 0.96$.

Solution

Key in $\sin^{-1} 0.96$. The solution is $\theta° = 74°$.   *$74°$ is called the **principal value** of the solution.*
Another solution is $\theta° = 180° - 74° = 106°$.

*These are the two solutions between $0°$ and $360°$. You can add or subtract
any multiple of $360°$ to get further angles whose sine is 0.96.*

The two angles between $0°$ and $-360°$ are $74° - 360° = -286°$ and $106° - 360° = -254°$.

The four solutions in the required interval are therefore $-286°$, $-254°$, $74°$ and $106°$.

Example 2

Find all the angles a, where $0 < a < 4\pi$, such that $\cos a = 0.5$.
Give your answers in radians.

Solution

$\cos a = 0.5 \Rightarrow$ one solution is $a = \dfrac{\pi}{3}$.　　　*You need to know that $\cos \dfrac{\pi}{3} = 0.5$ (see page 80).*

One way to find the other solutions is to sketch the graph of $y = \cos a$ over the required interval.

From the sketch, another solution is
$$a = 2\pi - \frac{\pi}{3} = \frac{5\pi}{3}.$$
The two solutions marked on the
right-hand side of the graph are each
2π radians bigger than the two solutions
already found.

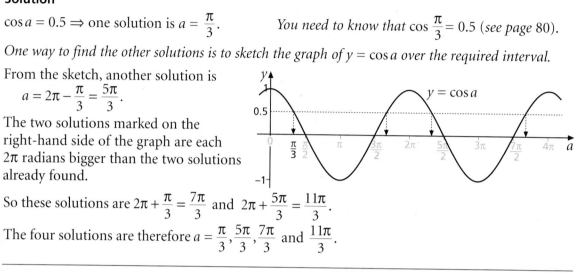

So these solutions are $2\pi + \dfrac{\pi}{3} = \dfrac{7\pi}{3}$ and $2\pi + \dfrac{5\pi}{3} = \dfrac{11\pi}{3}$.

The four solutions are therefore $a = \dfrac{\pi}{3}, \dfrac{5\pi}{3}, \dfrac{7\pi}{3}$ and $\dfrac{11\pi}{3}$.

Exercise A (answers p 146)

1 $\sin 70° = 0.94$ (to 2 s.f.).

　(a) Write down another angle between $0°$ and $360°$ whose sine is 0.94.

　(b) Write down two further angles between $360°$ and $720°$ whose sine is 0.94.

2 $\cos 1^c = 0.54$ (to 2 s.f.).　(Remember 1^c means 1 radian.)

　(a) Work out another angle (to 2 d.p.) in radians between
　　　0 and 2π whose cosine is 0.54.

　(b) Work out two further angles in radians between 2π and 4π whose cosine is 0.54.

3 (a) Solve each of these equations, giving all the solutions between $0°$ and $360°$.

　　(i) $\sin \theta° = 0.64$　　(ii) $\cos \theta° = 0.64$　　(iii) $\sin \theta° = -0.29$　　(iv) $\cos \theta° = -0.88$

　(b) Write down the solutions to each part of (a) between $360°$ and $720°$.

4 Solve each of these, giving solutions between 0 and 2π in terms of π.

　(a) $\sin \theta = \frac{1}{2}$　　　　(b) $\sin \theta = 1$　　　　(c) $\cos \theta = 0$

5 Solve each of these equations, giving all the solutions (in radians) between -2π and 2π.

　(a) $\sin \theta = \dfrac{1}{\sqrt{2}}$　　(b) $\sin \theta = -\dfrac{1}{\sqrt{2}}$　　(c) $\cos \theta = \dfrac{\sqrt{3}}{2}$　　(d) $\cos \theta = -\dfrac{1}{2}$

6 Solve each of these equations, giving answers to the nearest degree in the range specified.

　(a) $\sin \theta° = 0.1$ $(-360° \le \theta° < 360°)$　　(b) $\cos \theta° = -0.6$ $(0° \le \theta° < 720°)$

　(c) $4\sin \theta° = 3$ $(0° \le \theta° < 720°)$　　(d) $8\cos \theta° + 3 = 0$ $(-360° \le \theta° < 360°)$

B Transforming sine and cosine graphs (answers p 146)

The sine and cosine functions are **periodic**: they repeat themselves after an interval called the **period**.
The period for $y = \sin\theta°$ is 360°.
So $\sin\theta° = \sin(\theta + 360)° = \sin(\theta + 720)°\dots$ and so on.

For $y = \sin\theta°$, y takes values between -1 and 1.
The **amplitude** of $y = \sin\theta°$ is half this distance, so $y = \sin\theta°$ has an amplitude of 1.

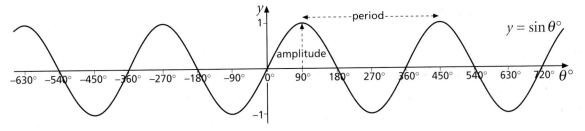

You need to be familiar with the graphs of the circular functions after various transformations.

B1 (a) Sketch the graph of $y = 2\sin\theta°$ for $-360° \le \theta° \le 360°$.

  (b) What is the period of $y = 2\sin\theta°$?

  (c) What is the amplitude of $y = 2\sin\theta°$?

  (d) Describe the transformation that maps the graph of $y = \sin\theta°$ on to $y = 2\sin\theta°$.

B2 (a) Sketch the graph of $y = a\sin\theta°$ for a value of a that you choose yourself (not 1 or 2!).

  (b) What is the period of $y = a\sin\theta°$?

  (c) What is the amplitude of $y = a\sin\theta°$?

  (d) Describe the transformation that maps the graph of $y = \sin\theta°$ on to $y = a\sin\theta°$.

B3 What is the value of $\sin 2\theta°$ when

  (a) $\theta° = 0°$ (b) $\theta° = 22\frac{1}{2}°$ (c) $\theta° = 45°$ (d) $\theta° = 90°$ (e) $\theta° = 135°$

B4 (a) Sketch the graph of $y = \sin 2\theta°$ for $-360° \le \theta° \le 360°$.

  (b) Write down the period and amplitude of $y = \sin 2\theta°$.

  (c) Describe the transformation that maps the graph of $y = \sin\theta°$ on to $y = \sin 2\theta°$.

B5 (a) What transformation maps the graph of $y = \sin\theta°$ on to $y = \sin b\theta°$?

  (b) Write down the period and amplitude of $y = \sin b\theta°$.

  (c) Check your answers for a value of b that you choose.

B6 (a) (i) For the graph of $y = \sin(\theta + 30)°$, find a negative value of $\theta°$ that makes $y = 0$.

　　(ii) Sketch the graph of $y = \sin(\theta + 30)°$.

　(b) Describe the transformation that maps $y = \sin\theta°$ on to $y = \sin(\theta + 30)°$.

　(c) What transformation maps $y = \sin\theta°$ on to $y = \sin(\theta + c)°$?

B7 (a) Describe the transformation that would map $y = \sin\theta°$ on to $y = (\sin\theta°) + d$.

　(b) What is the amplitude of $y = (\sin\theta°) + d$?

B8 (a) Sketch the graph of $y = \sin(-\theta)°$ for $-360° \le \theta° \le 360°$.

　(b) How is the graph of $y = \sin(-\theta)°$ related to that of $y = \sin\theta°$?

　(c) Sketch the graph of $y = -\sin\theta°$ for $-360° \le \theta° \le 360°$.

　(d) How is the graph of $y = -\sin\theta°$ related to that of $y = \sin\theta°$?

K If you start with the graph of $y = \sin\theta°$ (shown in grey in these diagrams)…

… the graph of $y = a\sin\theta°$ is obtained by a stretch in the y-direction, scale factor a

… the graph of $y = \sin b\theta°$ is obtained by a stretch in the θ-direction, scale factor $\dfrac{1}{b}$

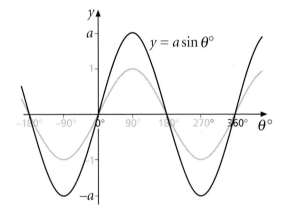

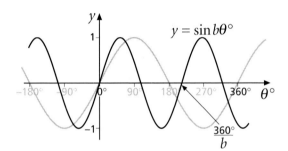

… the graph of $y = \sin(\theta + c)°$ is obtained by a translation of $\begin{bmatrix} -c \\ 0 \end{bmatrix}$

… the graph of $y = (\sin\theta°) + d$ is obtained by a translation of $\begin{bmatrix} 0 \\ d \end{bmatrix}$

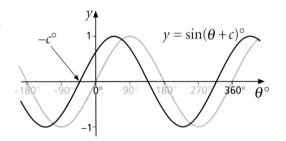

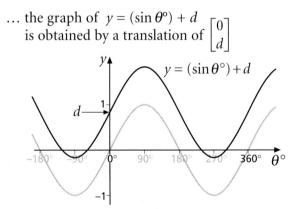

1 Each of these sketches shows the graph of $y = \sin\theta°$ after a single transformation. Identify each transformation and give the equation of the transformed graph.

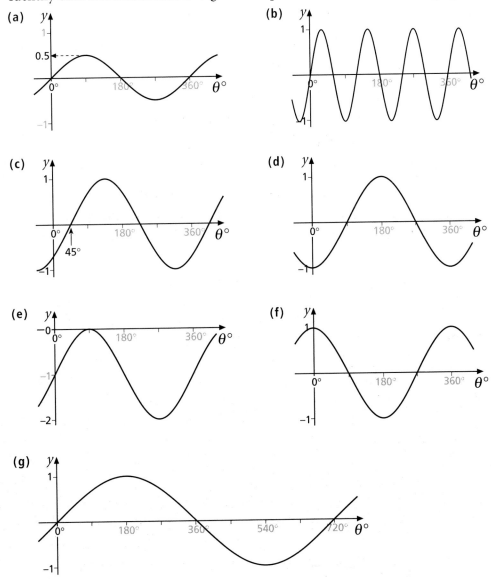

(a)

(b)

(c)

(d)

(e)

(f)

(g)

2 (a) By considering graph 1(f), write down a relationship between the sine and cosine ratios that is true for all $\theta°$.

(b) Write down a similar relationship based on graph 1(d).

3 For each of the following equations, where θ is measured in radians,
- sketch the graph of $y = \sin\theta \ (-2\pi \le \theta \le 2\pi)$
- superimpose the required graph

(a) $y = \sin\left(\theta - \dfrac{\pi}{3}\right)$ **(b)** $y = \sin\left(\theta + \dfrac{\pi}{6}\right)$ **(c)** $y = \sin\left(\theta - \dfrac{\pi}{2}\right)$

4 For each of the following graphs, first sketch the graph of $y = \cos\theta$ (where θ is measured in radians), labelling each θ-axis as shown on the right.

Then superimpose the required graph.

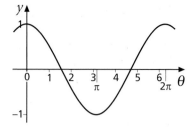

(a) $y = (\cos\theta) + 2$ (b) $y = 2\cos\theta$

(c) $y = \cos 2\theta$ (d) $y = \cos(\theta + 2)$

5 Each of these sketches shows the graph of $y = \cos\theta$ after a single transformation. In the graphs, θ is measured in radians.
Identify each transformation and give the equation of the transformed graph.

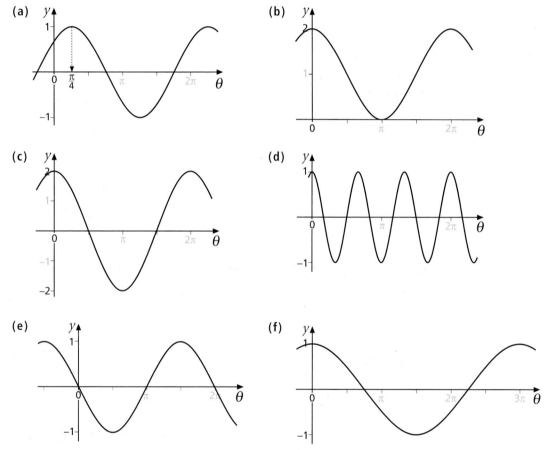

6 For each of the following, sketch the graph of $y = \cos\theta°$ for $-360° \leq \theta° \leq 360°$ and superimpose the required graph.

(a) $y = \cos(\theta + 60)°$ (b) $y = \cos(\theta - 180)°$ (c) $y = \cos(\theta + 180)°$

*7 Sketch each of these graphs for $-360° \leq \theta° \leq 360°$, labelling your axes carefully.

(a) $y = 2\sin(\theta + 60)°$ (b) $y = -\cos(\theta - 60)°$

*8 (a) For $y = \sin(2\theta + 120)°$ write down   **(i)** the period   **(ii)** the amplitude

(b) What value of $\theta°$ makes $\sin(2\theta + 120)° = 0$?

(c) Sketch the graph of $y = \sin(2\theta + 120)°$.

C Tangents (answers p 148)

You have seen how to define $\sin \theta°$ and $\cos \theta°$ in the unit circle shown on the right.

In triangle OQP, $\tan \theta° = \dfrac{QP}{OQ}$, so

K
$$\tan \theta° = \frac{\sin \theta°}{\cos \theta°}$$

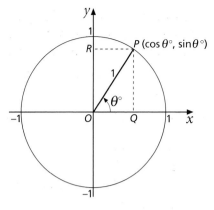

$\sin \theta°$ and $\cos \theta°$ are already defined for any angle, so you can use this relationship to define $\tan \theta°$ for any angle.

Note, however, that $\tan \theta°$ will not be defined if $\cos \theta° = 0$, that is if $\theta° = 90°$ or $270°$ or $450°$ and so on.

C1 This sketch shows the four quadrants, as $\theta°$ increases from $0°$ to $360°$, and whether $\sin \theta°$ is positive or negative in each of them.

(a) Copy the sketch and write whether $\cos \theta°$ is positive or negative in each quadrant.

(b) Use the fact that $\tan \theta° = \dfrac{\sin \theta°}{\cos \theta°}$ to write in each quadrant whether $\tan \theta°$ is positive or negative .

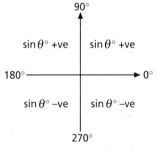

C2 Show that $\tan (-\theta)° = -\tan \theta°$ by simplifying $\dfrac{\sin(-\theta)°}{\cos(-\theta)°}$.

The graph of $\tan \theta°$, like that of $\sin \theta°$ and $\cos \theta°$, is periodic. Unlike these functions, the period of $\tan \theta°$ is $180°$, so $\tan (180 + \theta)° = \tan \theta°$.

$\tan (-\theta)° = -\tan \theta°$, so the graph has rotation symmetry about $(0, 0)$.

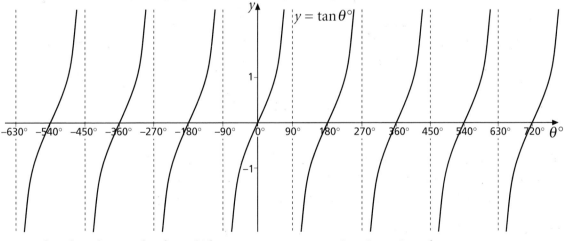

Note also that the graph of $\tan \theta°$ has asymptotes at $-90°$, $90°$, $270°$, and so on.

K
When you solve an equation such as $\tan \theta° = k$ (where k can have any value), you can see from the graph that there will always be one solution between $0°$ and $180°$. From this one solution, further solutions for $\theta°$ can be found by adding or subtracting multiples of $180°$.

Example 3

Find, to the nearest degree, all the angles $\theta°$ $(-360° \le \theta° \le 360°)$ such that $\tan \theta° = 1.19$.

Solution

Key in $\tan^{-1} 1.19$.

Since tan *has period* 180°, *add or subtract multiples of* 180° *to get the other solutions.*

One solution is $\theta° = 50°$.

Other solutions are $50° + 180° = 230°$, $50° - 180° = -130°$, and $50° - 2 \times 180° = -310°$
The solutions are $\theta° = -310°, -130°, 50°$ and $230°$.

Exercise C (answers p 148)

1 Solve each of these equations, giving all solutions between 0° and 360°, to the nearest degree.

   (a) $\tan x° = 3$ (b) $\tan x° = -3$ (c) $2 \tan x° = -1$ (d) $5 \tan x° = 8$

2 Solve these, giving answers in terms of π in the range specified.

   (a) $\tan a = \sqrt{3} \; (-\pi \le a \le \pi)$ (b) $\tan a = -\dfrac{1}{\sqrt{3}} \; (-\pi \le a \le \pi)$

   (c) $\tan a = -1 \; (-2\pi \le a \le 0)$ (d) $\tan a = 0 \; (\pi \le a \le 5\pi)$

3 The four graphs below show $y = \tan \theta°$ after a single transformation.
The graphs are (not in order) $y = \tan 2\theta°$, $y = \tan \frac{1}{2}\theta°$, $y = \tan(\theta + 45)°$, $y = \tan(\theta - 45)°$.
Identify which graph is which.

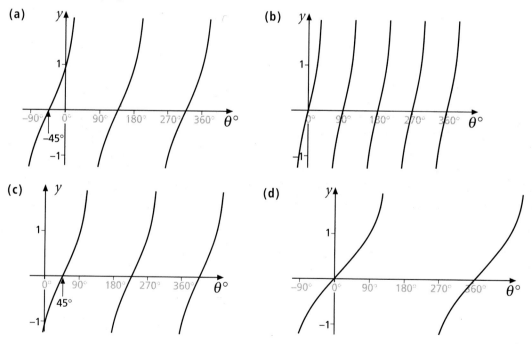

4 Sketch each of these graphs for $-2\pi < x < 2\pi$, labelling the axes clearly.

   (a) $\tan \dfrac{x}{3}$ (b) $\tan x + 0.5$ (c) $\tan\left(x + \dfrac{\pi}{2}\right)$ (d) $\tan\left(x - \dfrac{\pi}{6}\right)$

D Solving further equations (answers p 149)

You have solved simple equations such as $\sin \theta° = -0.6$, giving your answers for $\theta°$ within a specific range.

You sometimes need to go outside the given range to find a complete solution to a problem.

D1 Find the values of $\theta°$ to the nearest degree between $0°$ and $360°$ which satisfy the equation $\sin(\theta + 50)° = 0.4$.

Example 4

Solve $\sin(\theta + 70)° = 0.6$ to the nearest degree, for $0° \le \theta < 360°$

Solution

$\theta°$ is between $0°$ and $360°$, so $(\theta + 70)°$ is between $70°$ and $430°$.

$$\sin(\theta + 70)° = 0.6 \text{ gives } (\theta + 70)° = 37° \text{ (to the nearest degree)}$$
$$\text{and } (\theta + 70)° = 180° - 37° = \underline{143°}.$$

Since sine has period $360°$, we also have $(\theta + 70)° = 37° + 360° = \underline{397°}$
$$\text{and } (\theta + 70)° = 143° + 360° = 503°.$$

Adding or subtracting further multiples of $360°$ would clearly go outside the required range of $70°$ to $430°$.

The two underlined values above are within the range $70°$ to $430°$, and these lead to

$$(\theta + 70)° = 143° \implies \theta° = 73°$$
$$\text{and } (\theta + 70)° = 397° \implies \theta° = 327°.$$

Example 5

Solve $\tan 2\theta = -\sqrt{3}$, giving answers between 0 and 2π.

Solution

If θ is between 0 and 2π, then 2θ will be between 0 and 4π.

We know that $\tan \frac{\pi}{3} = \sqrt{3}$, therefore $\tan\left(-\frac{\pi}{3}\right) = -\sqrt{3}$.

So if $\tan 2\theta = -\sqrt{3}$, then one possibility is $2\theta = -\frac{\pi}{3}$.

This does not, however, lead to a solution in the range required.

Since tan has period π, other possibilities are
$$2\theta = -\frac{\pi}{3} + \pi = \frac{2\pi}{3} \implies \theta = \frac{\pi}{3}$$

Consider angles for 2θ from 0 to 4π.

$$\text{and } 2\theta = -\frac{\pi}{3} + 2\pi = \frac{5\pi}{3} \implies \theta = \frac{5\pi}{6}$$
$$\text{and } 2\theta = -\frac{\pi}{3} + 3\pi = \frac{8\pi}{3} \implies \theta = \frac{4\pi}{3}$$
$$\text{and } 2\theta = -\frac{\pi}{3} + 4\pi = \frac{11\pi}{3} \implies \theta = \frac{11\pi}{6}$$

So the solutions are $\theta = \frac{\pi}{3}, \frac{5\pi}{6}, \frac{4\pi}{3}$ and $\frac{11\pi}{6}$.

Example 6

Find all the solutions to $2 \sin \theta° - \cos \theta° = 0$ between $-180°$ and $180°$, to the nearest degree.

Solution

Reduce the equation to one just in $\tan \theta$.

$$2 \sin \theta° - \cos \theta° = 0$$
$$\Rightarrow \qquad 2 \sin \theta° = \cos \theta°$$

You can divide by $\cos \theta°$ because $\cos \theta° = 0$ is not a solution of the original equation.

$$\Rightarrow \qquad 2 \frac{\sin \theta°}{\cos \theta°} = 1$$
$$\Rightarrow \qquad 2 \tan \theta° = 1$$
$$\Rightarrow \qquad \tan \theta° = \tfrac{1}{2}$$

Key in $\tan^{-1} 0.5$ on the calculator.

So one value of $\theta°$ is $27°$.

tan has period $180°$.

Another value is $27° - 180° = -153°$.

So the two solutions are $\theta° = -153°$ and $27°$.
Other solutions are outside the required range

Example 7

Find the solutions to $2 \sin 3t = 1$ for $-\pi \leq t \leq \pi$.

Solution

If $-\pi \leq t \leq \pi$, then $-3\pi \leq 3t \leq 3\pi$, and so you need to find values of $3t$ from -3π to 3π.

If $2 \sin 3t = 1$, then $\sin 3t = \tfrac{1}{2}$.

One possibility is $3t = \dfrac{\pi}{6} \left(\text{since } \sin \dfrac{\pi}{6} = \tfrac{1}{2}\right)$

$\sin \theta = \sin(\pi - \theta)$

Another possibility is $3t = \pi - \dfrac{\pi}{6} = \dfrac{5\pi}{6}$

$\sin \theta$ has period 2π.

Other possibilities are $3t = \dfrac{\pi}{6} + 2\pi$

Add or subtract as many multiples of 2π as you need to be sure of including all the required solutions. Discard any solutions outside the required range at the end.

$$3t = \dfrac{5\pi}{6} + 2\pi$$
$$3t = \dfrac{\pi}{6} - 2\pi$$
$$3t = \dfrac{5\pi}{6} - 2\pi$$

If $3t = \dfrac{\pi}{6}, \ t = \dfrac{\pi}{18}$

If $3t = \dfrac{5\pi}{6}, \ t = \dfrac{5\pi}{18}$

$3t = \dfrac{\pi}{6} + 2\pi \ \Rightarrow 3t = \dfrac{13\pi}{6} \ \Rightarrow t = \dfrac{13\pi}{18}$

$3t = \dfrac{5\pi}{6} + 2\pi \Rightarrow 3t = \dfrac{17\pi}{6} \ \Rightarrow t = \dfrac{17\pi}{18}$

$3t = \dfrac{\pi}{6} - 2\pi \ \Rightarrow 3t = -\dfrac{11\pi}{6} \ \Rightarrow t = -\dfrac{11\pi}{18}$

$3t = \dfrac{5\pi}{6} - 2\pi \Rightarrow 3t = -\dfrac{7\pi}{6} \ \Rightarrow t = -\dfrac{7\pi}{18}$

So the solutions for t are $-\dfrac{11\pi}{18}, -\dfrac{7\pi}{18}, \dfrac{\pi}{18}, \dfrac{5\pi}{18}, \dfrac{13\pi}{18}$ and $\dfrac{17\pi}{18}$.

Exercise D (answers p 149)

1 Solve each of these equations to the nearest degree,
giving all solutions between 0° and 360°.

(a) $\cos(\theta + 80)° = 0.66$ (b) $\sin(\theta - 50)° = -0.9$ (c) $\tan(\theta + 120)° = 1.5$

(d) $\sin 2t° = 0.7$ (e) $\cos 3t° = 0.4$ (f) $5 \tan 2t° = 1$

2 Solve each of these, giving all answers between 0 and 2π.

(a) $\sin 2h = \frac{1}{2}$ (b) $\cos 4t = 1$ (c) $\tan 3f = 1$

3 Find the values of $t°$ in the range $0° \leq t° \leq 60°$ which satisfy

(a) $8 \sin 10t° = 5$ (b) $10 \cos \frac{1}{2}t° = 9$ (c) $5 \tan 5t° - 1 = 0$

4 Solve each of these, giving solutions to the nearest 0.1° in the range indicated.

(a) $\sin 3\theta° = 0.6$ $(-180° \leq \theta° \leq 180°)$ (b) $\cos 2\theta° = -0.38$ $(-360° \leq \theta° \leq 0°)$

(c) $\tan 5\theta° = -2$ $(-180° \leq \theta° \leq 180°)$ (d) $\sin \frac{\theta°}{2} = 0.76$ $(-360° \leq \theta° \leq 360°)$

5 Find the solutions to these, giving answers in radians between 0 and 2π.

(a) $\sin \theta - \sqrt{3} \cos \theta = 0$ (b) $\sqrt{3} \sin \theta + \cos \theta = 0$ (c) $\sin \theta + \sqrt{3} \cos \theta = 0$

*6 Find the values of $t°$ in the range $0° \leq t° \leq 360°$ which satisfy

(a) $4 - 7\cos(2t + 35)° = 0$ (b) $3 + 4\sin(4t - 21)° = 0$

(c) $3 \cos(0.5t + 20)° = 2$ (d) $\sin(2t + 20)° - 3\cos(2t + 20)° = 0$

E Further equations and identities (answers p 149)

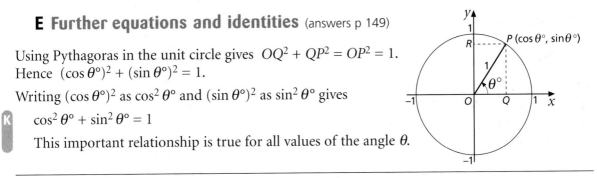

Using Pythagoras in the unit circle gives $OQ^2 + QP^2 = OP^2 = 1$.
Hence $(\cos \theta°)^2 + (\sin \theta°)^2 = 1$.

Writing $(\cos \theta°)^2$ as $\cos^2 \theta°$ and $(\sin \theta°)^2$ as $\sin^2 \theta°$ gives

$\cos^2 \theta° + \sin^2 \theta° = 1$

This important relationship is true for all values of the angle θ.

Example 8

Given that θ is an acute angle and $\sin \theta = \frac{1}{3}$, find (a) $\cos \theta$ (b) $\tan \theta$

Solution

(a) Using $\cos^2 \theta + \sin^2 \theta = 1$,

$$\cos^2 \theta + \left(\frac{1}{3}\right)^2 = 1, \quad \cos^2 \theta = 1 - \frac{1}{9} = \frac{8}{9}$$

$$\Rightarrow \quad \cos \theta = \sqrt{\frac{8}{9}} = \frac{\sqrt{8}}{\sqrt{9}} = \frac{\sqrt{8}}{3} = \frac{2\sqrt{2}}{3}$$

Take the positive root because θ is acute.

Note that the results are true whether θ is measured in degrees or radians.

(b) $\tan \theta = \dfrac{\sin \theta}{\cos \theta} = \dfrac{\frac{1}{3}}{\frac{2\sqrt{2}}{3}} = \dfrac{1}{2\sqrt{2}}$

(D) **E1** If θ is in the second quadrant and $\sin\theta = \frac{1}{3}$, find **(a)** $\cos\theta$ **(b)** $\tan\theta$

You can also solve equations involving the squares of the circular functions.

E2 Consider the equation $2\cos^2\theta° - 3\cos\theta° + 1 = 0$.

(a) Think of $\cos\theta°$ as a single letter, say c. Rewrite the equation replacing $\cos\theta°$ with c.

(b) You now have a quadratic equation in c. The equation factorises. Factorise it.

(c) Check that one of your factors is $(c - 1)$.

(d) If $c - 1 = 0$, then $c = 1$, that is, $\cos\theta° = 1$.
For what value of $\theta°$ ($0° \le \theta° \le 90°$) is $\cos\theta° = 1$?

(e) Similarly, use your second factor to find a solution for $\theta°$ between $0°$ and $90°$.

(f) Check that both solutions you have found work in the original equation.

(D) **E3** (a) Use the fact that $\cos^2\theta° + \sin^2\theta° = 1$ to rewrite the equation
$\sin^2\theta° - \cos\theta° - 1 = 0$ in terms of $\cos\theta°$ only.

(b) Factorise your new equation and thus solve $\sin^2\theta° - \cos\theta° - 1 = 0$ $(0 \le \theta° < 360°)$.

Example 9

Solve the equation $\cos^2\theta° + \cos\theta° - 1 = 0$, giving solutions between $-90°$ and $90°$ to the nearest $0.1°$.

Solution

The quadratic will not factorise so use the formula.

$$\cos^2\theta° + \cos\theta° - 1 = 0 \Rightarrow \cos\theta° = \frac{-1 \pm \sqrt{1^2 - 4\times 1\times -1}}{2\times 1}$$

$\cos\theta° = 0.618...$ or $-1.618...$

$\cos\theta° = -1.618...$ has no solution.

$\cos\theta° = 0.618... \Rightarrow \theta° = 51.8°$ or $-51.8°$ (to $0.1°$)

Example 10

Solve the equation $2\sin^2 x = 3\cos x$ for $0 \le x \le 2\pi$.

Solution

The range shows you are expected to give the solutions in radians.

$\cos^2 x + \sin^2 x = 1 \Rightarrow \sin^2 x = 1 - \cos^2 x$ so substitute for $\sin^2 x$.

$$2\sin^2 x = 3\cos x$$
$$2(1 - \cos^2 x) = 3\cos x$$
$$\Rightarrow \qquad 2 - 2\cos^2 x = 3\cos x$$

Rearrange.
Think of $\cos x$ as c and factorise.

$$2\cos^2 x + 3\cos x - 2 = 0$$
$$(2\cos x - 1)(\cos x + 2) = 0$$
$$\Rightarrow \cos x = \tfrac{1}{2} \text{ or } \cos x = -2$$

$\cos x = -2$ has no solution, so the only solutions are given by $\cos x = \frac{1}{2}$.

$\cos x = \frac{1}{2} \Rightarrow x = \dfrac{\pi}{3}$ or $2\pi - \dfrac{\pi}{3} = \dfrac{5\pi}{3}$ in the required range

so the solutions are $\dfrac{\pi}{3}$ and $\dfrac{5\pi}{3}$.

Example 11

Solve the equation $2\sin^2 x = 3\cos^2 x$ for $0 \le x \le 2\pi$, giving solutions to 2 d.p.

Solution

The range indicates you are expected to give the solutions in radians.

$$2\sin^2 x = 3\cos^2 x$$

You could write $2\sin^2 x = 2(1 - \cos^2 x)$ and solve for $\cos^2 x$ instead.

$$\Rightarrow \quad \frac{\sin^2 x}{\cos^2 x} = \frac{3}{2}$$

$$\Rightarrow \quad \tan^2 x = 1.5$$

$$\Rightarrow \quad \tan x = \pm\sqrt{1.5} = \pm 1.224\ldots$$

Set the calculator to radians, and use $\tan^{-1} 1.224\ldots$ $x = 0.886\ldots$

$$= 0.89 \text{ (2 d.p.)}$$

tan has period π.

Another solution is $x = 0.886\ldots + \pi$

$$= 4.03 \text{ (2 d.p.)}$$

If $\tan x = -1.224\ldots$, then $x = -0.886\ldots$ *Not within the required range*
and $-0.886\ldots + \pi = 2.26$ (2 d.p.)
and $-0.886\ldots + 2\pi = 5.40$ (2 d.p.)

So the required solutions are 0.89, 2.26, 4.03 and 5.40 (radians).
Check these by substituting back into the original equation.

Example 12

Prove that $\dfrac{2 - \sin^2 \theta}{\cos^2 \theta + 1} = 1$. *Note that this is not an equation; you have to prove it is true for all θ. Start with the more complex side and show it is equal to the other side.*

Solution

$$\frac{2 - \sin^2 \theta}{\cos^2 \theta + 1} = \frac{2 - (1 - \cos^2 \theta)}{\cos^2 \theta + 1} = \frac{2 - 1 + \cos^2 \theta}{\cos^2 \theta + 1} = \frac{1 + \cos^2 \theta}{\cos^2 \theta + 1} = 1$$

Example 13

Show that $(x - 1)$ is a factor of $x^3 - 2x^2 - x + 2$, and hence factorise $x^3 - 2x^2 - x + 2$.
Hence find all the values of θ (where $0 \le \theta < 2\pi$) such that $\sin^3 \theta - 2\sin^2 \theta - \sin \theta + 2 = 0$.

Solution

Use the factor theorem.

When $x = 1$, $x^3 - 2x^2 - x + 2 = 1 - 2 - 1 + 2 = 0$.
Hence $(x - 1)$ is a factor of $x^3 - 2x^2 - x + 2$.

$$x^3 - 2x^2 - x + 2 = (x - 1)(x^2 - x - 2)$$
$$= (x - 1)(x + 1)(x - 2)$$

To solve $\sin^3 \theta - 2\sin^2 \theta - \sin \theta + 2 = 0$, let $x = \sin \theta$.

$$\text{So } x^3 - 2x^2 - x + 2 = 0$$

$$\Rightarrow \quad (x - 1)(x + 1)(x - 2) = 0$$

Hence $x = \sin \theta = 1, -1$ or 2.

If $\sin \theta = 1, \theta = \dfrac{\pi}{2}$. If $\sin \theta = -1, \theta = \dfrac{3\pi}{2}$. $\sin \theta = -2$ has no solutions.

So the solutions are $\theta = \dfrac{\pi}{2}$ and $\theta = \dfrac{3\pi}{2}$.

Exercise E (answers p 149)

1 If $\sin\theta = \frac{1}{4}$, find $\cos\theta$ and $\tan\theta$ if   **(a)** θ is acute   **(b)** θ is in the second quadrant

2 (a) By replacing $\sin^2 x°$ by $1 - \cos^2 x°$, show that the equation
$1 + \cos x° = 3\sin^2 x°$ is equivalent to $3\cos^2 x° + \cos x° - 2 = 0$.

    (b) Factorise the left-hand side of this equation.

    (c) Solve the equation to find all values of $x°$ between $0°$ and $360°$.

3 Solve the following equations for $0 \le \theta \le 2\pi$.

    (a) $2\cos^2\theta = \cos\theta + 1$ **(b)** $\sqrt{3}\sin\theta - \cos\theta = 0$ **(c)** $2\sin^2\theta = 7\cos\theta - 2$

4 Solve the following equations for $0 \le x \le 2\pi$.

    (a) $\sin^2 x = 0.25$ **(b)** $\cos^2 x - \sin^2 x = 1$ **(c)** $\tan^2 x = 3$

    (d) $\cos^2 x - 4\sin^2 x = 0$ **(e)** $\cos^2 x - 4\sin^2 x = 1$ **(f)** $\cos^2 x = 2 + 2\sin x$

5 (a) Show that $(x - 1)$ is a factor of $x^3 - x^2 - 3x + 3$, and hence factorise $x^3 - x^2 - 3x + 3$.

    (b) Hence find all the values of θ $(0 \le \theta < 2\pi)$ such that $\tan^3\theta - \tan^2\theta - 3\tan\theta + 3 = 0$.

6 Show that   **(a)** $(\sin x + \cos x)^2 = 1 + 2\sin x \cos x$ **(b)** $\dfrac{6 - \cos^2\theta}{\sin^2\theta + 5} = 1$

*7 Show that $(1 + \sin\theta + \cos\theta)^2 = 2(1 + \sin\theta)(1 + \cos\theta)$.

*8 Find the relationship between y and x, given that $x = 3\cos\theta$ and $y = 2\sin\theta$.

Key points

- $\sin(-\theta) = -\sin\theta$, $\sin(180 - \theta)° = \sin\theta°$ (in radians, $\sin(\pi - \theta) = \sin\theta$)   (p 86)
- $\cos(-\theta) = \cos\theta$, $\cos(180 - \theta)° = -\cos\theta°$ (in radians, $\cos(\pi - \theta) = -\cos\theta$)   (p 87)
- The graphs of the sine and cosine functions are periodic, with period $360°$ or 2π. (pp 86–87)
- The graph of $y = a\sin\theta$ is obtained from that of $y = \sin\theta$ by a stretch in the y-direction, scale factor a. $y = -\sin\theta$ is obtained by a reflection in the θ-axis. The same applies for cos and tan.   (p 90)
- The graph of $y = \sin b\theta$ is obtained from that of $y = \sin\theta$ by a stretch in the θ-direction, scale factor $\dfrac{1}{b}$. $y = \sin(-\theta)$ is obtained by a reflection in the y-axis. The same applies for cos and tan.   (p 90)
- The graph of $y = \sin(\theta + c)$ is obtained from $y = \sin\theta$ by a translation of $\begin{bmatrix} -c \\ 0 \end{bmatrix}$. The same applies for cos and tan.   (p 90)
- The graph of $y = (\sin\theta) + d$ is obtained from $y = \sin\theta$ by a translation of $\begin{bmatrix} 0 \\ d \end{bmatrix}$. The same applies for cos and tan.   (p 90)
- $\tan\theta = \dfrac{\sin\theta}{\cos\theta}$ (p 93)
- $\tan(-\theta) = -\tan\theta$; the tangent function is periodic, with period $180°$ or π.   (p 93)
- $\cos^2\theta + \sin^2\theta = 1$ (p 97)

Test yourself (answers p 150)

1 Solve the equation $\cos\left(x + \dfrac{\pi}{6}\right) = -0.5$ in the interval $0 < x < 2\pi$,

leaving your answers in terms of π.   AQA 2002

2 Solve the following equations, giving solutions between $0°$ and $360°$ to the nearest $0.1°$.

    (a) $\sin(x + 60)° = 0.2$ **(b)** $\cos(x - 40)° = 0.78$ **(c)** $\tan(x + 70)° = -1.2$

3 Solve the following, giving solutions in radians between 0 and 2π to 2 d.p.

    (a) $\sin 2x = 0.2$ **(b)** $\cos 3x = -0.78$ **(c)** $\tan \frac{1}{2}x = 1.2$

4 (a) Given that $3\cos 5x = 4\sin 5x$, write down the value of $\tan 5x$.

    (b) Hence find all solutions of the equation $3\cos 5x = 4\sin 5x$ in the
        interval $0° \le x < 90°$, giving your answers correct to the nearest $0.1°$.   AQA 2001

5 Sketch the following graphs for $0° \le \theta° \le 720°$, labelling your axes clearly.

    (a) $y = \sin(\theta + 45)°$ **(b)** $y = \frac{1}{3}\cos\theta°$ **(c)** $y = 2 + \sin\theta°$ **(d)** $y = \tan 2\theta°$

6 Show that   **(a)** $\dfrac{3 - 2\cos^2\theta}{2\sin^2\theta + 1} = 1$ **(b)** $\tan\theta\sin\theta = \dfrac{1}{\cos\theta} - \cos\theta$

7 It is given that x satisfies the equation $2\cos^2 x = 2 + \sin x$.

    (a) Use an appropriate trigonometrical identity to show that $2\sin^2 x + \sin x = 0$.

    (b) Solve this quadratic equation and hence find all the possible values of x
        in the interval $0 \le x < 2\pi$.   AQA 2003

8 (a) Given that $2\cos^2\theta - \sin\theta = 1$, show that $2\sin^2\theta + \sin\theta - 1 = 0$.

    (b) Hence find all the values of θ in the interval $0 < \theta < 2\pi$ for which
        $2\cos^2\theta - \sin\theta = 1$, giving each answer in terms of π.

    (c) Write down all the values of x in the interval $0 < x < \pi$
        for which $2\cos^2 2x - \sin 2x = 1$.   AQA 2001

9 Solve the equation $8\sin^2 x - 7 = 2\cos x$, giving all answers for x in radians in
the interval $0 \le x \le 2\pi$.   AQA 2001

10 (a) Write down the exact values of   **(i)** $\sin\dfrac{\pi}{4}$ **(ii)** $\cos\dfrac{\pi}{6}$ **(iii)** $\tan\dfrac{\pi}{3}$

    The diagram shows the graphs of
    $y = \sin^2 x$ and $y = \frac{1}{2}$ for $0 \le x \le \pi$.

    (b) Solve $\sin^2 x = \frac{1}{2}$ for $0 \le x \le \pi$.

    (c) Hence solve $\sin^2 x > \frac{1}{2}$ for $0 \le x \le \pi$.

    (d) Prove that $\sin^2 x > \frac{1}{2} \Rightarrow \cos^2 x < \frac{1}{2}$.   AQA 2001

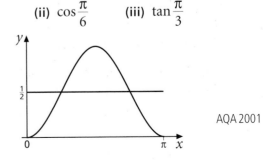

8 Exponentials and logarithms

In this chapter you will learn how to
- sketch the graphs of exponential functions
- use logarithmic notation
- use the laws of logarithms
- solve equations of the form $a^x = b$

A Graphs of exponential functions (answers p 151)

A1 Aquatic plants are growing on the surface of a pond.
Initially the plants cover an area of $1\,m^2$.

Each week the area covered by plants is doubled.

(a) Complete this table showing the area of pond, $A\,m^2$, covered by the plants t weeks after measurements were started.

t (weeks)	0	1	2	3	4
A (m²)	1				

(b) Plot the values of t and A on a graph with axes as shown.
Join the points with a curve.

(c) Write down a formula connecting the surface area, A, with the time, t.

(d) Use your formula and a calculator to find the value of A when $t = 0.5$.
Check that your graph gives the same result.

(e) Use your formula to calculate the value of A when $t = 1.7$.

(f) Assuming that the same rule for growth applied before the measurements were started, extend your graph back to $t = -3$.

The type of growth shown by these plants is called **exponential growth**.

> **K** A function of the form $y = a^x$ is called an **exponential function** ('exponential' is another word for 'power').
>
> The variable, x, is the index.

A2 Use a graph plotter to plot the graph of $y = 2^x$.

(a) What is the value of y when $x = 0$?

(b) What happens to y when x is large and positive?

(c) What happens to y when x is large and negative?

A3 (a) Investigate the shape of the graph of $y = a^x$ for positive values of a.

(b) Through which point do all graphs of the form $y = a^x$ pass?

K For all values of a, the graph of $y = a^x$
passes through the point $(0, 1)$.

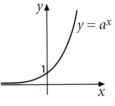

A4 Use a graph plotter to plot the graph of $y = (\frac{1}{2})^x$.

   (a) What happens to y when x is large and positive?

   (b) What happens to y when x is large and negative?

   (c) Use the laws of indices to show that the graph of $y = (\frac{1}{2})^x$ is the same as
   the graph of $y = 2^{-x}$.

   (d) What transformation maps the graph of $y = 2^x$ onto the graph of $y = (\frac{1}{2})^x$?

The type of growth shown by the function $y = a^x$, where $0 \le a \le 1$ is known as
exponential decay.

A5 The graph of $y = 2^x$ is translated by $\begin{bmatrix} 0 \\ 1 \end{bmatrix}$.

   (a) Show that the point $(3, 8)$ is on the graph of $y = 2^x$.

   (b) What is the image of the point $(3, 8)$ on the translated curve?

   (c) What is the y-intercept on the translated curve?

   (d) What is the equation of the translated curve?

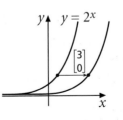

D **A6** The graph of $y = 2^x$ is translated by $\begin{bmatrix} 3 \\ 0 \end{bmatrix}$.

   What is the equation of the translated curve?

A7 The graph of $y = 2^x$ is translated by $\begin{bmatrix} -1 \\ 0 \end{bmatrix}$.

   What is the equation of the translated curve?

A8 The graph of $y = 2^x$ is transformed by a stretch of scale factor 3 in the
   direction of the y-axis.

   (a) Sketch the two graphs on the same set of axes, showing where each
   cuts the y-axis.

   (b) What is the equation of the transformed curve?

A9 The graph of $y = 2^x$ is transformed by a stretch of scale factor 3 in the
   direction of the x-axis.

   What is the equation of the transformed curve?

A10 (a) Use the laws of indices to show that the graph of $y = 16 \times 2^x$ is the same as the graph of $y = 2^{x+4}$.

(b) State two possible transformations which map the graph of $y = 2^x$ on to the graph of $y = 2^{x+4}$.

A11 State two possible transformations which map the graph of $y = 2^x$ on to the graph of $y = 2^{x+5}$.

Example 1

(a) Describe the transformation that maps the graph of $y = 3^x$ on to the graph of $y = 3^{x+2}$.

(b) On the same set of axes, sketch the graphs of $y = 3^x$ and $y = 3^{x+2}$.

Solution

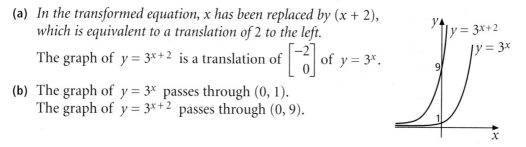

(a) *In the transformed equation, x has been replaced by (x + 2), which is equivalent to a translation of 2 to the left.*

The graph of $y = 3^{x+2}$ is a translation of $\begin{bmatrix} -2 \\ 0 \end{bmatrix}$ of $y = 3^x$.

(b) The graph of $y = 3^x$ passes through $(0, 1)$.
The graph of $y = 3^{x+2}$ passes through $(0, 9)$.

Exercise A (answers p 152)

1 On the same set of axes, sketch the graphs of $y = 2^x$, $y = 4^x$ and $y = (\frac{1}{2})^x$.

2 (a) Describe the transformation which maps the graph of $y = 5^x$ on to the graph of $y = 5^{x+1}$.

(b) On the same set of axes, sketch the graphs of $y = 5^x$ and $y = 5^{x+1}$.

3 (a) What is the equation of the image of the graph of $y = 6^x$ after a translation of $\begin{bmatrix} 3 \\ 0 \end{bmatrix}$?

(b) What is the equation of the image of the graph of $y = 6^x$ after a translation of $\begin{bmatrix} 0 \\ 3 \end{bmatrix}$?

4 The function f is defined by $f(x) = 4^x$.

(a) Write down $f(x - 2)$.

(b) What transformation maps the graph of $y = f(x)$ on to the graph of $y = f(x - 2)$?

5 The function g is defined by $g(x) = 7^x$.

(a) Write down $g(3x)$.

(b) What transformation maps the graph of $y = g(x)$ on to the graph of $y = g(3x)$?

6 Describe the transformation which maps the graph of $y = 3^x$ on to

(a) $y = 3^{-x}$ (b) $y = 3^x - 5$ (c) $y = 2 \times 3^x$ (d) $y = 3^{x+4}$

7 (a) Use the laws of indices to show that the graph of $y = 16 \times 4^x$ is the same as the graph of $y = 4^{x+2}$.

  (b) State two possible transformations which map the graph of $y = 4^x$ on to the graph of $y = 4^{x+2}$.

8 State two possible transformations which map the graph of $y = 5^x$ on to the graph of $y = 5^{x-1}$.

B Logarithms (answers p 152)

B1 Use your graph from question A1 to find after how long the area of the pond covered by plants will be $10\,\text{m}^2$.

In order to be able to solve problems like this exactly, we need to be able to find the inverse of an exponential function.

B2 Consider the function $y = 2^x$.

  (a) Find the value of y when

    (i) $x = 2$ (ii) $x = 5$ (iii) $x = -1$

  (b) Find the value of x when

    (i) $y = 1$ (ii) $y = 8$ (iii) $y = \frac{1}{4}$

The exponential function $y = 2^x$ expresses y in terms of x.
To find x given the value of y, we need to find the inverse function, x in terms of y.

For example, if $2^x = 8$, then $x = 3$ because $2^3 = 8$.

The index, 3, is known as the **logarithm** of 8 to base 2 or the log-to-base-2 of 8, written as $\log_2 8$.

Similarly, $\log_2 32 = 5$ because $2^5 = 32$.

> The 'log$_2$' of a number is the power to which you have to raise 2 in order to get the number.
>
> In symbols,
> $y = 2^x$ and $x = \log_2 y$ are equivalent statements.

B3 (a) Rewrite $2^6 = 64$ in logarithmic form.

  (b) Rewrite $\log_2 128 = 7$ in exponential form.

B4 (a) Given that $y = 5^x$, find the value of x when

    (i) $y = 5$ (ii) $y = 125$ (iii) $y = 0.2$

  (b) Given that $y = 10^x$, find the value of x when

    (i) $y = 1000$ (ii) $y = \frac{1}{100}$ (iii) $y = 0.001$

A logarithm can be defined with any positive base.

For example, log-to-base-5 of 25, or $\log_5 25$ is equal to 2 because $5^2 = 25$

> **K** If a number is expressed in exponential form as $y = a^x$, then the index x is known as $\log_a y$.
>
> $y = a^x$ and $x = \log_a y$ are equivalent statements.

$$\boxed{\begin{array}{c} \log_{\text{base}} \text{ number} = \text{index} \\ \text{is equivalent to} \\ \text{base}^{\text{index}} = \text{number} \end{array}}$$

This can also be written as

    $y = a^x \iff x = \log_a y$

where the symbol $\iff$ means 'implies and is implied by'.

B5 (a) Rewrite $5^4 = 625$ in logarithmic form.

  (b) Rewrite $\log_{10} 100 = 2$ in exponential form.

B6 Write the following in logarithmic form.

  (a) $3^4 = 81$ (b) $7^3 = 343$ (c) $8^{-1} = 0.125$

B7 Write the following in exponential form.

  (a) $\log_3 9 = 2$ (b) $\log_4 64 = 3$ (c) $\log_9 \frac{1}{9} = -1$

B8 (a) Write $\log_2 2 = x$ in index form.

  (b) What is the value of x?

B9 (a) Write $\log_2 1 = x$ in index form.

  (b) What is the value of x?

B10 (a) Write $\log_2 \frac{1}{2} = x$ in index form.

  (b) What is the value of x?

B11 Write down the values of the following.

  (a) $\log_a a$ (b) $\log_a 1$ (c) $\log_a \left(\dfrac{1}{a} \right)$

B12 (a) (i) Write $\log_5 5^2 = x$ in index form.

      (ii) What is the value of x?

  (b) What is the value of $\log_3 3^4$?

  (c) What is the value of $\log_a a^x$?

B13 (a) (i) Write $2^{\log_2 8} = x$ in log form.

      (ii) What is the value of x?

    (b) What is the value of $3^{\log_3 9}$?

    (c) What is the value of $a^{\log_a x}$?

You have now obtained the following properties of logarithms.

$$y = a^x \Leftrightarrow x = \log_a y$$

$$\log_a a = 1 \qquad\qquad \log_a 1 = 0$$

$$\log_a \left(\frac{1}{a} \right) = -1$$

$$\log_a a^x = x$$
$$a^{\log_a x} = x$$

Example 2

Write down these values.

(a) $\log_4 16$ (b) $\log_3 81$ (c) $\log_9 3$

Solution

(a) Since $4^2 = 16$, $\log_4 16 = 2$

(b) Since $3^4 = 81$, $\log_3 81 = 4$

(c) Since $9^{\frac{1}{2}} = 3$, $\log_9 3 = \frac{1}{2}$

Example 3

Find the value of x in $\log_x 625 = 4$.

Solution

First write $\log_x 625 = 4$ *in exponential form.* $\log_x 625 = 4$ is the same as $x^4 = 625$

$$5^4 = 625, \text{ so } x = 5$$

Exercise B (answers p 153)

1 (a) Write the following as powers of 2.

    (i) 64   (ii) $\sqrt{2}$ (iii) $\frac{1}{8}$ (iv) 0.25   (v) 1

    (b) Hence write down the values of the following.

        (i) $\log_2 64$ (ii) $\log_2 \sqrt{2}$ (iii) $\log_2 \frac{1}{8}$ (iv) $\log_2 0.25$ (v) $\log_2 1$

2 Write the following in index form.

    (a) $\log_3 \frac{1}{9} = -2$ (b) $\log_8 1 = 0$ (c) $\log_4 32 = 2.5$ (d) $\log_8 4 = \frac{2}{3}$

3 Write the following in logarithmic form.

    (a) $6^3 = 216$ **(b)** $3^5 = 243$ **(c)** $4^{-3} = \frac{1}{64}$ **(d)** $27^{\frac{2}{3}} = 9$

4 Write down the values of the following.

    (a) $\log_3 9$ **(b)** $\log_5 125$ **(c)** $\log_5 \frac{1}{25}$ **(d)** $\log_7 1$

    (e) $\log_3 \sqrt[4]{3}$ **(f)** $\log_4 2$ **(g)** $\log_{11} 11$ **(h)** $\log_{10} 0.1$

5 Find the values of the following.

    (a) $\log_a a^2$ **(b)** $\log_a \left(\frac{1}{a^2} \right)$ **(c)** $\log_a \sqrt{a}$ **(d)** $\log_a (a^3 \times a^4)$

6 Write $\log_3 p = 4$ in index form and hence find the value of p.

7 Write $\log_t 3 = \frac{1}{2}$ in index form and hence find the value of t.

8 Find the value of x in each of the following.

    (a) $\log_4 64 = x$ **(b)** $\log_x 8 = 3$ **(c)** $\log_3 x = 3$ **(d)** $\log_x 216 = 3$

    (e) $\log_x 0.04 = -2$ **(f)** $\log_4 x = -\frac{1}{2}$ **(g)** $\log_5 0.2 = x$ **(h)** $\log_3 x = \frac{1}{2}$

9 Here is a table of values and sketch of the graph of the function $y = 2^x$.

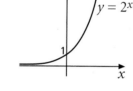

$y = 2^x$

x	-2	-1	0	1	2	3
$y = 2^x$	0.25	0.5	1	2	4	8

The table can be inverted to find values of the function $y = \log_2 x$.

(a) Complete this table of values for $y = \log_2 x$.

x	0.25	0.5	1	2	4	8
$y = \log_2 x$			0			

(b) Use the values in the table to draw the graph of $y = \log_2 x$.

(c) What is the relationship between the graph of $y = 2^x$ and the graph of $y = \log_2 x$?

C Laws of logarithms (answers p 153)

C1 (a) Write down the values of

    (i) $\log_2 8$ **(ii)** $\log_2 16$ **(iii)** $\log_2 128$

  (b) $8 \times 16 = 128$ can be written as $2^a \times 2^b = 2^c$.
     What are a, b and c? How is c related to a and b?

  (c) Use this to explain why $\log_2 8 + \log_2 16 = \log_2 (8 \times 16)$.

C2 $3^2 \times 3^3 = 3^5$.
    Show how this explains that $\log_3 9 + \log_3 27 = \log_3 (9 \times 27)$.

These results suggest that logs are related by the law

$$\log_a m + \log_a n = \log_a mn$$

In fact, it is possible to prove that this result is true for any positive base a.

Let $m = a^x$ so $x = \log_a m$ and let $n = a^y$ so $y = \log_a n$

Then $\log_a mn = \log_a (a^x \times a^y)$

$\Rightarrow \quad \log_a mn = \log_a (a^{x+y})$

$\Rightarrow \quad \log_a mn = x + y$

$\Rightarrow \log_a m + \log_a n = \log_a mn$

C3 Given that $\log_5 3 = 0.6826$ and $\log_5 4 = 0.8614$, use the law found above to find the value of $\log_5 12$.

C4 Using a similar method to that shown above, prove the result
$$\log_a m - \log_a n = \log_a \left(\frac{m}{n}\right)$$

C5 Given that $\log_8 3 = 0.5283$ and $\log_8 21 = 1.4641$, use the law found above to find the value of $\log_8 7$.

C6 Use the index law $(a^x)^2 = a^{2x}$ to prove the result
$$2\log_a m = \log_a m^2$$
(Hint: start by letting $m = a^x$ and consider $\log_a m^2$.)

C7 Use the index law $(a^x)^k = a^{kx}$ to prove the result
$$k\log_a m = \log_a m^k$$

C8 Given that $\log_3 2 = 0.6309$, find the values of
(a) $\log_3 4$ (b) $\log_3 16$ (c) $\log_3 \frac{1}{2}$ (d) $\log_3 \sqrt{2}$

K In summary, the laws of logarithms are

$$\log_a m + \log_a n = \log_a mn$$

$$\log_a m - \log_a n = \log_a \left(\frac{m}{n}\right)$$

$$k\log_a m = \log_a m^k$$

C9 Given that $\log_{10} 2 = 0.3010$ and $\log_{10} 3 = 0.4771$, use the laws of logs and the result that $\log_{10} 10 = 1$ to find the following.
(a) $\log_{10} \frac{1}{2}$ (b) $\log_{10} 1.5$ (c) $\log_{10} 4$ (d) $\log_{10} 5$
(e) $\log_{10} 6$ (f) $\log_{10} 9$ (g) $\log_{10} 16$ (h) $\log_{10} 20$

Example 4

Write $\log_a 3 + \log_a 8 - \log_a 2$ as a single logarithm.

Solution

Use the laws of logs to combine $\log_a 3$ and $\log_a 8$.

Now combine with $\log_a 2$.

$$\log_a 3 + \log_a 8 - \log_a 2 = \log_a 3 \times 8 - \log_a 2$$
$$= \log_a \frac{3 \times 8}{2}$$
$$= \log_a 12$$

Example 5

Express $\log_a \dfrac{x^2}{yz}$ in terms of $\log_a x$, $\log_a y$ and $\log_a z$.

Solution

Use $\log_a m - \log_a n$.

Use $k \log_a m$.

Use $\log_a m + \log_a n$.

$$\log_a \frac{x^2}{yz} = \log_a x^2 - \log_a yz$$
$$= 2 \log_a x - \log_a yz$$
$$= 2 \log_a x - (\log_a y + \log_a z)$$

so $\log_a \dfrac{x^2}{yz} = 2 \log_a x - \log_a y - \log_a z$

Exercise C (answers p 154)

1 Write each of the following as a single logarithm.

(a) $\log_a 5 + \log_a 2$
(b) $\log_a 12 - \log_a 3$
(c) $2 \log_a 3$
(d) $1 + \log_a 8$
(e) $3 \log_a 4 - \log_a 2$
(f) $\log_a 6 + 2 \log_a 2 - \log_a 3$

2 Given that $\log_5 3 = 0.6826$, use the laws of logs to find the values of the following.

(a) $\log_5 5$
(b) $\log_5 9$
(c) $\log_5 \frac{1}{3}$
(d) $\log_5 \sqrt{3}$
(e) $\log_5 15$
(f) $\log_5 25$
(g) $\log_5 0.6$
(h) $\log_5 \frac{9}{25}$

3 Express the following in terms of $\log_a x$ and $\log_a y$.

(a) $\log_a \dfrac{x}{y}$
(b) $\log_a xy$
(c) $\log_a \dfrac{x^2}{y}$
(d) $\log_a \dfrac{\sqrt[a]{y}}{x}$

4 The notation 4! means $4 \times 3 \times 2 \times 1$ and is read as '4 factorial'.
Given that $\log_5 4! = 1.9746$, write down the value of $\log_5 5!$.

5 Write each of the following as a single logarithm.

(a) $2 \log_a p + \log_a q$
(b) $1 + 3 \log_a p$
(c) $\frac{1}{2} \log_a p - 4 \log_a q$

6 A colony of bacteria doubles in size every hour.

   (a) Explain why the time t hours for the colony to increase in size 1000-fold is given by $2^t = 1000$.

   (b) Express t as a logarithm to base 2 and explain why $9 < t < 10$.

   (c) By using trial and improvement and the power key on your calculator, find an approximate value of t to two decimal places.

7 Solve these equations for x.

   (a) $\log_x 4 + \log_x 16 = 3$

   (b) $\log_2 96 - \log_2 6 = x$

   (c) $\log_6 4 + \log_6 x = 2$

   (d) $\log_4 (x + 1) - \log_4 3 = 1$

   (e) $\log_2 2x - \log_2 (3x - 4) = 1$

   (f) $\log_2 x^2 = 2 + \log_2 (x + 3)$

D Equations of the form $a^x = b$ (answers p 154)

Logarithms are useful for a variety of purposes, one of which is met in this section. Originally, however, they were used as a way of easing multiplication and division, by replacing them with addition and subtraction.
In 1615, the Scottish mathematician John Napier discussed the idea of using logarithms with the Oxford professor Henry Briggs. Two years later, Briggs published his first table of logarithms (to 14 decimal places!) and after much further work published his *Arithmetica Logarithmica* in 1624.

Logarithms can now be found directly from a calculator. 'Log' is usually taken to mean $\log_{10}$, and you will find that the $\boxed{\log}$ key on calculators evaluates logarithms to the base 10.

   D1 Use the log key on your calculator to check your answers to C9.

In answering question 6 in Exercise C about a colony of bacteria you used trial and improvement to solve the equation $2^t = 1000$.

Problems concerning growth often lead to such equations, in which the unknown appears as an index. These equations can be solved using logarithms.

   D2 (a) What is the relationship between $\log 2^t$ and $\log 2$?

      (b) Solve the equation $2^t = 1000$ by first taking logs to base 10 of both sides and then using the relationship you stated in (a). Compare your answer with the answer you obtained using trial and improvement.

   D3 £1000 is invested in an account which earns 1% interest per month, all interest being reinvested.

      (a) Explain why the number m of months taken for the total investment to reach £2000 is given by the equation $1.01^m = 2$.

      (b) Use logs to find m.

D4 The population of a village is decreasing at a rate of 5% each year.

(a) By what factor is the population multiplied each year?
(This is known as the growth factor.)

(b) After t years, the population of the village is $\frac{3}{5}$ of its original value.
Show that $0.6 = 0.95^t$.

(c) Find the value of t.

Example 6

Solve $4^x = 28$.

Solution

$$4^x = 28$$

Take logs of both sides.

$$\log 4^x = \log 28$$

Use the laws of logs.

$$x \log 4 = \log 28$$

$$\Rightarrow \quad x = \frac{\log 28}{\log 4} = 2.4036...$$

$$\Rightarrow \quad x = 2.40 \text{ to 3 s.f.}$$

Example 7

Solve $5^{2x+1} = 8$.

Solution

$$5^{2x+1} = 8$$

Take logs of both sides.

$$\log 5^{2x+1} = \log 8$$

Use the laws of logs.

$$(2x+1) \log 5 = \log 8$$

$$\Rightarrow \quad 2x + 1 = \frac{\log 8}{\log 5}$$

$$\Rightarrow \quad x = \frac{1}{2}\left(\frac{\log 8}{\log 5} - 1\right)$$

$$\Rightarrow \quad x = 0.146 \text{ to 3 s.f.}$$

Example 8

Solve $5^{2x} - 3(5^x) + 2 = 0$.

Solution

As $5^{2x} = (5^x)^2$, this is a quadratic expression.
$$5^{2x} - 3(5^x) + 2 = 0$$

This quadratic factorises.
so $\quad (5^x - 1)(5^x - 2) = 0$

Either $(5^x - 1) = 0$ or $(5^x - 2) = 0$.
giving $5^x = 1$ and $5^x = 2$

Use the result $a^0 = 1$.
When $5^x = 1$, then $x = 0$

When $5^x = 2$,

Take logs of both sides.
then $\quad \log 5^x = \log 2$

Use the laws of logs.
$$x \log 5 = \log 2$$

$$\Rightarrow \quad x = \frac{\log 2}{\log 5} = 0.4306...$$

so the solutions are $x = 0$ and $x = 0.431$ to 3 s.f.

Exercise D (answers p 154)

1 Solve these equations for x.

  (a) $2^x = 32$ (b) $9^x = 243$ (c) $8^x = 256$

  (d) $3^x = 10.05$ (e) $5^x = 9.2$ (f) $2.073^x = 7.218$

2 The number, n, of years needed for an investment of £4000 to grow to £5000 at 8% per annum compound interest is given by $1.08^n = 1.25$. Find n using logarithms.

3 The half-life, t days, of bismuth-210 is given approximately by the equation $10 \times (0.87)^t = 5$. Find its half-life in days, correct to two significant figures.

4 A colony of bacteria has a growth factor of 3.7 per hour and initially there are 250 bacteria.

  (a) Write down an expression for the number of bacteria, n, after t hours.

  (b) Find the time (to the nearest minute) after which there are 10 000 bacteria.

5 The charge of a capacitor has a growth factor of 0.9 per second.
After how long will there be $\frac{1}{5}$ of the original charge?
Give your answer in seconds to 2 d.p.

6 Find the smallest possible integer satisfying the inequality $2^n > 50^{132}$.

7 The population of a city is predicted to rise at a rate of 6% per year.
In 2003 the population was 250 000.

  (a) What is the growth factor for the population?

  (b) Write down an expression for the population, P, after t years.

  (c) Use this model to predict the number of years it will take for the population to reach 400 000.

8 A radioactive isotope is decaying at a rate of 7.5% per year.

  (a) After t years, the amount of isotope present has decayed by a half. Show that $0.5 = 0.925^t$.

  (b) Find the value of t.

9 A savings account has an interest rate of 3.25% per annum.
After how long will an investment have increased by $\frac{1}{4}$ of its original value?

10 Solve these equations for x.

  (a) $3^{x-1} = 5$ (b) $7^{2x+1} = 5$ (c) $5(3^x) + 1 = 3$

  (d) $4^{x+2} = 5^x$ (e) $4(7^x) - 2 = 3$ (f) $6^{x-4} = 2^{x+3}$

11 A population of red squirrels is introduced into a forest. The population P at time t years after the squirrels have been introduced is modelled by

$$P = \frac{300a^t}{5 + a^t}$$

where a is constant. Given that there are 80 squirrels in the park after 5 years,

(a) calculate, to four decimal places, the value of a;

(b) use the model to predict the number of years needed for the population of squirrels to increase from 80 to 120.

12 (a) Solve the equation $y^2 - 5y + 6 = 0$.

(b) Hence solve the equation $2^{2x} - 5(2^x) + 6 = 0$.

13 Solve these equations.

(a) $3^{2x} - 4(3^x) + 3 = 0$ (b) $5^{2x} - 6(5^x) + 8 = 0$ (c) $2^{2x} + 3(2^x) - 10 = 0$

*14 (a) In 1980, the population of Africa was 470 million and growing at a rate of 2.9% per annum. In what year will its population reach one thousand million according to this model?

(b) In 1980, the population of China was 995 million and growing at a rate of 1.4% per annum. After how many years will the two populations be equal?

Key points

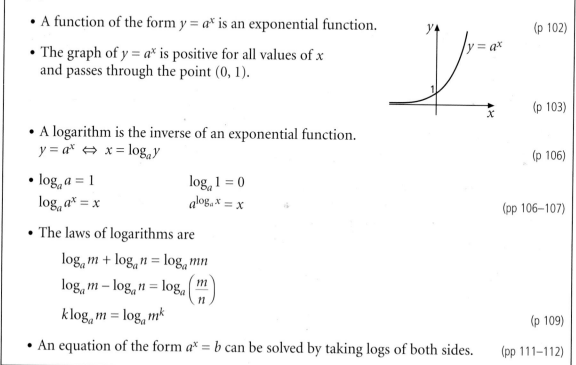

- A function of the form $y = a^x$ is an exponential function.   (p 102)

- The graph of $y = a^x$ is positive for all values of x and passes through the point $(0, 1)$.   (p 103)

- A logarithm is the inverse of an exponential function.
  $y = a^x \Leftrightarrow x = \log_a y$ (p 106)

- $\log_a a = 1$ $\log_a 1 = 0$
  $\log_a a^x = x$ $a^{\log_a x} = x$ (pp 106–107)

- The laws of logarithms are

  $$\log_a m + \log_a n = \log_a mn$$
  $$\log_a m - \log_a n = \log_a \left(\frac{m}{n}\right)$$
  $$k \log_a m = \log_a m^k$$
     (p 109)

- An equation of the form $a^x = b$ can be solved by taking logs of both sides.   (pp 111–112)

Test yourself (answers p 155)

1 Describe, in each of the following cases, a single transformation which maps the graph of $y = 3^x$ on to the graph of the function given.

   (a) $y = 3^{x+2}$ **(b)** $y = 3^{-x}$ **(c)** $y = 4 \times 3^x$ **(d)** $y = 3^x - 1$

2 (a) Show that $\log_5 125 = 3$.

   (b) Find the value of

   (i) $\log_5 (125^4)$ **(ii)** $\log_5 \left(\dfrac{1}{\sqrt{125}} \right)$

3 (a) Describe a geometrical transformation by which the graph of $y = 2^{x+3}$ can be obtained from that of $y = 2^x$.

   (b) The graph of $y = 2^{x+3}$ passes through the point $(0, p)$. What is the value of p?

4 (a) Write down the value of $\log_2 8$.

   (b) Express $\log_2 9$ in the form $n \log_2 3$.

   (c) Hence show that $\log_2 72 = m + n \log_2 3$, where m and n are integers.   AQA 2002

5 (a) Given that $\log_a x = \log_a 5 + 2 \log_a 3$, where a is a positive constant, show that $x = 45$.

   (b) (i) Write down the value of $\log_2 2$.

   (ii) Given that $\log_2 y = \log_4 2$, find the value of y.   AQA 2002

6 Given that $\log_a x = 2(\log_a k - \log_a 2)$ where a is a positive constant, show that $k^2 = 4x$.   AQA 2003

7 (a) Simplify $\dfrac{x^2 + 8x + 12}{x^2 + 2x}$.

   (b) Find the value of x for which $\log_5 (x^2 + 8x + 12) - \log_5 (x^2 + 2x) = 2$.

8 Solve these equations for x.

   (a) $4^x = 24$ **(b)** $2^{x-3} = 9$ **(c)** $3^{2x+1} = 12$

9 A radioactive isotope decays at a rate of 12% per year.
After t years the amount of isotope has decreased to half of its original value. This is the half-life of the isotope.

   Form and solve an equation to find the value of t.

10 Find the possible values of x for which $3^{2x} - 5(3^x) + 4 = 0$.

9 Differentiation and integration

In this chapter you will learn how to
- differentiate x^n, where n is a rational number
- integrate x^n, where n is a rational number ($n \neq -1$)
- use the trapezium rule to find an approximate value for a definite integral

Key points from Core 1

- The derivative of x^n, where n is a positive integer, is nx^{n-1}.

- The value of the derivative at a point P on a graph tells you the gradient of the tangent at P.

- The normal to a curve at a point P is the line through P perpendicular to the tangent at P.

- If the gradient of the tangent is m, the gradient of the normal is $-\dfrac{1}{m}$.

- If the value of $\dfrac{dy}{dx}$ is positive at $x = a$, then y is increasing at $x = a$.

  If the value of $\dfrac{dy}{dx}$ is negative at $x = a$, then y is decreasing at $x = a$.

  (Alternative notation: if $f'(a) > 0$, then $f(x)$ is increasing at $x = a$; if $f'(a) < 0$, then $f(x)$ is decreasing at $x = a$.)

- Points where $\dfrac{dy}{dx} = 0$ are called stationary points.

  At a local maximum, $\dfrac{dy}{dx}$ goes from positive to negative.

  At a local minimum, $\dfrac{dy}{dx}$ goes from negative to positive.

- The second derivative, $\dfrac{d^2y}{dx^2}$ or $f''(x)$, is the derivative of $\dfrac{dy}{dx}$ or $f'(x)$.

- If at a stationary point $\dfrac{d^2y}{dx^2}$ is positive, the point is a local minimum; if $\dfrac{d^2y}{dx^2}$ is negative, the point is a local maximum.

- If $\dfrac{dy}{dx} = f(x)$ then $y = \int f(x)\, dx$.

- $\int x^n\, dx = \dfrac{x^{n+1}}{n+1} + c$ for positive integers n.

- The area under the graph of $y = f(x)$ between $x = a$ and $x = b$ is found by evaluating the definite integral $\int_a^b f(x)\, dx$.

- An area below the x-axis has a negative value.

A Differentiating x^n, where n is negative or a fraction

K If $y = x^n$, where n is a positive integer, then $\dfrac{dy}{dx} = nx^{n-1}$.

This rule also applies when n is negative or a fraction. (The proof of this is beyond the scope of this book.)

Example 1

Given that $y = \dfrac{1}{x^2}$, find $\dfrac{dy}{dx}$.

Solution

Write the function as a negative power.

Then use the rule for differentiating a power.

$y = x^{-2}$

$\dfrac{dy}{dx} = -2x^{-2-1} = -2x^{-3} \left(\text{or} -\dfrac{2}{x^3} \right)$

Example 2

Given that $f(x) = 5x^{\frac{2}{3}}$, find $f'(x)$.

Solution

$f'(x) = 5\left(\frac{2}{3}x^{\frac{2}{3}-1}\right) = \frac{10}{3}x^{-\frac{1}{3}}$

Example 3

Given that $y = x^3\sqrt{x}$, find $\dfrac{dy}{dx}$.

Solution

Use the rules of indices to write $x^3\sqrt{x}$ as a single power of x.

$y = x^3\sqrt{x} = x^3 \times x^{\frac{1}{2}} = x^{\frac{7}{2}}$

$\dfrac{dy}{dx} = \frac{7}{2}x^{\frac{7}{2}-1} = \frac{7}{2}x^{\frac{5}{2}}$

Example 4

Given that $f(x) = \dfrac{1+x}{\sqrt{x}}$, find $f'(x)$.

Solution

Write the expression as the sum of two separate fractions.

$f(x) = \dfrac{1}{\sqrt{x}} + \dfrac{x}{\sqrt{x}} = x^{-\frac{1}{2}} + x^{\frac{1}{2}}$

$f'(x) = -\frac{1}{2}x^{-\frac{3}{2}} + \frac{1}{2}x^{-\frac{1}{2}}$

Exercise A (answers p 156)

1 Differentiate each of these with respect to x.

(a) x^{-3} (b) $\dfrac{1}{x}$ (c) $x^{\frac{1}{3}}$ (d) $\sqrt{x}$ (e) $x^{\frac{3}{4}}$

2 Find $\dfrac{dy}{dx}$ for each of the following functions.

(a) $y = (\sqrt{x})^3$ (b) $y = x - \dfrac{1}{x}$ (c) $y = \dfrac{3}{x^2}$ (d) $y = \dfrac{1}{4x^3}$ (e) $y = \dfrac{2}{3\sqrt{x}}$

3 (a) Write the expression $5x(1 + \sqrt{x})$ without brackets.

(b) Given that $f(x) = 5x(1 + \sqrt{x})$, find $f'(x)$.

4 Find $f'(x)$ for each of the following functions.

(a) $\sqrt{x}\,(3 - x^2)$ **(b)** $x^2(1 + \sqrt{x})$ **(c)** $3x(x - \sqrt{x})$ **(d)** $(x + 3)(\sqrt{x} - 1)$

5 Find $f'(x)$ for each of the following functions.

(a) $f(x) = \dfrac{x + 1}{x}$ **(b)** $f(x) = \dfrac{x^2 - 3}{x}$ **(c)** $f(x) = \dfrac{3x + 2}{\sqrt{x}}$ **(d)** $f(x) = \dfrac{1 + \sqrt{x} + x}{x^2}$

6 (a) Express $x^2\sqrt{x}$ in the form x^p.

(b) Given that $y = x^2\sqrt{x}$, find the value of $\dfrac{dy}{dx}$ at the point where $x = 9$.   AQA 2001

7 (a) Expand $\left(\sqrt{x} + \dfrac{1}{\sqrt{x}}\right)^2$.

(b) Given that $f(x) = \left(\sqrt{x} + \dfrac{1}{\sqrt{x}}\right)^2$, find $f'(x)$.

8 The graph of $y = 3\sqrt{x}$ goes through the point $P\,(9, 9)$. Find

(a) the gradient of the tangent at P **(b)** the equation of the tangent at P

9 Find the equation of the normal to the graph of $y = \dfrac{x^2 + 4}{x}$ at the point where $x = 1$.

10 The graph of $y = x + 4x^{-2}$ has a stationary point.

(a) Find $\dfrac{dy}{dx}$.

(b) Find the coordinates of the stationary point.

(c) Find the value of $\dfrac{d^2y}{dx^2}$ at the stationary point and hence determine whether

the stationary point is a maximum or minimum.   AQA 2003

11 Find the x-coordinates of the stationary points on the graph of $y = 3x^3 + \dfrac{1}{9x}$ and determine the type of each stationary point.

12 An open box is made of sheet metal.
The base of the box is a rectangle x cm by $2x$ cm.
The height of the box is h cm.

(a) Find an expression, in terms of x and h, for

     (i) the volume V cm^3 of the box

     (ii) the area A cm^2 of the metal

(b) Given that the volume of the box is 288 cm^3, show that
$$A = 2x^2 + \frac{864}{x}$$

(c) Find the value of x for which A is a minimum, showing that it is a minimum.

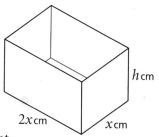

B Integrating x^n, where n is negative or a fraction

The rule for integrating x^n also works when n is negative or a fraction, except for the case $n = -1$.

$$\int x^n \, dx = \frac{x^{n+1}}{n+1} + c \qquad (n \neq -1)$$

Example 5

Find $\int \frac{1}{x^4} \, dx$.

Solution

$$\int \frac{1}{x^4} \, dx = \int x^{-4} \, dx = \frac{x^{-4+1}}{-4+1} + c = \frac{x^{-3}}{-3} + c = -\frac{1}{3x^3} + c$$

Example 6

Find $\int_1^8 x^{\frac{2}{3}} \, dx$.

Solution

$$\int_1^8 x^{\frac{2}{3}} \, dx = \left[\frac{x^{\frac{2}{3}+1}}{\frac{2}{3}+1} \right]_1^8 = \left[\frac{x^{\frac{5}{3}}}{\frac{5}{3}} \right]_1^8 = \left[\tfrac{3}{5} x^{\frac{5}{3}} \right]_1^8$$

$$= \tfrac{3}{5} \times 8^{\frac{5}{3}} - \tfrac{3}{5} \times 1^{\frac{5}{3}}$$

$$= \tfrac{3}{5} \times 32 - \tfrac{3}{5} \times 1 = \tfrac{93}{5} = 18.6$$

Example 7

Find $\int \sqrt{x}\left(x + \frac{1}{x}\right) dx$.

Solution

$$\int \sqrt{x}\left(x + \frac{1}{x}\right) dx = \int \left(x\sqrt{x} + \frac{1}{\sqrt{x}} \right) dx = \int \left(x^{\frac{3}{2}} + x^{-\frac{1}{2}} \right) dx$$

$$= \tfrac{2}{5} x^{\frac{5}{2}} + 2 x^{\frac{1}{2}} + c$$

Exercise B (answers p 156)

1 Find the following indefinite integrals.

(a) $\int x^{-3} \, dx$ (b) $\int x^{\frac{3}{4}} \, dx$ (c) $\int x\sqrt{x} \, dx$ (d) $\int x^{-\frac{3}{4}} \, dx$

(e) $\int x(1 + \sqrt{x}) \, dx$ (f) $\int \left(\frac{x^2 - 1}{x^2} \right) dx$ (g) $\int \left(\frac{1 + \sqrt{x}}{\sqrt{x}} \right) dx$ (h) $\int \left(\frac{1 + x}{\sqrt{x}} \right) dx$

(i) $\int \left(\frac{1 + x^2}{\sqrt{x}} \right) dx$ (j) $\int (1 + \sqrt{x})^2 \, dx$

2 (a) Write $x^2 \sqrt{x}$ in the form x^k, where k is a fraction.

  (b) The gradient of a curve at the point (x, y) is given by $\dfrac{dy}{dx} = 7x^2 \sqrt{x}$.

    Use integration to find the equation of the curve, given that the curve passes through the point $(1, 1)$.   AQA 2002

3 (a) Express $\dfrac{x^5 + 1}{x^2}$ in the form $x^p + x^q$, where p and q are integers.

  (b) Hence find $\int_1^2 \left(\dfrac{x^5 + 1}{x^2} \right) dx$.   AQA 2002

4 Evaluate   (a) $\int_1^3 \frac{1}{x^3} \, dx$ (b) $\int_{16}^{25} \frac{1}{x\sqrt{x}} \, dx$ (c) $\int_1^4 (x + \sqrt{x})^2 \, dx$

5 The diagram shows the graph of $y = x^2 - \sqrt{x}$.
Find the shaded area.

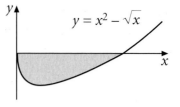

6 Find the area under the graph of $y = \dfrac{x-1}{x^3}$ between $x = 1$ and $x = 3$.

C Numerical integration: the trapezium rule (answers p 156)

The shaded area is the area under the graph of
$y = \dfrac{5x - 7}{x - 1}$ from $x = 1.5$ to $x = 3.5$.

$$\text{Area} = \int_{1.5}^{3.5}\left(\frac{5x-7}{x-1}\right) dx$$

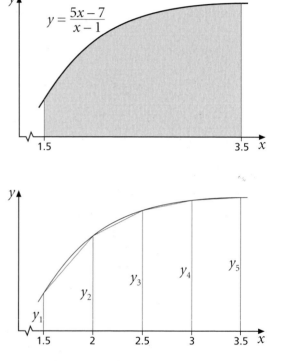

The function $\dfrac{5x - 7}{x - 1}$ is one that cannot be
integrated by the methods you have met so far.

However, it is possible to get a good numerical
approximation to the area. One of the simplest
methods is called the **trapezium rule**.

The area is divided into vertical strips of equal width.
The heights of the vertical lines are called **ordinates**.
In the diagram on the right there are five ordinates
at $x = 1.5, 2.0, 2.5, 3.0$ and 3.5.

To get an approximation to the area, the curve is
replaced by straight line segments and each strip
becomes a trapezium. The total area of the trapezia
is an estimate of the area under the curve.

C1 Will the estimate obtained in this way be too large or too small?
How can you tell from the diagram?

The first ordinate, labelled y_1, is $\dfrac{5 \times 1.5 - 7}{1.5 - 1} = \dfrac{7.5 - 7}{1.5 - 1} = 1.$

Similarly, y_2 is $\dfrac{10 - 7}{2 - 1} = 3.$

The area of a trapezium is found by using the formula $\frac{1}{2}h(a + b)$, where
a and b are the parallel sides and h is the distance between them.

C2 (a) Calculate the area of the first trapezium.

(b) Calculate the area of each of the other four trapezia (rounding to 2 d.p.
where necessary) and hence find an estimate of the area under the curve
between $x = 1.5$ and $x = 3.5$.

When the area calculation is set out using the symbols h, y_1, y_2 and so on, a pattern appears that leads to a short cut.

$$\text{Total area} = \tfrac{1}{2}h(y_1 + y_2) + \tfrac{1}{2}h(y_2 + y_3) + \tfrac{1}{2}h(y_3 + y_4) + \tfrac{1}{2}h(y_4 + y_5)$$
$$= \tfrac{1}{2}h(y_1 + y_2 + y_2 + y_3 + y_3 + y_4 + y_4 + y_5)$$
$$= \tfrac{1}{2}h(y_1 + y_5 + 2[y_2 + y_3 + y_4])$$
$$= \tfrac{1}{2}h(\text{end ordinates} + \text{twice sum of 'interior' ordinates})$$

There is nothing special about using five ordinates – any number may be used.

C3 (a) Use this form of the trapezium rule to estimate the area under the curve. Check that you get the same result as before.

(b) How could you improve on the estimate of the area, still using the trapezium rule?

Example 8

(a) Sketch the graph of $y = \dfrac{12}{x}$ for $0.5 \le x \le 3$.

(b) Use the trapezium rule with six ordinates to calculate an approximation to $\displaystyle\int_{0.5}^{3} \dfrac{12}{x}\, dx$, stating, with a reason, whether your result is an overestimate or underestimate.

Solution

(a) The sketch is shown on the right.

(b) Using six ordinates means five trapezia.
The width of each trapezium is 0.5.
The values of x and y are shown in this table.

x	0.5	1	1.5	2	2.5	3
y	24	12	8	6	4.8	4

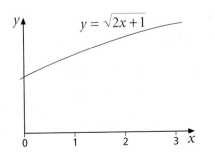

Estimate of area $= \dfrac{0.5}{2}(24 + 4 + 2[12 + 8 + 6 + 4.8]) = 22.4$

As the curve is below the line segments, this is an overestimate.

The trapezium rule can easily be set up in a spreadsheet.
The estimate will be improved if you use a larger number of narrower strips.

Exercise C (answers p 156)

1 The diagram shows part of the graph of $y = \sqrt{2x+1}$.

(a) Use the trapezium rule with four ordinates to calculate an approximation to $\displaystyle\int_{0}^{3} \sqrt{2x+1}\, dx$.

(b) State, with a reason, whether your result is an overestimate or underestimate.

2 (a) Use the trapezium rule, with ordinates spaced at intervals of 0.5, to estimate the area under the graph of $y = \sqrt{1 + x^2}$ from $x = 0$ to $x = 2$.

(b) By reducing the interval between ordinates to 0.25, calculate a better estimate.

3 (a) Use the trapezium rule with four ordinates to calculate an approximate value for $\int_1^4 \sqrt{x}\, dx$.

(b) Find the exact value of the same integral.

4 (a) Copy and complete this table of values for the function $y = \sqrt{x + \dfrac{1}{x}}$, giving y to 2 d.p.

x	2	2.2	2.4	2.6	2.8	3
y	1.58					

(b) Use the trapezium rule, with the values in the table, to estimate $\int_2^3 \sqrt{x + \dfrac{1}{x}}\, dx$.

Key points

- If $y = x^n$, then $\dfrac{dy}{dx} = nx^{n-1}$ for all values of n.   (p 117)

- $\int x^n\, dx = \dfrac{x^{n+1}}{n+1} + c$ for all values of n except $n = -1$.   (p 119)

- The trapezium rule gives an approximation to the area under a graph. If the gap between ordinates is h, then

$$\text{Area} = \tfrac{1}{2}h(\text{end ordinates} + \text{twice sum of 'interior' ordinates})$$

To improve the estimate, use a smaller value of h (and hence more ordinates).   (p 121)

Mixed questions (answers p 157)

1 It is given that $y = x^{\frac{1}{3}}$.

(a) Find $\dfrac{dy}{dx}$.

(b) (i) Find $\int y\, dx$.   **(ii)** Hence evaluate $\int_0^8 y\, dx$.   AQA 2002

2 The gradient of a curve at the point (x, y) is given by $\dfrac{dy}{dx} = \dfrac{3}{x\sqrt{x}}$.
The curve goes through the point $(4, 6)$. Find the equation of the curve.

3 (a) Sketch the graph of $y = \dfrac{1}{x} + 1$ for values of x from 1 to 4.

(b) Use the trapezium rule with seven ordinates to estimate $\int_1^4 \left(\dfrac{1}{x} + 1\right) dx$.

(c) By referring to the graph, determine whether the estimate is greater or less than the actual area.

4 (a) It is given that $y = 2\pi x^2 + \dfrac{1000}{x}$.

(i) Find $\dfrac{dy}{dx}$.

(ii) Show that $\dfrac{dy}{dx} = 0$ when $x^3 = \dfrac{250}{\pi}$.

(iii) Find $\dfrac{d^2y}{dx^2}$.

(iv) Verify that $\dfrac{d^2y}{dx^2} = 12\pi$ when $x^3 = \dfrac{250}{\pi}$.

(v) Find, to one decimal place, the value of x for which y has a stationary value and state whether this stationary value is a maximum or a minimum.

(b) A closed cylindrical tin can contains $500\,\text{cm}^3$ of liquid when full. The can has base radius r cm and total external surface area $A\,\text{cm}^2$.

It is given that $A = 2\pi r^2 + \dfrac{1000}{r}$.

Use your results from part (a) to find the smallest possible value for the total surface area of the can. Give your answer to the nearest square centimetre.   AQA 2002

5 A curve has equation $y = \dfrac{x^4}{4} + \dfrac{32}{x^2}$

and is sketched on the right.

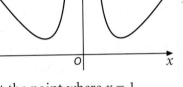

(a) (i) Find $\dfrac{dy}{dx}$.

(ii) Hence find the gradient of the curve at the point where $x = 1$.

(iii) Show that the stationary points of the curve occur when $x^6 = 64$.

(iv) Hence find the x-coordinates of the stationary points.

(b) (i) Find $\displaystyle\int \left(\dfrac{x^4}{4} + \dfrac{32}{x^2} \right) dx$.

(ii) Hence find the area of the region bounded by the curve, the lines $x = 1$, $x = 2$ and the x-axis.   AQA 2002

6 The diagram shows a prism whose cross-section is a right-angled triangle with sides $3x$, $4x$ and $5x$ cm. The height is h cm.

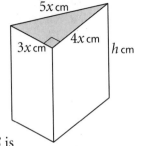

(a) (i) Show that the volume $V\,\text{cm}^3$ is given by $V = 6x^2 h$.

(ii) Show that the surface area $S\,\text{cm}^2$ is given by $S = 12x^2 + 12xh$.

(b) Given the volume of the prism is $100\,\text{cm}^3$, show that

$$S = 12x^2 + \dfrac{200}{x}$$

(c) Find, correct to three significant figures, the value of x for which S is a minimum, showing that this value does give a minimum for S.

7 The diagram shows part of the graph of the function $y = \sqrt{x} - x$.

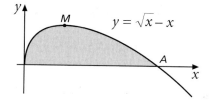

(a) Find the gradient of the curve at the point A.

(b) M is the maximum point on the graph. Find the coordinates of M.

(c) Show that to the right of the point M the function is always decreasing .

(d) Calculate the shaded area.

8 The diagram shows a sketch of the curve
$$y = 14 - x^2 - \frac{9}{x^2}$$
and the line $y = 4$.

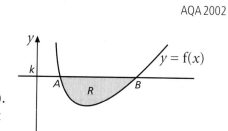

(a) Find the x-coordinates of the two stationary points P and Q on the curve.

(b) (i) Show that the curve intersects the line $y = 4$ when
$$(x^2 - 9)(x^2 - 1) = 0$$

(ii) Hence find the x-coordinates of the four points where the curve intersects the line $y = 4$.

(iii) Show that the shaded region has area $5\frac{1}{3}$.

AQA 2002

9 The function f is defined for all positive values of x by $f(x) = x^2 + \frac{16}{x^2}$.

The diagram shows the curve with equation $y = f(x)$. The line with equation $y = k$ intersects the curve at the points A and B.

(a) Determine the coordinates of the minimum point of the curve.

The x-coordinate of A is 1 and the x-coordinate of B is 4.

(b) (i) Verify that the y-coordinate of A and the y-coordinate of B are equal.

(ii) The shaded region R is bounded by the curve and the line with equation $y = k$. Calculate the area of the region R.

(c) The curve with equation $y = 2^x$ intersects the curve with equation $y = f(x)$ at the point where $x = \alpha$. Show that α lies between 4.2 and 4.3.

AQA 2001

Test yourself (answers p 157)

1 The diagram shows the graph of

$$y = x^{\frac{3}{2}}, \ 0 \leq x \leq 4$$

and a straight line joining the origin to the point P which has coordinates $(4, 8)$.

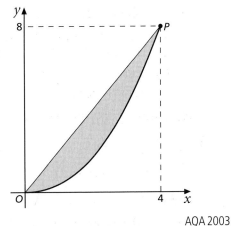

(a) (i) Find $\int x^{\frac{3}{2}} \, dx$.

   (ii) Hence find the value of $\int_0^4 x^{\frac{3}{2}} \, dx$.

(b) Calculate the area of the shaded region.

AQA 2003

2 A box made from sheet metal is in the shape of a square-based prism, open at the top.

The volume of the box is $256 \, \text{cm}^3$.

The base is a square of side x cm.

(a) Find an expression in terms of x for the height of the box.

(b) Show that the area $A \, \text{cm}^2$ of the metal is given by

$$A = x^2 + \frac{1024}{x}$$

(c) Find the value of x for which A is a minimum.

x cm x cm

3 The curve with equation $y = 2x + \dfrac{27}{x^2} - 7$ is defined

for $x > 0$, and is sketched on the right.

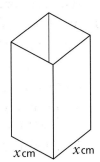

(a) (i) Find $\dfrac{dy}{dx}$.

   (ii) The curve has a minimum point M.
Find the x-coordinate of M.

(b) (i) Find $\int \left(2x + \dfrac{27}{x^2} - 7 \right) dx$.

   (ii) Hence determine the area of the region bounded by the curve, the lines $x = 1$, $x = 2$ and the x-axis.

AQA 2003

4 (a) Use the trapezium rule with five ordinates to find an approximate

value for $\int_0^2 \dfrac{2}{1+x} \, dx$.

(b) By sketching a graph, determine whether the result in (a) is an overestimate or underestimate.

Answers

1 Indices

A Positive and negative indices

Exercise A (p 7)

1 (a) 243 (b) -32 (c) $\frac{1}{32}$ (d) 1 (e) $-\frac{1}{10}$

2 (a) 0.09 (b) 0.25 (c) 0.125

   (d) 0.0001 (e) 0.000001

3 (a) $\frac{1}{27}$ (b) $\frac{16}{49}$ (c) $\frac{3}{2}$ (d) $\frac{16}{9}$ (e) $\frac{8}{125}$

4 (a) 2^5 (b) 2^{-3} (c) 2^{-1} (d) 2^0 (e) 2^{-6}

5 (a) 2^8 (b) 5^{-3} (c) 2^{-4} (d) 3^{-4} (e) 5^{-1}

6 (a) 3^3 (b) 3^{-2} (c) 3^{-7} (d) 3^{10} (e) 3^{10}

7 (a) 2^4 (b) 2^9 (c) 2^9 (d) 2^{-4} (e) 2^{-13}

8 (a) 5^{-2}

   (b) $\left(\frac{1}{25}\right)^{-4} = (5^{-2})^{-4} = 5^{-2 \times -4} = 5^8$

9 (a) 2^{-10} (b) 2^{-6} (c) 2^4 (d) 2^3 (e) 2^{10}

10 (a) n^{-1} or $\frac{1}{n}$ (b) $3n^{-2}$ or $\frac{3}{n^2}$ (c) n^8

   (d) $5n^6$ (e) n^{20} (f) $2n^7$

   (g) $\frac{1}{2}n$ or $\frac{n}{2}$ (h) $\frac{1}{3}n^5$ or $\frac{n^5}{3}$ (i) $\frac{5}{3}n^{-2}$ or $\frac{5}{3n^2}$

   (j) $\frac{4}{3}n^5$ or $\frac{4n^5}{3}$

11 (a) $5^5 + 5^4$ (b) $5 + 5^2$ (c) $5^6 - 5$

   (d) $5^{-1} + 5$ (e) $5^2 - 5^{-1} + 5^{-5}$

12 (a) $x^2 + x^5$ (b) $x^7 - x$ (c) $x^{-4} + x^{-2}$

   (d) $x + x^{-3} - x^{-4}$ (e) $x^{-4} - x$

13 (a) $x = 9$ (b) $x = -2$ (c) $x = -2$

   (d) $x = -5$ (e) $x = -4$

14 (a) $x = \frac{5}{2}$ (b) $x = \frac{5}{2}$ (c) $x = \frac{10}{3}$

   (d) $x = 2$ (e) $x = \frac{4}{3}$

B Roots and fractional indices

Exercise B (p 10)

1 (a) 6 (b) 5 (c) 2 (d) 2 (e) 1

2 (a) 27 (b) 16 (c) 243 (d) 27 (e) 4

3 $125^{\frac{2}{3}} = \left(\sqrt[3]{125}\right)^2 = 5^2 = 25$

   so $125^{-\frac{2}{3}} = \frac{1}{25}$

4 (a) $\frac{1}{3}$ (b) $\frac{1}{4}$ (c) $\frac{1}{32}$ (d) $\frac{1}{9}$ (e) $\frac{1}{8}$

5 $\left(\frac{1}{9}\right)^{\frac{3}{2}} = \left(\sqrt{\frac{1}{9}}\right)^3 = \left(\frac{1}{3}\right)^3 = \frac{1}{27}$

6 $\left(\frac{4}{9}\right)^{\frac{3}{2}} = \left(\sqrt{\frac{4}{9}}\right)^3 = \left(\frac{2}{3}\right)^3 = \frac{8}{27}$

   so $\left(\frac{4}{9}\right)^{-\frac{3}{2}} = \frac{1}{\left(\frac{8}{27}\right)} = \frac{27}{8}$

7 (a) $\frac{1}{9}$ (b) $\frac{3}{2}$ (c) $\frac{1}{32}$ (d) $\frac{4}{25}$ (e) 16

8 (a) $a^{\frac{5}{2}}$ (b) $a^{\frac{5}{2}}$ (c) $a^{\frac{3}{4}}$ (d) a (e) $a^{\frac{3}{2}}$

   (f) a^{-2} (g) $a^{-\frac{2}{3}}$ (h) $a^{-\frac{1}{8}}$

9 (a) $2^{\frac{1}{2}}$ (b) $2^{\frac{1}{5}}$ (c) $2^{-\frac{1}{2}}$ (d) $2^{\frac{1}{2}}$ (e) $2^{\frac{3}{2}}$

   (f) $2^{\frac{9}{2}}$ (g) $2^{\frac{3}{2}}$ (h) $2^{-\frac{1}{2}}$ (i) $2^{-\frac{9}{2}}$ (j) $2^{\frac{1}{6}}$

   (k) 2^4 (l) $2^{\frac{3}{2}}$ (m) 2^2 (n) 2^3 (o) $2^{\frac{15}{2}}$

10 $x^{\frac{9}{2}}$

11 (a) $x + x^{\frac{9}{2}}$ (b) $x^{\frac{3}{2}} - x^{\frac{7}{2}}$ (c) $x^{\frac{5}{2}} - x$

   (d) $x^{-\frac{1}{2}} + x^{\frac{1}{2}}$ (e) $x^3 + x^{\frac{11}{2}}$

12 (a) $4x$ (b) $5x^{\frac{3}{2}}$ (c) $2x^{\frac{1}{2}}$

   (d) $\frac{1}{2}x^{\frac{3}{2}}$ (e) $\frac{4}{3}x^{-\frac{1}{2}}$

13 (a) $6x - 8x^{\frac{1}{2}}$ (b) $5x^3 + 2x^2$

   (c) $2x^{\frac{1}{2}} + 3x^{\frac{7}{2}}$ (d) $\frac{1}{9}x^{\frac{3}{2}} - \frac{2}{3}x^{-\frac{1}{2}}$

14 (a) $x = 27$ (b) $x = \frac{1}{49}$ (c) $x = 1$

   (d) $x = 32$ (e) $x = \frac{8}{125}$

15 (a) $x = 25$ (b) $x = 16$ (c) $x = \frac{8}{27}$ (d) $x = 1$

   (e) $x = 27$ (f) $x = 32$ (g) $x = 81$ (h) $x = 9$

   (i) $x = \frac{1}{27}$ (j) $x = \frac{1}{4}$

C Further problems

Exercise C (p 13)

1 (a) $x = 1$ (b) $x = \frac{2}{3}$ (c) $x = -\frac{1}{2}$

   (d) $x = 2$ (e) $x = -2$

2 (a) 3^{2x} (b) 3^{x+1} (c) 3^{3x+2}

   (d) 3^{x-2} (e) $3^{\frac{x}{2}}$

3 (a) 2^{2x} (b) 2^{3x} (c) 2^{-4x} (d) 2^{5x-1}
   (e) $2^{x-\frac{1}{2}}$ (f) 2^{3x-2} (g) 2^{10-x} (h) $2^{\frac{x}{2}}$
   (i) $2^{4x-\frac{3}{2}}$ (j) 2^{x}

4 (a) $x=\frac{1}{2}$ (b) $x=-\frac{1}{2}$ (c) $x=-\frac{1}{3}$ (d) $x=\frac{2}{3}$
   (e) $x=\frac{1}{3}$ (f) $x=-\frac{3}{5}$ (g) $x=\frac{2}{3}$ (h) $x=-\frac{3}{4}$
   (i) $x=-2$ (j) $x=-\frac{3}{4}$

5 (a) $x=\frac{1}{5}$ (b) $x=\frac{1}{6}$ (c) $x=\frac{3}{2}$ (d) $x=-\frac{3}{2}$
   (e) $x=\frac{5}{2}$ (f) $x=-\frac{1}{2}$ (g) $x=-6$ (h) $x=\frac{1}{2}$
   (i) $x=-\frac{1}{2}$ (j) $x=-3$

6 (a) $y=\frac{1}{2}$ (b) $x=\frac{1}{3}$ (c) $p=6$ (d) $n=-\frac{3}{5}$

7 $3^{2x}=(3^x)^2=y^2$

8 $8^x=(2^3)^x=2^{3x}=(2^x)^3=u^3$

9 $5^{n+2}=5^n\times 5^2=25\times 5^n=25x$

10 (a)
$$2^{2x}-5\times 2^x+4=0$$
$$\Rightarrow (2^x)^2-5\times 2^x+4=0$$
$$\Rightarrow y^2-5y+4=0 \text{ where } y=2^x$$
   (b) $x=0,\,2$

11 (a)
$$25^x-6\times 5^x+5=0$$
$$\Rightarrow (5^2)^x-6\times 5^x+5=0$$
$$\Rightarrow 5^{2x}-6\times 5^x+5=0$$
$$\Rightarrow (5^x)^2-6\times 5^x+5=0$$
$$\Rightarrow n^2-6n+5=0 \text{ where } n=5^x$$
   (b) $x=0,\,1$

12 (a)
$$9^x-4\times 3^{x+1}+27=0$$
$$\Rightarrow (3^2)^x-4\times 3^1\times 3^x+27=0$$
$$\Rightarrow 3^{2x}-12\times 3^x+27=0$$
$$\Rightarrow (3^x)^2-12\times 3^x+27=0$$
$$\Rightarrow u^2-12u+27=0 \text{ where } u=3^x$$
   (b) $x=1,\,2$

13 (a) $y^2-4y+3=0$ (b) $x=0,\,\frac{1}{2}$

14 (a)
$$5^{2x+1}-6\times 5^x+1=0$$
$$\Rightarrow 5^1\times 5^{2x}-6\times 5^x+1=0$$
$$\Rightarrow 5\times (5^x)^2-6\times 5^x+1=0$$
$$\Rightarrow 5n^2-6n+1=0 \text{ where } n=5^x$$
   (b) $x=-1,\,0$

15 (a)
$$4^{x+1}-33\times 2^x+8=0$$
$$\Rightarrow (2^2)^{x+1}-33\times 2^x+8=0$$
$$\Rightarrow 2^{2x+2}-33\times 2^x+8=0$$
$$\Rightarrow 2^2\times 2^{2x}-33\times 2^x+8=0$$
$$\Rightarrow 4\times (2^x)^2-33\times 2^x+8=0$$
$$\Rightarrow 4u^2-33u+8=0 \text{ where } u=2^x$$
   (b) $x=-2,\,3$

16 (a)
$$4^{x-1}-2^x+1=0$$
$$\Rightarrow (2^2)^{x-1}-2^x+1=0$$
$$\Rightarrow 2^{2x-2}-2^x+1=0$$
$$\Rightarrow 2^{-2}\times 2^{2x}-2^x+1=0$$
$$\Rightarrow \tfrac{1}{4}\times (2^x)^2-2^x+1=0$$
$$\Rightarrow \tfrac{1}{4}y^2-y+1=0 \text{ where } y=2^x$$
$$\Rightarrow y^2-4y+4=0$$
   (b) $x=1$

17 (a) $\frac{1}{4}u^2-u+1=0$ or $u^2-4u+4=0$
   (b) $x=\frac{1}{2}$

Test yourself (p 15)

1 (a) $\frac{1}{16}$ (b) 7 (c) $\frac{1}{2}$ (d) 125 (e) $\frac{1}{8}$

2 (a) $x=0$ (b) $x=3$ (c) $x=-2$
   (d) $x=25$ (e) $x=-\frac{2}{3}$

3 a

4 $x^{-\frac{1}{2}}+x^{\frac{3}{2}}$

5 A proof such as
$$\frac{\sqrt{x}\left(5-6x^3\sqrt{x}\right)}{10x}=\frac{5\sqrt{x}-6x^4}{10x}$$
$$=\frac{5\sqrt{x}}{10x}-\frac{6x^4}{10x}$$
$$=\frac{\sqrt{x}}{2x}-\frac{3x^4}{5x}$$
$$=\frac{x^{\frac{1}{2}}}{2x^1}-\frac{3x^4}{5x^1}$$
$$=\tfrac{1}{2}x^{\frac{1}{2}-1}-\tfrac{3}{5}x^{4-1}$$
$$=\tfrac{1}{2}x^{-\frac{1}{2}}-\tfrac{3}{5}x^3$$

6 $25^{y+2}=(5^2)^{y+2}=5^{2(y+2)}=5^{2y+4}$.
   Hence $5^x=25^{y+2}\Rightarrow x=2y+4$.

7 $x=\frac{1}{3}$

8 (a) (i) $3^{\frac{1}{2}}$ **(ii)** $3^{x-\frac{1}{2}}$

(b) $x = -\frac{1}{2}$

9 (a) $2^{\frac{1}{2}}$ **(b)** $2^{\frac{5}{2}}$ **(c)** $x = -\frac{1}{2}$

10 (a) (i) 3^{-3} **(ii)** 3^{2x}

(b) $x = -4$

11 $x = \frac{3}{5}$

12 (a)
$$7^{2x+1} - 8 \times 7^x + 1 = 0$$
$$\Rightarrow \quad 7^1 \times 7^{2x} - 8 \times 7^x + 1 = 0$$
$$\Rightarrow \quad 7 \times (7^x)^2 - 8 \times 7^x + 1 = 0$$
$$\Rightarrow \quad 7u^2 - 8u + 1 = 0 \quad \text{where } u = 7^x$$

(b) $x = -1, 0$

2 Graphs and transformations

A Further graphs (p 16)

A1 (a) (i) **(ii)**

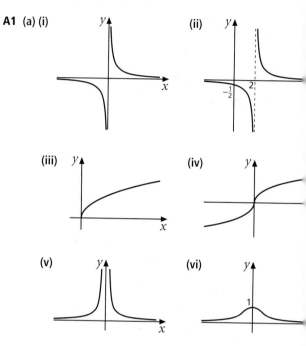

(iii) **(iv)**

(v) **(vi)**

Exercise A (p 17)

1 (a) (i) The value of y gets closer and closer to 1.

(ii) $y = 1$

(b) $x = 2$

(c) $\frac{1}{2}$

(d) 1

2 (a) B **(b)** F **(c)** H **(d)** A **(e)** I

(f) C **(g)** G **(h)** D **(i)** E

3

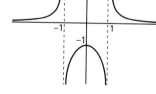

B Translating

Exercise B (p 19)

1 (a) $y = \dfrac{1}{x-5} - 1$

(b)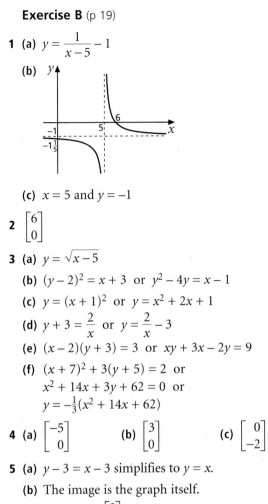

(c) $x = 5$ and $y = -1$

2 $\begin{bmatrix} 6 \\ 0 \end{bmatrix}$

3 (a) $y = \sqrt{x-5}$

(b) $(y-2)^2 = x + 3$ or $y^2 - 4y = x - 1$

(c) $y = (x+1)^2$ or $y = x^2 + 2x + 1$

(d) $y + 3 = \dfrac{2}{x}$ or $y = \dfrac{2}{x} - 3$

(e) $(x-2)(y+3) = 3$ or $xy + 3x - 2y = 9$

(f) $(x+7)^2 + 3(y+5) = 2$ or
$x^2 + 14x + 3y + 62 = 0$ or
$y = -\frac{1}{3}(x^2 + 14x + 62)$

4 (a) $\begin{bmatrix} -5 \\ 0 \end{bmatrix}$ (b) $\begin{bmatrix} 3 \\ 0 \end{bmatrix}$ (c) $\begin{bmatrix} 0 \\ -2 \end{bmatrix}$

5 (a) $y - 3 = x - 3$ simplifies to $y = x$.

(b) The image is the graph itself.

The vector $\begin{bmatrix} 3 \\ 3 \end{bmatrix}$ makes an angle of 45° with
the x-axis, as does the straight line $y = x$.
Hence the vector will not change the position
of the line.

6 (a) $y - 1 = x$ simplifies to $y = x + 1$.

(b) $y - 4 = x - 3$ simplifies to $y = x + 1$.

(c) The translations give the same image.

Both translations have the form $\begin{bmatrix} k \\ k+1 \end{bmatrix}$.

So the image of $y = x$ will be of the form
$y - (k + 1) = x - k$, simplifying to $y = x + 1$.

C Reflecting (p 20)

C1 (a) Each reflection is shown by a dotted graph.

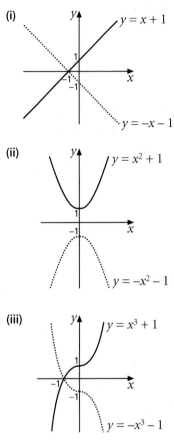

(b) A comment such as: The equation of each
image can be found by multiplying the
right-hand side by –1.

(c) $y = -x^4 - 1$

C2 (a) (i)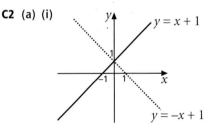

(ii) The image here is the same as the original
graph.

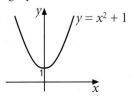

(iii)

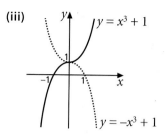

$y = x^3 + 1$

$y = -x^3 + 1$

(b) A comment such as: The equation of each image can be found by replacing x with $-x$.

(c) $y = x^4 + 1$

C3 (a)

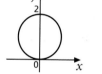

$y = (x - 1)^2$

(b) $y = -(x - 1)^2$ or $y = -x^2 + 2x - 1$

(c) $y = (x + 1)^2$ or $y = (-x - 1)^2$
    or $y = x^2 + 2x + 1$

C4 (a)

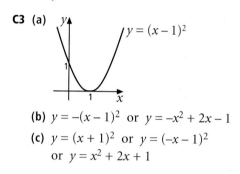

(b) $x^2 + (y + 1)^2 = 1$ or $x^2 + (-y - 1)^2 = 1$

(c) $x^2 + (y - 1)^2 = 1$

C5 (a) $y = -x^2 - x$

(b)

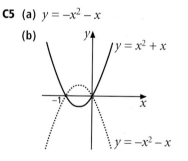

$y = x^2 + x$

$y = -x^2 - x$

C6 Using notation similar to that on page 21, on any curve the image of (x_1, y_1) is $(x_2, y_2) = (-x_1, y_1)$, which implies that $x_1 = -x_2$ and that $y_1 = y_2$. So the equation of the image can be found by replacing x by $-x$.

C7 (a) $y = x^2 - x$

(b)

$y = x^2 + x$ $y = x^2 - x$

C8 (a) Replace x by y and replace y by x.

(b) (i) $x = y + 6$ or $y = x - 6$

(ii) $y + x = 10$ or $x + y = 10$

(iii) $y^2 + (x - 3)^2 = 9$

Exercise C (p 22)

1 (a) $y = -x + 5$

(b) $y = -\dfrac{1}{x} - 3$

(c) $y = -x^3 - x$

(d) $x - y = 10$ or $y = x - 10$

(e) $-xy = 10$ or $y = -\dfrac{10}{x}$

(f) $x^2 + y^2 = 5$

2 (a) $y = -x + 2$ **(b)** $y = -\dfrac{1}{x} - 1$

(c) $y = x^2 - 2x$ **(d)** $y = 2x^2 + 5x$

(e) $x^2 - y^2 = 4$ **(f)** $y = x^2 + 3x + 5$

3 Replacing x by $-x$ gives $y = (-x)^4 + (-x)^2 - 9$ which simplifies to give the original equation $y = x^4 + x^2 - 9$. Since the graph is unchanged after reflection in the y-axis, it must have the y-axis as a line of symmetry.

4 Replacing y by $-y$ gives $(x + 2)^2 + (-y - 3)^2 = 1$. Now $(-y - 3)^2 = (-(y + 3))^2 = (y + 3)^2$ so the equation can be written as $(x + 2)^2 + (y + 3)^2 = 1$.

D Stretching (p 22)

D1 (a), (b) The image is shown by dotted lines.

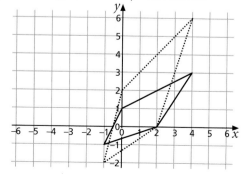

D2 (a), (b) The image is shown by dotted lines.

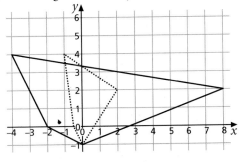

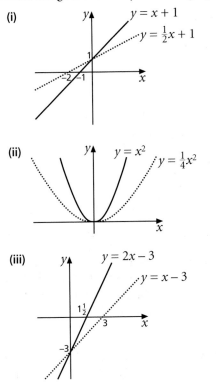

D3 (a) Each image is shown by a dotted graph.

(i)

$y = x + 1$
$y = \frac{1}{2}x + 1$

(ii)

$y = x^2$ $y = \frac{1}{4}x^2$

(iii)

$y = 2x - 3$
$y = x - 3$

(b) A comment such as: The equation of each image can be found by replacing x by $\frac{1}{2}x$.

D4 (a) Each image is shown by a dotted graph.

(i)

$y = 3x + 3$
$y = x + 1$

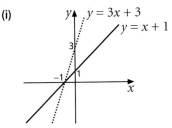

(ii)

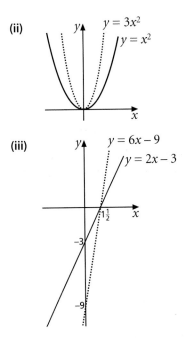

$y = 3x^2$
$y = x^2$

(iii)

$y = 6x - 9$
$y = 2x - 3$

(b) A comment such as: The equation of each image can be found by multiplying the right-hand side by 3.

D5 (a) $y = \frac{1}{3}x$ (b) $y = \frac{1}{4}x^2 - 4$
    (c) $y^2 + \frac{1}{25}x^2 = 7$ (d) $y = 3x + 6$
    (e) $y = 4x^2 + 3$

D6 (a) $\frac{1}{3}y + x = 4$ or $y = -3x + 12$
    (b) $y = x^2 + \frac{3}{4}$ or $4y = 4x^2 + 3$

D7 (a) Factor 3 in the y-direction
    (b) Factor $\frac{1}{3}$ in the x-direction
    (c) Factor $\frac{1}{3}$ in the x-direction

Exercise D (p 24)

1   (a) $y = \frac{1}{2}x + 3$ (b) $y = 2x - 1$
    (c) $y = \frac{1}{4}x^2 - 2$ (d) $y = \frac{1}{4}x^2 + x + 1$
    (e) $\frac{1}{2}xy = 4$ or $xy = 8$ (f) $\frac{1}{4}x^2 + y^2 = 1$

2   (a) $y = 3x - 1$ (b) $y = 27x^3 + 5$
    (c) $y = \dfrac{1}{3x}$

3   (a) $\frac{1}{4}y = x + 6$ or $y = 4x + 24$
    (b) $\frac{1}{4}y = 3x - 2$ or $y = 12x - 8$
    (c) $\frac{1}{2}y + x = 10$ or $y + 2x = 20$ or $y = -2x + 20$

4   (a) Factor 5 in the y-direction
    (b) Factor $\frac{1}{5}$ in the x-direction

(c) Factor 5 in the *x*-direction

(d) Factor $\frac{1}{2}$ in the *x*-direction

(e) Factor 4 in the *y*-direction

E Function notation

Exercise E (p 27)

1 (a) A translation of $\begin{bmatrix} 0 \\ 6 \end{bmatrix}$ (b) A translation of $\begin{bmatrix} -6 \\ 0 \end{bmatrix}$

(c) A translation of $\begin{bmatrix} 0 \\ -1 \end{bmatrix}$ (d) A translation of $\begin{bmatrix} 1 \\ 0 \end{bmatrix}$

(e) A stretch of factor 2 in the *y*-direction

(f) A stretch of factor $\frac{1}{2}$ in the *x*-direction

(g) A stretch of factor $\frac{1}{3}$ in the *y*-direction

(h) A stretch of factor 3 in the *x*-direction

2 (a)
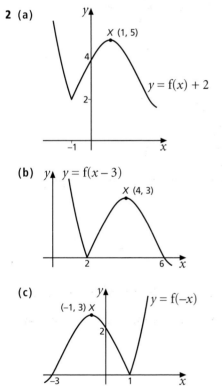

(b)

(c)

(d)

(e)
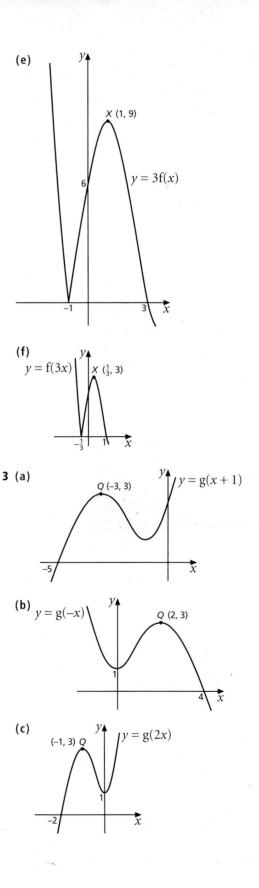

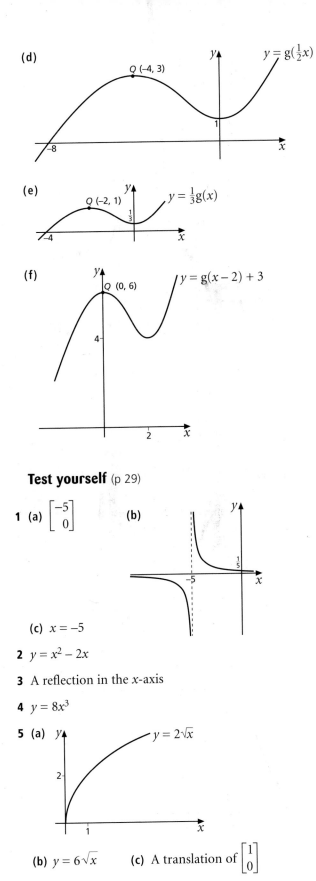

(d) $y = g(\tfrac{1}{2}x)$, $Q\,(-4, 3)$, -8, 1

(e) $y = \tfrac{1}{3}g(x)$, $Q\,(-2, 1)$, $\tfrac{1}{3}$, -4

(f) $y = g(x - 2) + 3$, $Q\,(0, 6)$, 4, 2

Test yourself (p 29)

1 (a) $\begin{bmatrix} -5 \\ 0 \end{bmatrix}$ **(b)** $\tfrac{1}{5}$, -5

(c) $x = -5$

2 $y = x^2 - 2x$

3 A reflection in the x-axis

4 $y = 8x^3$

5 (a) $y = 2\sqrt{x}$, 2, 1

(b) $y = 6\sqrt{x}$ **(c)** A translation of $\begin{bmatrix} 1 \\ 0 \end{bmatrix}$

6 (a) $y = f(-x)$, -1, 1, 5, 2, $P\,(3, -2)$

(b) $y = f(x + 3)$, -8, -4, -2, 2, $P\,(-6, -2)$

7 (a) (i) $y = f(2x)$, 2, -2, 2, -2

(ii) $y = 2f(x)$, 4, -4, 4, -4

(b) A stretch by scale factor $\tfrac{1}{2}$ in the x-direction

8 A stretch by scale factor 2 in the y-direction

3 Sequences and series 1

A Using a rule for the *n*th term (p 30)

Values are given to four significant figures where appropriate.

A1 (a) (i) $5, 11, 17, 23, 29, 35$

(ii) $a_{10} = 59, a_{25} = 149, a_{100} = 599$

(iii) The terms increase at a steady rate.

(b) (i) $2, -1, -4, -7, -10, -13$

(ii) $b_{10} = -25, b_{25} = -70, b_{100} = -295$

(iii) The terms decrease at a steady rate.

(c) (i) $5, 7, 11, 19, 35, 67$

(ii) $c_{10} = 1027, c_{25} = 33\,554\,435,$
$c_{100} = 1.268 \times 10^{30}$

(iii) The terms increase at a faster and faster rate.

(d) (i) $-1, 3, 9, 17, 27, 39$

(ii) $d_{10} = 107, d_{25} = 647, d_{100} = 10\,097$

(iii) The terms increase at a faster and faster rate (though not as fast as the sequence in part (c)).

(e) (i) $5.1, 5.01, 5.001, 5.0001, 5.000\,01, 5.000\,001$

(ii) $e_{10} = 5 + 1 \times 10^{-10}, e_{25} = 5 + 1 \times 10^{-25},$
$e_{100} = 5 + 1 \times 10^{-100}$

(iii) The terms get closer and closer to 5.

(f) (i) $4, 2.5, 2, 1.75, 1.6, 1.5$

(ii) $f_{10} = 1.3, f_{25} = 1.12, f_{100} = 1.03$

(iii) The terms get closer and closer to 1.

(g) (i) $1, 1.333, 1.5, 1.6, 1.667, 1.714$

(ii) $g_{10} = 1.818, g_{25} = 1.923, g_{100} = 1.980$

(iii) The terms get closer and closer to 2.

(h) (i) $-2, 4, -8, 16, -32, 64$

(ii) $h_{10} = 1024, h_{25} = -33\,554\,432,$
$h_{100} = 1.268 \times 10^{30}$

(iii) The terms get larger and larger in size, alternating between positive and negative values.

(i) (i) $-0.1, 0.01, -0.001, 0.0001, -0.000\,01,$
$0.000\,001$

(ii) $i_{10} = 1 \times 10^{-10}, i_{25} = -1 \times 10^{-25},$
$i_{100} = 1 \times 10^{-100}$

(iii) The terms get closer and closer to 0, alternating between positive and negative values.

Exercise A (p 31)

1 (a) $u_1 = 5, u_2 = 9, u_3 = 13$ (b) $u_{100} = 401$

(c) $n = 20$ (d) 24

2 (a) $a_1 = 37, a_2 = 34, a_3 = 31$ (b) $a_{16} = -8$

(c) 13

3 (a) $p_1 = 6, p_2 = 18, p_3 = 54, p_{10} = 118\,098$

(b) The terms increase at a faster and faster rate.

4 (a) $h_{30} = 9.7 \times 10^{-15}$ (to 2 s.f.)

(b) The terms get closer and closer to 0.

5 (a) B: The terms increase at a faster and faster rate.

(b) A: The terms decrease at a steady rate.

(c) D: The terms increase but at a slower and slower rate, converging to a limit of 2.

(d) E: The terms decrease but converge to a limit of 2.

(e) C: The terms go up and down but get closer and closer to a limit of 2.

6 (a) B   (b) C   (c) A

7 (a) $u_n = \dfrac{1}{n}$ (b) $u_n = \dfrac{n+1}{n}$ or $u_n = 1 + \dfrac{1}{n}$

8 (a) $u_n = 3.007$ (b) $\dfrac{3n+7}{n} = \dfrac{3n}{n} + \dfrac{7}{n} = 3 + \dfrac{7}{n}$

(c) As n gets larger $\dfrac{7}{n}$ converges to 0 so $3 + \dfrac{7}{n}$ converges to 3.

9 $(-1)^n \times \left(\dfrac{n+5}{n} \right)$

B Inductive definition

Exercise B (p 33)

1 $2, 1, -2, -11, -38, -119$

2 (a) $6, 5, 4.5, 4.25$ (b) $10, 9, 7.7, 6.01$

3 $n = 6$

4 (a) $u_2 = pu_1 + q$ so $4 = 2p + q$

$u_3 = pu_2 + q$ so $7.2 = 4p + q$

(b) $p = 1.6, q = 0.8; u_{n+1} = 1.6u_n + 0.8$

5 $a = 2, b = -5; u_{n+1} = 2u_n - 5$

6 (a) $k = 0.4; u_{n+1} = 0.4u_n + 0.4$

(b) $u_4 = 1.2$

7 $p = 4$

8 (a) (i) $u_2 = 8 + k$ **(ii)** $u_3 = 16 + 3k$

(b) $16 + 3k = 20.5, k = 1.5$

9 (a) (i) $u_2 = 2p + 1$ **(ii)** $u_3 = 2p^2 + p + 1$

(b) $2p^2 + p - 10 = 0, p = -2\frac{1}{2}, 2$

10 (a) $u_2 = 4p + 7$

So $u_3 = p(4p + 7) + 7 = 4p^2 + 7p + 7$

Hence, $4p^2 + 7p + 7 = 9 \Rightarrow 4p^2 + 7p - 2 = 0$

$\Rightarrow (4p - 1)(p + 2) = 0 \Rightarrow p = \frac{1}{4}, -2$

(b) $p = \frac{1}{4}: u_1 = 4, u_2 = 8, u_3 = 9, u_4 = 9\frac{1}{4}$

$p = -2: u_1 = 4, u_2 = -1, u_3 = 9, u_4 = -11$

C Inductive definition and limits (p 35)

C1 (a) (i) 3, 8, 13, 18, 23, 28

(ii) The terms increase at a steady rate.

(b) (i) 0, 0, 0, 0, 0, 0

(ii) The terms are all the same.

(c) (i) −2, −6, −18, −54, −162, −486

(ii) The terms decrease at a faster and faster rate.

(d) (i) 3, 1, $\frac{1}{3}$, $\frac{1}{9}$, $\frac{1}{27}$, $\frac{1}{81}$

(ii) The terms decrease at a slower and slower rate, converging towards a limit of 0.

(e) (i) 5, 9, 17, 33, 65, 129

(ii) The terms increase at a faster and faster rate.

(f) (i) 3, 2.5, 2.25, 2.125, 2.0625, 2.03125

(ii) The terms decrease at a slower and slower rate, converging to a limit of 2.

(g) (i) 0.9, 0.9487, 0.9740, 0.9869, 0.9934, 0.9967

(ii) The terms increase at a slower and slower rate, converging to a limit of 1.

(h) (i) 2, 5.5, 5.1818, 5.1930, 5.1926, 5.1926

(ii) The terms increase at a slower and slower rate, converging to a limit of 5.192 582 403 6 (to 10 d.p.)

(i) (i) 3, 3, 3, 3, 3, 3

(ii) The terms are all the same.

(j) (i) −5, −5, −5, −5, −5, −5

(ii) The terms are all the same.

C2 1

C3 (a) If the sequence is constant then $u_{n+1} = u_n = c$. So the recurrence relation gives $c = 3c - 10$.

(b) $c = 5$

C4 (a) $c = \frac{c}{3} + 6$ **(b)** $c = 9$

C5 (a) $u_1 = 4$ **(b)** $u_1 = -3$ **(c)** $u_1 = -2$ **(d)** $u_1 = 5$

C6 For all values of a, the sequences converge to 6. $u_1 = 6$ is the only starting value that gives a constant sequence.

C7 For all values of b, the sequences converge to $-1\frac{1}{3}$. $u_1 = -1\frac{1}{3}$ is the only starting value that gives a constant sequence.

Exercise C (p 37)

Where appropriate, values are given correct to 4 d.p.

1 The letter l is used for the limit in each equation. Any letter may, of course, be used.

(a) $l = \frac{l}{3} + 5$ gives $l = 7.5$

6, 7, 7.3333, 7.4444, 7.4815, 7.4938, 7.4979, … is converging to 7.5.

(b) $l = 0.5l - 1$ gives $l = -2$

−8, −5, −3.5, −2.75, −2.375, −2.1875, −2.0938, −2.0469, … is converging to −2.

(c) $l = \frac{l}{8} + 1$ gives $l = 1\frac{1}{7}$

0.6, 1.075, 1.1344, 1.1418, 1.1427, 1.1428, 1.1429, … is converging to $1\frac{1}{7}$.

(d) $l = 0.6l + 2$ gives $l = 5$

10, 8, 6.8, 6.08, 5.648, 5.3888, 5.2333, 5.1400, 5.0840, 5.0504, 5.0302, 5.0181, 5.0109, 5.0065, … is converging to 5.

2 (a) $p_2 = 43.4375$ so about 43 birds

(b) 80

3 (a) A value for a that generates a constant sequence must satisfy the equation $a = \dfrac{6}{a} + 1$ which rearranges to give the quadratic equation $a^2 - a - 6 = 0$.
This factorises to $(a - 3)(a + 2) = 0$ and has two solutions, $a = 3$ and $a = -2$.

(b) (i) $u_2 = \dfrac{6}{5} + 1 = 1.2 + 1 = 2.2$

(ii) $u_3 = 3.7273$, $u_4 = 2.6098$, $u_5 = 3.2991$, $u_6 = 2.8187$, $u_7 = 3.1286$, $u_8 = 2.9178$, $u_9 = 3.0564$, $u_{10} = 2.9631$

(iii) 3

(c) (i) An hypothesis about the limit

(ii) $-1.9, -2.1579, -1.7805, -2.3699, -1.5318,$ $-2.9170, -1.0569, -4.6769, -0.2829,$ $-20.2081, 0.7031, 9.5338$ are the first twelve terms.
It doesn't appear to be converging to -2. In fact, it converges to 3.

4 This investigation yields many interesting results. For example, if $1 < r < 3$ then the sequences converge to a limit $1 - \dfrac{1}{r}$.

D Arithmetic sequences (p 37)

D1 (a) 10, 13, 16, 19, 22

(b) $u_{10} = 37$, $u_{100} = 307$, $u_{1000} = 3007$

(c) $u_n = 10 + 3(n - 1)$ or $u_n = 7 + 3n$

D2 (a) $x_{10} = -17$, $x_{100} = -287$, $x_{1000} = -2987$

(b) $x_n = 10 - 3(n - 1)$ or $x_n = 13 - 3n$

D3 (a) $x_n = 6 + 7(n - 1)$ or $x_n = 7n - 1$

(b) $x_{100} = 699$

D4 The nth term is $11 + 3(n - 1)$ or $3n + 8$.

Exercise D (p 39)

1 (a) 5, 14, 23, 32

(b) $u_n = 5 + 9(n - 1)$ or $u_n = 9n - 4$

(c) $u_{50} = 446$

2 (a) 61.5

(b) The nth term is $90 - 1.5(n - 1)$ or $91.5 - 1.5n$.

(c) $n = 33$

3 8

4 (a) 47 **(b)** 19 **(c)** 31 **(d)** 100

5 402

6 $-2 + 0.5(n - 1)$ or $0.5n - 2.5$

7 -134

8 First term 7; common difference $2\frac{1}{2}$

9 $2 + 3(n - 1)$ or $3n - 1$

10 -71

E Arithmetic series (p 40)

E1 (a) 10 **(b)** 5050

E2 1275

E3 (a) (i) 20 100 **(ii)** 11 325

(b) 8775

E4 29 605

E5 (a) 210 **(b)** $210 \times 7 = 1470$

E6 (a) 329 **(b)** 15 250

Exercise E (p 42)

1 20 100

2 10 962

3 60 300

4 166 833

5 5820

6 $a = 10$, $d = \frac{1}{2}$, $n = 100$ and so the sum is
$\frac{1}{2} \times 100 \times (2 \times 10 + (100 - 1) \times \frac{1}{2})$
$= 50 \times (20 + 49.5)$
$= 3475$

7 (a) 24 **(b)** -150

8 The first term is 1 so $a = 1$.
The tenth term is 7 so $a + 9d = 7 \Rightarrow 1 + 9d = 7$
$\Rightarrow d = \frac{2}{3}$.
$n = 40$ and so the sum is
$\frac{1}{2} \times 40 \times (2 \times 1 + (40 - 1) \times \frac{2}{3})$
$= 20 \times (2 + 26)$
$= 560$

9 5040

10 $4\frac{1}{2}$

11 9

12 (a) 255 m   **(b)** 31 seconds

13 (a) £875   **(b)** £12 750

14 n^2

15 First term −1.35; common difference 0.3

16 118.8 m^2

17 587 full turns

F Sigma notation

Exercise F (p 44)

1 (a) 30   **(b)** 36   **(c)** 36   **(d)** 21
   (e) 33   **(f)** 126   **(g)** 68   **(h)** $1\frac{1}{12}$

2 (a) 1081   **(b)** 2460   **(c)** 615   **(d)** 4080
   (e) 290   **(f)** 362.5   **(g)** −2325   **(h)** 6360

3 (a) (i) 1275   **(ii)** 465
   (b) 810

4 (a) 28
   (b) The first term is 23 and the last term is 77.
   The number of terms is 28 so the sum is
   $\frac{1}{2} \times 28 \times (23 + 77) = 14 \times 100 = 1400$.

5 (a) 473   **(b)** 1324.6   **(c)** −9637

6 (a) The first term is 2 and the last term is 59.
   The number of terms is 20 so the sum is
   $\frac{1}{2} \times 20 \times (2 + 59) = 10 \times 61 = 610$.
   (b) The first term is 2 and the last term is $3n - 1$.
   The number of terms is n so the sum is
   $\frac{1}{2} \times n \times (2 + 3n - 1) = \frac{1}{2}n(3n + 1)$.

Mixed questions (p 46)

1 $-2.6 + 0.4(n - 1)$ or $0.4n - 3$

2 −0.525

3 $k = 0.2k + 4$ gives $k = 5$

4 11 325

5 75 150

6 4100

7 (a) 3.8   **(b)** 897

8 (a) 7.2   **(b)** 14 110

9 (a) $1\frac{1}{2}$, 65   **(b)** $n = 75$

10 (a) The sum of the first 19 terms is 266 so
   $\frac{1}{2} \times 19 \times (2a + 18d) = 266$
   $\Rightarrow 19 \times (a + 9d) = 266$
   $\Rightarrow a + 9d = 266 \div 19$
   $\Rightarrow a + 9d = 14$
   (b) $a = -13, d = 3$

Test yourself (p 47)

1 (a) (i) $a = 12, b = 0.2$ **(ii)** 14.92
   (b) $w = 12 + 0.2w$ gives $w = 15$

2 (a) $u_1 = 10.5, u_2 = 11$ **(b)** 0.5
   (c) $n = 30$ **(d)** 532.5

3 45 150

4 3775

5 (a) 392
   (b) (i) $u_1 = 47, u_2 = 44, u_3 = 41, u_4 = 38$
   (ii) The first 16 terms of this sequence will
   form the sequence in part (a) in reverse.
   The next term will be −1 so there are just
   16 positive terms.

6 (a) 18
   (b) The sum is $\frac{1}{2} \times 400 \times (12 + 399 \times 1\frac{1}{3}) = 200 \times$
   $544 = 108\,800$.

7 3875

8 (a) 16   **(b)** 890

9 (a) $15 + 3(n-1)$ or $3n + 12$

(b) The total time will be
$15 + 18 + 21 + \ldots + (3n + 12)$.

The first term is 15, the last term is $3n + 12$ and the number of terms is n.
So the sum is $\frac{1}{2} \times n \times (15 + 3n + 12)$
$= \frac{1}{2}n(3n + 27) = \frac{3}{2}n(n + 9)$.

(c) 16 miles

4 Sequences and series 2

A Geometric sequences (p 48)

A1 (a) £6553.60 **(b)** $5 \times 2^{n-1}$ pence

A2 A, C, D and E are geometric sequences.
The common ratios are 3, 0.4, $\frac{4}{3}$ and -2 respectively.

A3 $40\frac{1}{2}$, $60\frac{3}{4}$

A4 0.419 904

A5 $\frac{3}{32}$

A6 1 572 864

A7 12

A8 (a) $16, 4, 1, \frac{1}{4}, \frac{1}{16}$ **(b)** 2, **10**, 50, **250**, **1250**

(c) **9**, 18, **36**, 72, **144** **(d)** 2, **8**, 32, 128, **512**

A9 -8

Exercise A (p 50)

1 (a) 57 344 **(b)** $3\frac{1}{2} \times 2^{n-1}$

2 (a) 2, 10, 50, 250 **(b)** 5

3 0.002 44

4 $\frac{1}{2}$

5 (a) 2nd term $\times (-3)^3 = -12 \times -27 = 324$
$= $ 5th term, so -3 is the common ratio.

(b) 4

6 $\frac{2}{3}$

7 2, -2

8 (a) 743 hedgehogs **(b)** 2%

9 (a) To increase an amount by 3%, multiply by 1.03. So on Ken's 5th birthday he will have $1000 \times (1.03)^4 = $ £1125.51 (to the nearest 1p)

(b) £1304.77

(c) $1000 \times (1.03)^{n-1}$

10 1.2

11 6, -7

12 With a as the first term and r as the common ratio, we have

$$\frac{ar^3}{a} = \frac{3}{81} = \frac{1}{27}$$

$$\Rightarrow r^3 = \frac{1}{27} \Rightarrow r = \frac{1}{3}$$

So the nth term is $81 \times \left(\frac{1}{3}\right)^{n-1} = 3^4 \times \frac{1}{3^{n-1}}$

$= 3^{4-(n-1)} = 3^{5-n}$

B Geometric series (p 51)

B1 (a) An estimate of the total on the board

(b) £327.68

(c) £655.35

B2 (a) Let $S = 1 + 3 + 3^2 + \ldots + 3^{10}$

Then $3S = 3 + 3^2 + \ldots + 3^{10} + 3^{11}$

So $3S - S = (3 + 3^2 + \ldots + 3^{10} + 3^{11})$

$-(1 + 3 + 3^2 + \ldots + 3^{10}) = 3^{11} - 1$

Hence $2S = 3^{11} - 1$ and finally $S = \dfrac{3^{11} - 1}{2}$

(b) 88 573

B3 $\dfrac{3^{13} - 1}{2} = 797\,161$

B4 9

B5 n

Exercise B (p 53)

1 357 913 941

2 20 475

3 12 093 235

4 The first term is 8 and the common ratio is $\frac{1}{2}$ so the sum of the first 10 terms is

$$\frac{8\left(\left(\frac{1}{2}\right)^{10} - 1\right)}{\frac{1}{2} - 1} = 15.98 \text{ (to 2 d.p.)}$$

5 The first term is 1 and the common ratio is -3 so the sum of the first 12 terms is

$$\frac{(-3)^{12} - 1}{-3 - 1} = \frac{531\,440}{-4} = -132\,860$$

6 (a) 47.9985   (b) 32 769

(c) 17.9589   (d) 28.8000

7 2.286

8 7 174 453

9 (a) 1.845×10^{19} (to 4 s.f.)

(b) $3.689 \times 10^{14}\,\text{kg}$ (to 4 s.f.)

10 6141

11 9.333

12 (a) £2.19   (b) £438.22

13 $x = 9$

C Sum to infinity (p 54)

C1 (a) $S_{10} = 1023, S_{11} = 2047, S_{12} = 4095$

(b) As n gets larger and larger, S_n gets larger and larger without limit.

C2 (a) $S_{10} = -14\,762, S_{11} = 44\,287, S_{12} = -132\,860$

(b) As n gets larger and larger, S_n alternates between positive and negative values but gets larger and larger in size without limit.

C3 (a) To four decimal places, $S_{10} = 11.9883$, $S_{11} = 11.9941, S_{12} = 11.9971, S_{13} = 11.9985$, $S_{14} = 11.9993$

(b) As n gets larger and larger, S_n increases but gets closer and closer to 12.

C4 (a) To four decimal places, $S_{10} = 0.5896$, $S_{11} = 0.6069, S_{12} = 0.5954, S_{13} = 0.6031$, $S_{14} = 0.5979$

(b) As n gets larger and larger, S_n gets closer and closer to 0.6, alternating above and below it.

Exercise C (p 55)

1 (a) The common ratio is $\frac{1}{2}$.
The sum to infinity is 28.

(b) The common ratio is $\frac{1}{10}$.
The sum to infinity is 10.

(c) The common ratio is -2 which is less than -1 so no sum to infinity exists.

(d) The common ratio is $-\frac{3}{4}$.
The sum to infinity is $2\frac{2}{7}$ or $\frac{16}{7}$.

2 $6\frac{1}{4}$ or $\frac{25}{4}$

3 $\frac{1}{6}$

4 27

5 12

6 $9 + 6$

Mixed questions (p 56)

1 (a) 2nd term $\times \left(\frac{1}{2}\right)^3 = 24 \times \frac{1}{8} = 3$

= 5th term, so $\frac{1}{2}$ is the common ratio.

(b) 48

(c) 96

2 (a) $\frac{3}{5}$ or 0.6 **(b)** $\frac{3}{5} \times 5^{n-1}$

(c) 46 875 **(d)** $58\,593\frac{3}{5}$ or $58\,593.6$

3 (a) 8737.88 (to 2 d.p.) **(b)** 246

(c) −29 524

4 (a) (i) $p\%$ as a fraction is $\frac{p}{100}$. The result of

increasing a by $p\%$ is $a + \frac{p}{100} \times a$

$= a\left(1 + \frac{p}{100}\right)$ so $\left(1 + \frac{p}{100}\right)$ is the common

ratio.

(ii) $b = 2000\left(1 + \frac{p}{100}\right)$

$c = 2000\left(1 + \frac{p}{100}\right)^2$

(b) (i) $2000 \times \left(1 + \frac{8}{100}\right)^2 = £2332.80$ so $p = 8$

(ii) $u_n = 2000 \times (1.08)^n$

(iii) £4317.85

5 (a) (i) 2 min 43 seconds **(ii)** 18 min 21 seconds

(b) 3 hours 10 minutes (to the nearest minute)

6 (a) 3rd term $\times \left(\frac{2}{3}\right)^3 = 81 \times \frac{8}{27} = 24$

= 6th term, so $\frac{2}{3}$ is the common ratio.

(b) $546\frac{3}{4}$

7 The common ratio is $\frac{2}{5}$ and the sum to infinity is $\frac{125}{3}$ or $41\frac{2}{3}$.

8 (a) The 2nd term of the series is −12 so $ar = -12$.

The sum to infinity is 16 so

$\frac{a}{1-r} = 16$

$\Rightarrow a = 16(1 - r) \Rightarrow ar = 16r(1 - r)$

$\Rightarrow -12 = 16r - 16r^2$

$\Rightarrow 16r^2 - 16r - 12 = 0$

$\Rightarrow 4r^2 - 4r - 3 = 0$

(b) $-\frac{1}{2}$

9 524 287.75

10 −24

11 (a) The number of dots in P_5 is
$9 + 8 + 7 + 6 + 5 = 35$

(b) The number of dots in P_n is $\frac{1}{2}n(3n - 1)$.
(One method is to consider the number of
dots in P_n as the arithmetic series
$n + (n + 1) + \ldots + (2n - 1)$.)

(c) P_{10}

12 (a) Let S_n be the number of black squares in B_n.
So $S_0 = 1$. At each stage, each black square is
transformed into 5 black squares so $S_n = 5^n$.

Let A_n be the total black area in B_n.
So $A_0 = 1$.
$A_1 = S_1 \times \frac{1}{9}$ (as the area of each smaller square
is $\frac{1}{9}$ of the larger one) $= 5 \times \frac{1}{9}$.
$A_2 = S_2 \times \left(\frac{1}{9}\right)^2$ (as the area of each smaller
square is $\frac{1}{9}$ of $\frac{1}{9}$ now) $= 5^2 \times \left(\frac{1}{9}\right)^2 = \left(\frac{5}{9}\right)^2$.
$A_3 = S_3 \times \left(\frac{1}{9}\right)^3 = 5^3 \times \left(\frac{1}{9}\right)^3 = \left(\frac{5}{9}\right)^3$ and so on
giving
$A_n = S_n \times \left(\frac{1}{9}\right)^n = 5^n \times \left(\frac{1}{9}\right)^n = \left(\frac{5}{9}\right)^n$
Now as $\left|\frac{5}{9}\right| < 1$ then, as n tends to infinity,
$\left(\frac{5}{9}\right)^n$ tends to 0.

(b) (i) The area of B_0 is 1 square unit so the
length of one side of B_0 is $\sqrt{1} = 1$ unit.

(ii) The length of one side of B_0 is 1. At each
stage the length of each side is divided by 3
so the length of each side in B_n is $\left(\frac{1}{3}\right)^n$.
Hence the perimeter of each black square
in B_n is $4 \times \left(\frac{1}{3}\right)^n$.
So the total perimeter of B_n is
$S_n \times 4 \times \left(\frac{1}{3}\right)^n = 5^n \times 4 \times \left(\frac{1}{3}\right)^n = 4 \times \left(\frac{5}{3}\right)^n$.
Now as $\left|\frac{5}{3}\right| > 1$ then, as n tends
to infinity, $\left(\frac{5}{3}\right)^n$ tends to infinity.

13 (a) Let E_n be the number of edges in F_n.
So $E_0 = 3$. At each stage, each edge is
transformed into 4 edges so $E_n = 3 \times 4^n$.

Let A_n be the total area of F_n.
$A_1 = A_0 + E_0 \times \frac{1}{9}$ (as each smaller triangle is $\frac{1}{9}$
of the larger one) $= 1 + 3 \times \frac{1}{9}$.

$A_2 = A_1 + E_1 \times \left(\frac{1}{9}\right)^2$ (as each smaller triangle is $\frac{1}{9}$ of $\frac{1}{9}$ now) $= 1 + 3 \times \frac{1}{9} + 3 \times 4^1 \times \left(\frac{1}{9}\right)^2$

$A_3 = A_2 + E_2 \times \left(\frac{1}{9}\right)^3$
$= 1 + 3 \times \frac{1}{9} + 3 \times 4^1 \times \left(\frac{1}{9}\right)^2 + 3 \times 4^2 \times \left(\frac{1}{9}\right)^3$

and so on giving

$A_n = 1 + 3 \times \frac{1}{9} + 3 \times 4^1 \times \left(\frac{1}{9}\right)^2 + 3 \times 4^2 \times \left(\frac{1}{9}\right)^3$
$+ 3 \times 4^3 \times \left(\frac{1}{9}\right)^4 + \ldots + 3 \times 4^{n-1} \times \left(\frac{1}{9}\right)^n$
$= 1 + \frac{3}{4}\left(\frac{4}{9} + \left(\frac{4}{9}\right)^2 + \left(\frac{4}{9}\right)^3 + \left(\frac{4}{9}\right)^4 + \ldots + \left(\frac{4}{9}\right)^n\right)$

Now $\left(\frac{4}{9} + \left(\frac{4}{9}\right)^2 + \left(\frac{4}{9}\right)^3 + \left(\frac{4}{9}\right)^4 + \ldots + \left(\frac{4}{9}\right)^n\right)$ is a geometric series with n terms where the common ratio of $\frac{4}{9}$ is between -1 and 1, so its sum to infinity exists and is $\dfrac{\frac{4}{9}}{1 - \frac{4}{9}} = \frac{4}{5}$.

Hence, as n tends to infinity, then A_n tends to $1 + \frac{3}{4} \times \frac{4}{5} = 1\frac{3}{5}$.

(b) The length of one side of F_0 is x. At each stage the length of each side is divided by 3 so the length of each side in F_n is $x \times \left(\frac{1}{3}\right)^n$.

So the total perimeter of F_n is
$E_n \times x \times \left(\frac{1}{3}\right)^n = 3 \times 4^n \times x \times \left(\frac{1}{3}\right)^n = 3x\left(\frac{4}{3}\right)^n$.

Now as $\left|\frac{4}{3}\right| > 1$ then, as n tends to infinity, $\left(\frac{4}{3}\right)^n$ tends to infinity. Hence the perimeter of F_n does not converge to a limit.

Test yourself (p 59)

1 (a) 3rd term $\times 3^3 = 54 \times 27 = 1458$
= 6th term, so 3 is the common ratio.

(b) 43 046 718

2 The common ratio is $\frac{2}{3}$ and the sum to infinity is 243.

3 (a) Each term in the sequence is double the one before. Hence there is a common ratio of 2. So the sequence is geometric.

(b) 5×2^n is the prime factorisation of each term and, as the index of 5 is an odd number (1), then none can be a square number.

(c) 10 230

4 $3^n - 1$

5 (a) 118 096   **(b)** 600   **(c)** $10\,922\frac{1}{3}$

6 (a) 2nd term $\times \left(\dfrac{1}{\sqrt{2}}\right)^6 = 4 \times \frac{1}{8} = \frac{1}{2}$
= 8th term, so $\dfrac{1}{\sqrt{2}}$ is the common ratio.

(b) $8\left(\sqrt{2} + 1\right)$ so $k = 8$

7 (a) The 2nd term is $1200r$ and the 3rd term is $1200r^2$.

(b) (i) As the total is more than £3600, r must be greater than 1 and so the smallest share is the first term. The total of the three shares is $1200 + 1200r + 1200r^2$ so
$1200 + 1200r + 1200r^2 = 11\,700$
$\Rightarrow 1200r^2 + 1200r - 10\,500 = 0$
$\Rightarrow 12r^2 + 12r - 105 = 0$
$\Rightarrow 4r^2 + 4r - 35 = 0$

(ii) £7500

8 49.70 (to 2 d.p.)

9 (a) 650   **(b)** 65

5 Binomial expansion

A Pascal's triangle (p 60)

A1 (a) $(a + b)^4 = a^4 + 4a^3b + 6a^2b^2 + 4ab^3 + b^4$

(b) Multiply the expansion in (a) by $(a + b)$.

A2 (a) Each number is the sum of the two numbers above it in the previous row.

(b) 1, 6, 15, 20, 15, 6, 1
$a^6 + 6a^5b + 15a^4b^2 + 20a^3b^3 + 15a^2b^4 + 6ab^5 + b^6$

(c) In the table for expanding $(a + b)^5$, the coefficients in the 'a' row are the row 1, 4, 6, 4, 1 from Pascal's triangle. So are the coefficients in the 'b' row. When like terms are combined, the coefficients are added, like this: 1 4 6 4 1
1 4 6 4 1

Exercise A (p 61)

1 $1 + 3x + 3x^2 + x^3$

2 (a) $1 + 6x + 12x^2 + 8x^3$

(b) $1 + 10x + 40x^2 + 80x^3 + 80x^4 + 32x^5$

(c) $1 - 6x + 15x^2 - 20x^3 + 15x^4 - 6x^5 + x^6$

(d) $1 - 18x + 135x^2 - 540x^3 + 1215x^4 - 1458x^5 + 729x^6$

(e) $1 + \frac{7}{2}x + \frac{21}{4}x^2 + \frac{35}{8}x^3 + \frac{35}{16}x^4 + \frac{21}{32}x^5 + \frac{7}{64}x^6 + \frac{1}{128}x^7$

3 (a) $1 - \frac{5}{2}x + \frac{5}{2}x^2 - \frac{5}{4}x^3 + \frac{5}{16}x^4 - \frac{1}{32}x^5$

(b) $8 + 12x + 6x^2 + x^3$

(c) $81 - 216x + 216x^2 - 96x^3 + 16x^4$

4 (a) $1 + 8x + 28x^2 + 56x^3$ (b) 2.136 (c) 0.424

B Arrangements (p 62)

B1 (a) 120 (b) $5 \times 4 \times 3 \times 2 \times 1$

B2 (a) 720 (b) 3 628 800

B3 (a) 12

(b) Because the two As can be put in two different orders

B4 (a) 120 (b) 6 (c) 20

B5 84

B6 (a) 15 (b) 126 (c) 184 756

B7 (a) 1 (b) 1

C The binomial theorem (p 65)

C1 $aaa + aab + aba + baa + abb + bab + bba + bbb$

C2 (a) $1 + 10x + 45x^2 + 120x^3$

(b) $1 - 10x + 45x^2 - 120x^3$

Exercise C (p 67)

1 $1 + 12x + 66x^2 + 220x^3$

2 (a) 252 (b) 1140

3 1.23

4 (a) $1 + 18x + 144x^2 + 672x^3$

(b) $1 - 24x + 252x^2 - 1512x^3$

(c) $1 + \frac{15}{2}x + \frac{105}{4}x^2 + \frac{455}{8}x^3$

(d) $1 - \frac{7}{5}x + \frac{21}{25}x^2 - \frac{7}{25}x^3$

5 (a) $1 - 10x + 40x^2$ (b) 159

6 (a) 5376 (b) −5376 (c) 145 152

7 (a) Coefficient of $x^3 = \dfrac{n(n-1)(n-2)}{6}k^3$

Coefficient of $x^2 = \dfrac{n(n-1)}{2}k^2$

So $\dfrac{n(n-1)(n-2)}{6}k^3 = \dfrac{2n(n-1)}{2}k^2$

$\Rightarrow \qquad (n-2)k = 6$

$\Rightarrow \qquad n - 2 = \dfrac{6}{k}$

$\Rightarrow \qquad n = 2 + \dfrac{6}{k}$

(b) $k = 1, n = 8$; $k = 2, n = 5$; $k = 3, n = 4$; $k = 6, n = 3$

Test yourself (p 67)

1 $1 + 20x + 190x^2 + 1140x^3$

2 (a) 2240 (b) −960

3 $1 + 6x + 7x^2$

6 Trigonometry 1

All answers for this chapter are given to 1 d.p.
unless otherwise required.

A Sine and cosine: revision (p 68)

A1 $OQ = 1 \times \cos\theta° = \cos\theta°$
$OR = PQ = 1 \times \sin\theta° = \sin\theta°$
Hence coordinates of P are $(\cos\theta°, \sin\theta°)$.

A2 (a) 1   (b) 0   (c) 1   (d) 0
(e) 0   (f) 0   (g) −1   (h) 0

A3 (a) Positive   (b) Positive   (c) Negative
(d) Negative   (e) Negative   (f) Positive
(g) Negative   (h) Negative

A4 (a) Negative; $\cos\theta°$ is negative.
(b) $\sin\theta°$ is positive.

A5

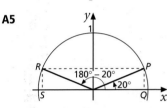

A proof such as:
$\sin 160° = SR = QP$ by symmetry
$= \sin 20°$

A6 A similar proof to A5

A7

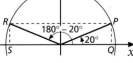

A8

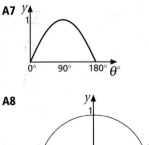

A proof such as:
$\cos 160° = OS = -OQ$ by symmetry
$= -\cos 20°$

A9 A similar proof to A8

A10

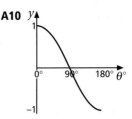

A11 $\theta° = 39°$; another angle is 141°.

A12 $\theta° = 51°$; the obtuse angle is 129°.

Exercise A (p 69)

1 (a) Positive   (b) Negative
(c) Positive   (d) Negative

2 (a) 20°   (b) 20° and 160°

3 (a) 64° and 116°   (b) 26°
(c) 27° and 153°   (d) 117°
(e) 32° and 148°   (f) 58°
(g) 4° and 176°   (h) 94°

4 An explanation such as: the line $y = k$ meets
$y = \sin\theta°$ at either two or no points; it meets
$y = \cos\theta°$ at one point.

B Cosine rule (p 70)

B1 (a) $PB = c - x$ (b) $h^2 = a^2 - (c - x)^2$
(c) $h^2 = b^2 - x^2$ (d) $a^2 = b^2 - x^2 + (c - x)^2$
(e) $a^2 = b^2 + c^2 - 2cx$ (f) $x = b\cos A$
(g) $a^2 = b^2 + c^2 - 2bc\cos A$

B2 $PB = c + x$
In $\triangle CPB$, $h^2 = a^2 - (c + x)^2$
In $\triangle CPA$, $h^2 = b^2 - x^2$
Hence $a^2 = b^2 - x^2 + (c + x)^2$
   i.e. $a^2 = b^2 + c^2 + 2cx$
In $\triangle CPA$, $x = b\cos\angle CAP$
            $= b\cos(180° - A)$
            $= -b\cos A$
Hence $a^2 = b^2 + c^2 - 2bc\cos A$

Exercise B (p 71)

1 (a) 4.1 cm   (b) 8.9 cm   (c) 6.0 cm

2 (a) 34.8°   (b) 106.1°   (c) 38.7°

3 8.9 cm

4 34.0°, 101.5°, 44.4° or 44.5°

5 5.4 km

6 (a) $AC^2 = 4^2 + AM^2 - 2 \times 4 \times AM \times \cos\theta°$

(b) $AB^2 = 4^2 + AM^2 - 2 \times 4 \times AM \times \cos(180° - \theta°)$
$= 4^2 + AM^2 + 2 \times 4 \times AM \times \cos\theta°$

(c) $AC^2 + AB^2 = 2(4^2 + AM^2)$
$6^2 + 7^2 = 2(4^2 + AM^2)$
$AM = 5.1$

C Sine rule (p 72)

C1 (a) $h = b\sin A$ (b) $h = a\sin B$

(c) $b\sin A = a\sin B$ (d) $\dfrac{a}{\sin A} = \dfrac{b}{\sin B}$

C2 (a) $h = b\sin\angle PAC$

(b) $\angle PAC = 180° - A$
$h = b\sin(180° - A)$

(c) $h = b\sin A$

(d) $h = a\sin B$

(e) $\dfrac{a}{\sin A} = \dfrac{b}{\sin B}$

Exercise C (p 74)

1 (a) 3.8 cm   (b) 10.5 cm   (c) 17.7 cm

2 (a)

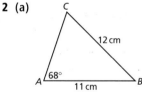

(b) $\sin C = 0.849\ldots$

(c) 58° and 122°

(d) If $C = 58°$, $B = 54°$
If $C = 122°$, $B = -10°$

(e) $C = 58°$ is the only possible answer.

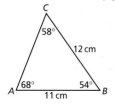

3 (a) 35.9° (144.1° is impossible)

(b) 48.7° (131.3° is impossible)

(c) 59.2° or 24.8°

D Both rules

Exercise D (p 76)

1 (a) $E = 38.0°$, $F = 62.0°$, $DE = 7.2$ cm

(b) $Q = 27.4°$, $R = 22.6°$, $PQ = 10.0$ mm

(c) $M = 66.8°$, $N = 63.2°$, $LM = 11.7$ m or
$M = 113.2°$, $N = 16.8°$, $LM = 3.8$ m

2 (a) $RS = 11.4$ cm, $R = 30.3°$, $S = 114.7°$

(b) $EF = 100.3$ m, $E = 58.6°$, $F = 49.4°$

3 (a) $BC = 43.2$ m, $C = 46.8°$, $B = 33.2°$

(b) $DE = 24$ mm, $E = 16.3°$, $F = 73.7°$

(c) $J = 41.9°$, $K = 73.1°$, 40.1 cm

(d) $X = 58.4°$, $Y = 48.2°$, $Z = 73.4°$

E Area of a triangle

Exercise E (p 78)

1 (a) 5.6 cm²   (b) 38.6 mm²   (c) 11.8 m²

2 (a) $R = 61.1°$ (or $S = 74.4°$ or $T = 44.5°$)

(b) Area = 38.5 cm²

3 (a) 11.2 cm²   (b) 59.6 mm²

(c) 1270 m² (3 s.f.)

F Radians and arcs (p 79)

F1 (a) π (b) $\dfrac{\pi}{2}$ (c) $\dfrac{\pi}{3}$

(d) $\dfrac{\pi}{6}$ (e) $\dfrac{3\pi}{2}$ (f) $\dfrac{\pi}{180}$

F2 57.3°

F3 (a) $2r$ (b) $\frac{1}{2}r$ (c) θr

F4 2 cm

F5 (a)

(b) $\sin 30° = \frac{1}{2}$ $\cos 30° = \frac{\sqrt{3}}{2}$ $\tan 30° = \frac{1}{\sqrt{3}}$

$\sin 60° = \frac{\sqrt{3}}{2}$ $\cos 60° = \frac{1}{2}$ $\tan 60° = \sqrt{3}$

Exercise F (p 81)

1 (a) $\frac{7\pi}{6}$ **(b)** $\frac{3\pi}{4}$ **(c)** $\frac{2\pi}{3}$

(d) $\frac{11\pi}{6}$ **(e)** $\frac{5\pi}{3}$

2 (a) $22\frac{1}{2}°$ **(b)** $18°$ **(c)** $1°$ **(d)** $45°$

(e) $150°$ **(f)** $225°$ **(g)** $75°$ **(h)** $315°$

(i) $40°$ **(j)** $240°$

3

Radians	Degrees	$\sin\theta$	$\cos\theta$	$\tan\theta$
$\frac{\pi}{6}$	$30°$	$\frac{1}{2}$	$\frac{\sqrt{3}}{2}$	$\frac{1}{\sqrt{3}}$
$\frac{2\pi}{3}$	$120°$	$\frac{\sqrt{3}}{2}$	$-\frac{1}{2}$	$-\sqrt{3}$
$\frac{3\pi}{4}$	$135°$	$\frac{1}{\sqrt{2}}$	$-\frac{1}{\sqrt{2}}$	-1
$\frac{5\pi}{6}$	$150°$	$\frac{1}{2}$	$-\frac{\sqrt{3}}{2}$	$-\frac{1}{\sqrt{3}}$

4 (a) $\frac{2\pi}{3}$ m **(b)** $4 + \frac{2\pi}{3}$ m

5 (a) 11.5 cm **(b)** 9.8 cm **(c)** 21.3 cm

6 $81.9°$

7 4.3 cm

G Area of a sector

Exercise G (p 83)

1 (a) 81.3 cm^2 **(b)** 69.8 m^2

(c) 52.8 cm^2 **(d)** 335.8 mm^2

2 (a) 8π **(b)** $\frac{100\pi}{3}$

3 $35.8°$

4 (a) $\theta = \frac{18}{r} - 2$ **(b)** Area $= 9r - r^2$

5 (a) 1600 m **(b)** $80\,000$ people

6 (a) $r\sin\theta$ **(b)** $\frac{1}{2}r^2\sin\theta$

(c) $\frac{1}{2}r^2\theta$ **(d)** $\frac{1}{2}r^2(\theta - \sin\theta)$

7 (a) A proof such as:
By symmetry $BP = 10$ cm and $OP = 10$ cm
(radius), so $\angle BOP = 60°$.
Hence $\angle AOB = 120°$.

(b) 104.7 cm^2 **(c)** 43.3 cm^2 **(d)** 61.4 cm^2

8 (a) (i) $\alpha = \frac{\pi}{3}$

(ii) 2π cm

(iii) Area $\triangle ABC$
$= \frac{1}{2} \times AB \times AC \times \sin\alpha$
$= 18\sin\frac{\pi}{3} = 18 \times \frac{\sqrt{3}}{2}$
$= 9\sqrt{3}$ cm^2

(iv) Area sector ABC
$= \frac{1}{2} \times AB^2 \times \alpha$
$= \frac{1}{2} \times 6^2 \times \frac{\pi}{3}$
$= 6\pi$ cm^2

(b) (i) 19 cm **(ii)** 25 cm^2

Test yourself (p 85)

1 (a) 3.2 cm **(b)** $55.4°$ or $124.6°$ **(c)** $117.3°$

2 (a) 4.7 cm^2 **(b)** 17.5 cm^2 or 5.8 cm^2 **(c)** 21.3 cm^2

3 (a) 6.8 cm **(b)** 16.8 cm **(c)** 17.0 cm^2

4 15 cm

5 (a) Area of sector $= \frac{1}{2} \times 6^2 \times \theta$
$= 18\theta = \frac{1}{3} \times$ area of square $= \frac{1}{3} \times 36$
So $18\theta = 12$, $\theta = \frac{2}{3}$

(b) Perimeter of square $= 4 \times 6 = 24$
Perimeter of sector $= 6 + 6 + $ arc
$= 12 + 6 \times \theta = 12 + 6 \times \frac{2}{3} = 16$.
Perimeter of sector $\times 1\frac{1}{2} = 16 \times 1\frac{1}{2} = 24$
$=$ perimeter of square

6 (a) (i) $PM = 3$ cm, $OM = \sqrt{27} = 3\sqrt{3}$

(ii) 2π cm **(iii)** 6π cm^2

(b) Shaded area
$= $ area sector $POQ - $ area $\triangle POQ$
$= 6\pi - \frac{1}{2} \times OM \times PQ$
$= 6\pi - \frac{1}{2} \times 3\sqrt{3} \times 6$
$= 6\pi - 9\sqrt{3} = 3(2\pi - 3\sqrt{3})$
Hence $m = 3$

7 Trigonometry 2

A Sines and cosines (p 86)

A1 (a) Same   (b) Not   (c) Not   (d) Not

(e) Same   (f) Same   (g) Same   (h) Same

A2 Let R be the reflection of P in the x-axis. By symmetry, the coordinates of R are $(\cos \theta°, -\sin \theta°)$, and $\angle QOR = -\theta°$. Hence $QR = \sin(-\theta)°$ $= -\sin \theta°$.

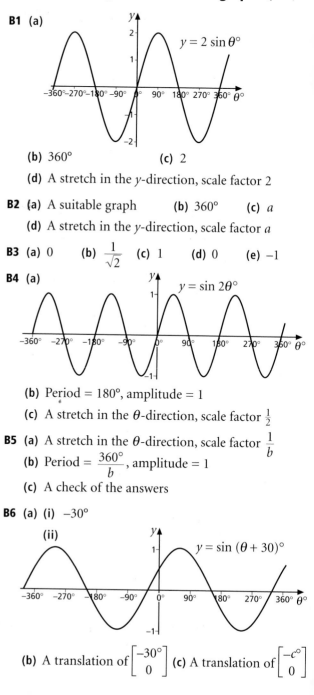

A3 (a) $\sin 20°$ (b) $-\sin 20°$ (c) $-\sin 20°$

(d) $-\sin 20°$ (e) $-\sin 20°$ (f) $\sin 20°$

(g) $\sin 20°$ (h) $-\sin 20°$ (i) $-\sin 20°$

(j) $\sin 20°$

A4 (a) Not   (b) Not   (c) Same   (d) Same

(e) Same   (f) Not   (g) Same   (h) Not

A5 In the diagram for A2, in $\triangle OQP$, $OQ = \cos \theta°$, and in $\triangle OQR$, $OQ = \cos(-\theta)°$. So $\cos \theta° = \cos(-\theta)°$.

A6 (a) $-20°$ (b) $160°$ (c) $340°$ (d) $-200°$

A7 (a) $317°$ (b) $260°$

(c) If one solution is $\theta° = \alpha°$, then the other solution is $\theta° = 360° - \alpha°$.

Exercise A (p 88)

1 (a) $110°$ (b) $430°$ and $470°$

2 (a) 5.28^c (b) 7.28^c and 11.57^c

3 (a) (i) $40°, 140°$ (ii) $50°, 310°$

(iii) $197°, 343°$ (iv) $152°, 208°$

(b) (i) $400°, 500°$ (ii) $410°, 670°$

(iii) $557°, 703°$ (iv) $512°, 568°$

4 (a) $\dfrac{\pi}{6}, \dfrac{5\pi}{6}$ (b) $\dfrac{\pi}{2}$ (c) $\dfrac{\pi}{2}, \dfrac{3\pi}{2}$

5 (a) $-\dfrac{7\pi}{4}, -\dfrac{5\pi}{4}, \dfrac{\pi}{4}, \dfrac{3\pi}{4}$ (b) $-\dfrac{3\pi}{4}, -\dfrac{\pi}{4}, \dfrac{5\pi}{4}, \dfrac{7\pi}{4}$

(c) $-\dfrac{11\pi}{6}, -\dfrac{\pi}{6}, \dfrac{\pi}{6}, \dfrac{11\pi}{6}$ (d) $-\dfrac{4\pi}{3}, -\dfrac{2\pi}{3}, \dfrac{2\pi}{3}, \dfrac{4\pi}{3}$

6 (a) $-354°, -186°, 6°, 174°$

(b) $127°, 233°, 487°, 593°$

(c) $49°, 131°, 409°, 491°$

(d) $-248°, -112°, 112°, 248°$

B Transforming sine and cosine graphs (p 89)

B1 (a)

[graph: $y = 2 \sin \theta°$]

(b) $360°$ (c) 2

(d) A stretch in the y-direction, scale factor 2

B2 (a) A suitable graph   (b) $360°$ (c) a

(d) A stretch in the y-direction, scale factor a

B3 (a) 0 (b) $\dfrac{1}{\sqrt{2}}$ (c) 1 (d) 0 (e) -1

B4 (a)

[graph: $y = \sin 2\theta°$]

(b) Period $= 180°$, amplitude $= 1$

(c) A stretch in the θ-direction, scale factor $\frac{1}{2}$

B5 (a) A stretch in the θ-direction, scale factor $\dfrac{1}{b}$

(b) Period $= \dfrac{360°}{b}$, amplitude $= 1$

(c) A check of the answers

B6 (a) (i) $-30°$

(ii)

[graph: $y = \sin(\theta + 30)°$]

(b) A translation of $\begin{bmatrix} -30° \\ 0 \end{bmatrix}$ (c) A translation of $\begin{bmatrix} -c° \\ 0 \end{bmatrix}$

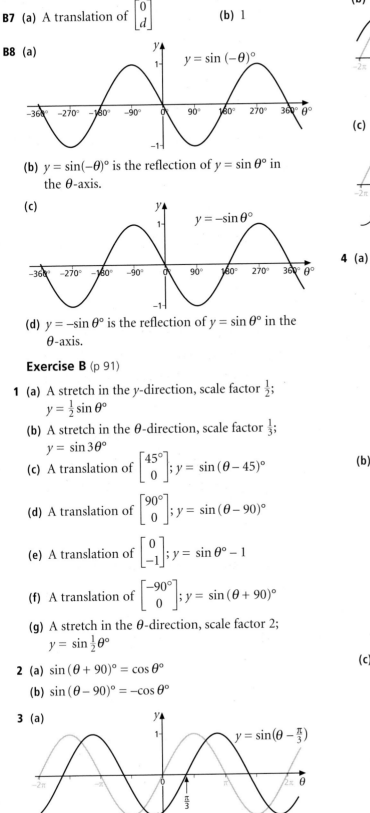

B7 (a) A translation of $\begin{bmatrix} 0 \\ d \end{bmatrix}$ **(b)** 1

B8 (a)

$y = \sin(-\theta)^\circ$

(b) $y = \sin(-\theta)^\circ$ is the reflection of $y = \sin\theta^\circ$ in the θ-axis.

(c)

$y = -\sin\theta^\circ$

(d) $y = -\sin\theta^\circ$ is the reflection of $y = \sin\theta^\circ$ in the θ-axis.

Exercise B (p 91)

1 (a) A stretch in the y-direction, scale factor $\frac{1}{2}$; $y = \frac{1}{2}\sin\theta^\circ$

(b) A stretch in the θ-direction, scale factor $\frac{1}{3}$; $y = \sin 3\theta^\circ$

(c) A translation of $\begin{bmatrix} 45^\circ \\ 0 \end{bmatrix}$; $y = \sin(\theta - 45)^\circ$

(d) A translation of $\begin{bmatrix} 90^\circ \\ 0 \end{bmatrix}$; $y = \sin(\theta - 90)^\circ$

(e) A translation of $\begin{bmatrix} 0 \\ -1 \end{bmatrix}$; $y = \sin\theta^\circ - 1$

(f) A translation of $\begin{bmatrix} -90^\circ \\ 0 \end{bmatrix}$; $y = \sin(\theta + 90)^\circ$

(g) A stretch in the θ-direction, scale factor 2; $y = \sin\frac{1}{2}\theta^\circ$

2 (a) $\sin(\theta + 90)^\circ = \cos\theta^\circ$

(b) $\sin(\theta - 90)^\circ = -\cos\theta^\circ$

3 (a)

$y = \sin(\theta - \frac{\pi}{3})$

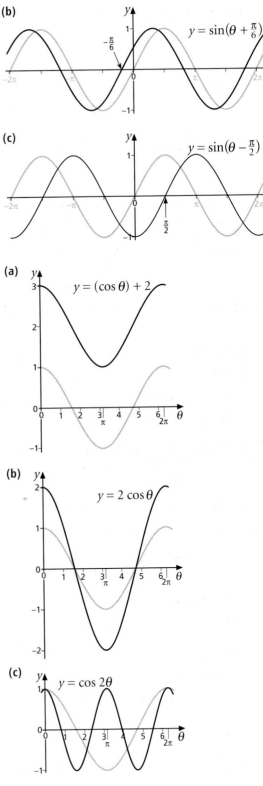

(b) $y = \sin(\theta + \frac{\pi}{6})$

(c) $y = \sin(\theta - \frac{\pi}{2})$

4 (a) $y = (\cos\theta) + 2$

(b) $y = 2\cos\theta$

(c) $y = \cos 2\theta$

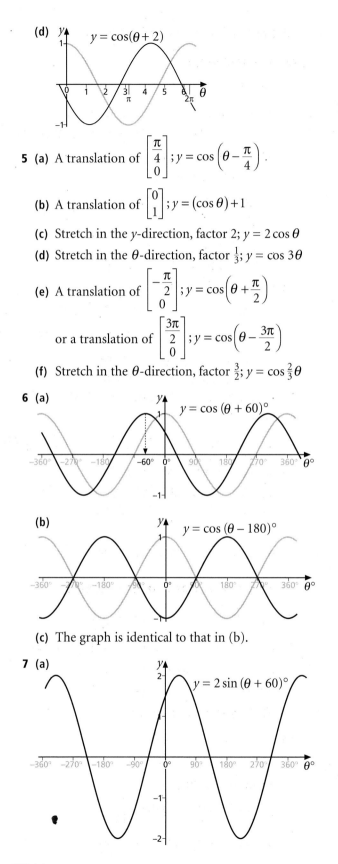

(d) $y = \cos(\theta + 2)$

5 (a) A translation of $\begin{bmatrix} \frac{\pi}{4} \\ 0 \end{bmatrix}$; $y = \cos\left(\theta - \frac{\pi}{4}\right)$.

(b) A translation of $\begin{bmatrix} 0 \\ 1 \end{bmatrix}$; $y = (\cos\theta) + 1$

(c) Stretch in the y-direction, factor 2; $y = 2\cos\theta$

(d) Stretch in the θ-direction, factor $\frac{1}{3}$; $y = \cos 3\theta$

(e) A translation of $\begin{bmatrix} -\frac{\pi}{2} \\ 0 \end{bmatrix}$; $y = \cos\left(\theta + \frac{\pi}{2}\right)$

or a translation of $\begin{bmatrix} \frac{3\pi}{2} \\ 0 \end{bmatrix}$; $y = \cos\left(\theta - \frac{3\pi}{2}\right)$

(f) Stretch in the θ-direction, factor $\frac{3}{2}$; $y = \cos\frac{2}{3}\theta$

6 (a) $y = \cos(\theta + 60)°$

(b) $y = \cos(\theta - 180)°$

(c) The graph is identical to that in (b).

7 (a) $y = 2\sin(\theta + 60)°$

(b) $y = -\cos(\theta - 60)°$

8 (a) (i) 180° **(ii)** 1

(b) −60°

(c) $y = \sin(2\theta + 120)°$

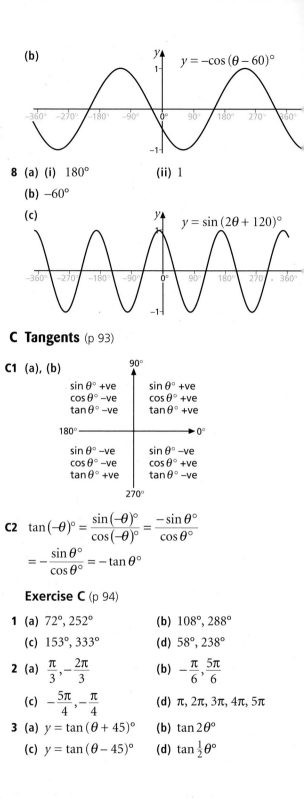

C Tangents (p 93)

C1 (a), (b)

$\sin\theta°$ +ve $\cos\theta°$ −ve $\tan\theta°$ −ve	$\sin\theta°$ +ve $\cos\theta°$ +ve $\tan\theta°$ +ve
$\sin\theta°$ −ve $\cos\theta°$ −ve $\tan\theta°$ +ve	$\sin\theta°$ −ve $\cos\theta°$ +ve $\tan\theta°$ −ve

C2 $\tan(-\theta)° = \dfrac{\sin(-\theta)°}{\cos(-\theta)°} = \dfrac{-\sin\theta°}{\cos\theta°}$

$= -\dfrac{\sin\theta°}{\cos\theta°} = -\tan\theta°$

Exercise C (p 94)

1 (a) 72°, 252° **(b)** 108°, 288°

(c) 153°, 333° **(d)** 58°, 238°

2 (a) $\dfrac{\pi}{3}, -\dfrac{2\pi}{3}$ **(b)** $-\dfrac{\pi}{6}, \dfrac{5\pi}{6}$

(c) $-\dfrac{5\pi}{4}, -\dfrac{\pi}{4}$ **(d)** $\pi, 2\pi, 3\pi, 4\pi, 5\pi$

3 (a) $y = \tan(\theta + 45)°$ **(b)** $\tan 2\theta°$

(c) $y = \tan(\theta - 45)°$ **(d)** $\tan\frac{1}{2}\theta°$

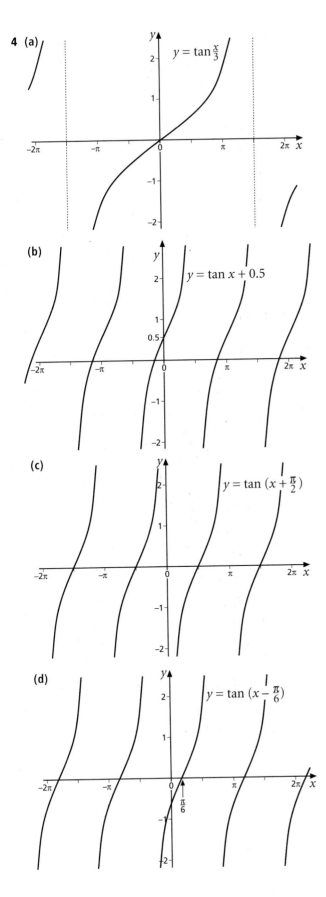

4 (a) $y = \tan \frac{x}{3}$

(b) $y = \tan x + 0.5$

(c) $y = \tan\left(x + \frac{\pi}{2}\right)$

(d) $y = \tan\left(x - \frac{\pi}{6}\right)$

D Solving further equations (p 95)

D1 $\theta° = 106°$ or $334°$

Exercise D (p 97)

1 (a) $231°$ or $329°$ **(b)** $294°$ or $346°$

(c) $116°$ or $296°$ **(d)** $22°, 68°, 202°$ or $248°$

(e) $22°, 98°, 142°, 218°, 262°$ or $338°$

(f) $6°, 96°, 186°$ or $276°$

2 (a) $\dfrac{\pi}{12}, \dfrac{5\pi}{12}, \dfrac{13\pi}{12}$ or $\dfrac{17\pi}{12}$

(b) $0, \dfrac{\pi}{2}, \pi, \dfrac{3\pi}{2}$ or 2π

(c) $\dfrac{\pi}{12}, \dfrac{5\pi}{12}, \dfrac{9\pi}{12}, \dfrac{13\pi}{12}, \dfrac{17\pi}{12}$ or $\dfrac{21\pi}{12}$

3 (a) $3.9°, 14.1°, 39.9°$ or $50.1°$

(b) $51.7°$ **(c)** $2.3°$ or $38.3°$

4 (a) $-107.7°, -72.3°, 12.3°, 47.7°, 132.3°$ or $167.7°$

(b) $-303.8°, -236.2°, -123.8°$ or $-56.2°$

(c) $-156.7°, -120.7°, -84.7°, -48.7°, -12.7°,$
$23.3°, 59.3°, 95.3°, 131.3°$ or $167.3°$

(d) $98.9°$ or $261.1°$

5 (a) $\dfrac{\pi}{3}$ or $\dfrac{4\pi}{3}$ **(b)** $\dfrac{5\pi}{6}$ or $\dfrac{11\pi}{6}$ **(c)** $\dfrac{2\pi}{3}$ or $\dfrac{5\pi}{3}$

6 (a) $10.1°, 134.9°, 190.1°$ or $314.9°$

(b) $62.4°, 83.1°, 152.4°, 173.1°,$
$242.4°, 263.1°, 332.4°$ or $353.1°$

(c) $56.4°$

(d) $25.8°, 115.8°, 205.8°$ or $295.8°$

E Further equations and identities (p 97)

E1 (a) $-\dfrac{2\sqrt{2}}{3}$ **(b)** $-\dfrac{1}{2\sqrt{2}}$

E2 (a) $2c^2 - 3c + 1 = 0$ **(b)** $(2c - 1)(c - 1) = 0$

(c) A check that one factor is $(c - 1)$

(d) $\theta° = 0°$ **(e)** $\theta° = 60°$

(f) A check of the solutions

E3 (a) $\cos^2 \theta° + \cos \theta° = 0$

(b) $\theta° = 90°, 180°$ or $270°$

Exercise E (p 100)

1 (a) $\cos \theta = \dfrac{\sqrt{15}}{4}$, $\tan \theta = \dfrac{1}{\sqrt{15}}$

(b) $\cos \theta = -\dfrac{\sqrt{15}}{4}$, $\tan \theta = -\dfrac{1}{\sqrt{15}}$

2 (a) $1 + \cos x° = 3\sin^2 x°$

$\Rightarrow 1 + \cos x° = 3(1 - \cos^2 x°)$

$\Rightarrow 1 + \cos x° = 3 - 3\cos^2 x°$

$\Rightarrow 3\cos^2 x° + \cos x° - 2 = 0$

(b) $(3\cos x° - 2)(\cos x° + 1) = 0$

(c) $x° = 48.2°, 180°$ or $311.8°$

3 (a) $\dfrac{2\pi}{3}, \dfrac{4\pi}{3}, 0$ or 2π **(b)** $\dfrac{\pi}{6}$ or $\dfrac{7\pi}{6}$

(c) $\dfrac{\pi}{3}$ or $\dfrac{5\pi}{3}$

4 (a) $\dfrac{\pi}{6}, \dfrac{5\pi}{6}, \dfrac{7\pi}{6}$ or $\dfrac{11\pi}{6}$ **(b)** $0, \pi$ or 2π

(c) $\dfrac{\pi}{3}, \dfrac{2\pi}{3}, \dfrac{4\pi}{3}$ or $\dfrac{5\pi}{3}$ **(d)** $0.46, 2.68, 3.61$ or 5.82

(e) $0, \pi$ or 2π **(f)** $\dfrac{3\pi}{2}$

5 (a) When $x = 1$, $x^3 - x^2 - 3x + 3$

$= 1 - 1 - 3 + 3 = 0$. Hence $(x - 1)$ is a factor by the factor theorem.

$x^3 - x^2 - 3x + 3 = (x - 1)(x^2 - 3)$

(b) $\dfrac{\pi}{4}, \dfrac{\pi}{3}, \dfrac{2\pi}{3}, \dfrac{5\pi}{4}, \dfrac{4\pi}{3}$ or $\dfrac{5\pi}{3}$

6 (a) $(\sin x + \cos x)^2$

$= \sin^2 x + 2\sin x \cos x + \cos^2 x$

$= \sin^2 x + \cos^2 x + 2\sin x \cos x$

$= 1 + 2\sin x \cos x$

(b) $\dfrac{6 - \cos^2\theta}{\sin^2\theta + 5} = \dfrac{6 - (1 - \sin^2\theta)}{\sin^2\theta + 5} = \dfrac{6 - 1 + \sin^2\theta}{\sin^2\theta + 5}$

$= \dfrac{5 + \sin^2\theta}{\sin^2\theta + 5} = 1$

7 $(1 + \sin\theta + \cos\theta)^2$

$= 1(1 + \sin\theta + \cos\theta) + \sin\theta(1 + \sin\theta + \cos\theta)$

  $+ \cos\theta(1 + \sin\theta + \cos\theta)$

$= 1 + \sin\theta + \cos\theta + \sin\theta + \sin^2\theta + \sin\theta\cos\theta$

  $+ \cos\theta + \cos\theta\sin\theta + \cos^2\theta$

$= 1 + 2\sin\theta + 2\cos\theta + 2\sin\theta\cos\theta + \sin^2\theta + \cos^2\theta$

$= 1 + 2\sin\theta + 2\cos\theta + 2\sin\theta\cos\theta + 1$

$= 2 + 2\sin\theta + 2\cos\theta + 2\sin\theta\cos\theta$

$= 2(1 + \sin\theta + \cos\theta + \sin\theta\cos\theta)$

$= 2(1 + \sin\theta)(1 + \cos\theta)$

8 $\dfrac{x^2}{9} + \dfrac{y^2}{4} = 1$

Test yourself (p 101)

1 $x = \dfrac{\pi}{2}$ or $\dfrac{7\pi}{6}$

2 (a) $108.5°$ or $311.5°$ **(b)** $1.3°$ or $78.7°$

(c) $59.8°$ or $239.8°$

3 (a) $0.10, 1.47, 3.24$ or 4.61

(b) $0.82, 1.27, 2.92, 3.37, 5.01$ or 5.46

(c) 1.75

4 (a) 0.75 **(b)** $7.4°, 43.4°$ or $79.4°$

5 (a)

$y = \sin(\theta + 45)°$

(b)

$y = \tfrac{1}{3}\cos\theta°$

(c)

$y = 2 + \sin\theta°$

(d)

$y = \tan 2\theta°$

6 (a) $\dfrac{3 - 2\cos^2\theta}{2\sin^2\theta + 1} = \dfrac{3 - 2(1 - \sin^2\theta)}{2\sin^2\theta + 1} = \dfrac{3 - 2 + 2\sin^2\theta}{2\sin^2\theta + 1}$

$= \dfrac{1 + 2\sin^2\theta}{2\sin^2\theta + 1} = 1$

(b) $\tan\theta\sin\theta = \dfrac{\sin\theta}{\cos\theta}\sin\theta = \dfrac{\sin^2\theta}{\cos\theta} = \dfrac{1 - \cos^2\theta}{\cos\theta}$

$= \dfrac{1}{\cos\theta} - \cos\theta$

7 (a) $2\cos^2 x = 2 + \sin x$
$\Rightarrow \quad 2(1 - \sin^2 x) = 2 + \sin x$
$\Rightarrow \quad 2 - 2\sin^2 x = 2 + \sin x$
$\Rightarrow 2\sin^2 x + \sin x = 0$

(b) $x = 0, \pi, \dfrac{7\pi}{6}$ or $\dfrac{11\pi}{6}$

8 (a) $2\cos^2 \theta - \sin \theta = 1$
$\Rightarrow \quad 2(1 - \sin^2 \theta) - \sin \theta = 1$
$\Rightarrow \quad 2 - 2\sin^2 x - \sin \theta - 1 = 0$
$\Rightarrow \quad 1 - 2\sin^2 \theta - \sin \theta = 0$
$\Rightarrow \quad 2\sin^2 \theta + \sin \theta - 1 = 0$

(b) $\theta = \dfrac{\pi}{6}, \dfrac{5\pi}{6}$ or $\dfrac{3\pi}{2}$ **(c)** $x = \dfrac{\pi}{12}, \dfrac{5\pi}{12}$ or $\dfrac{3\pi}{4}$

9 1.32, 2.09, 4.19 or 4.97

10 (a) (i) $\dfrac{1}{\sqrt{2}}$ **(ii)** $\dfrac{\sqrt{3}}{2}$ **(iii)** $\sqrt{3}$

(b) $x = \dfrac{\pi}{4}$ or $\dfrac{3\pi}{4}$ **(c)** $\dfrac{\pi}{4} < x < \dfrac{3\pi}{4}$

(d) $\sin^2 x > \frac{1}{2} \Rightarrow 1 - \cos^2 x > \frac{1}{2} \Rightarrow -\cos^2 x > -\frac{1}{2}$
$\Rightarrow \cos^2 x < \frac{1}{2}$

8 Exponentials and logarithms

A Graphs of exponential functions (p 102)

A1 (a)

t (weeks)	0	1	2	3	4
A (m²)	1	2	4	8	16

(b), (f)

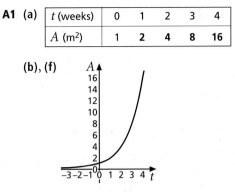

(c) The formula is $A = 2^t$.

(d) $A = 1.414$ to 3 d.p.

(e) $A = 3.249$ to 3 d.p.

A2 (a) $y = 1$

(b) y is large and positive.

(c) y approaches zero and is positive.

A3 (a) The family of graphs is shown.

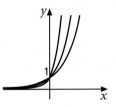

(b) All graphs of $y = a^x$ pass through $(0, 1)$.

A4 (a) y approaches zero and is positive.

(b) y is large and positive.

(c) $y = \left(\frac{1}{2}\right)^x = \dfrac{1}{2^x} = 2^{-x}$ as required

(d) The graph of $y = \left(\frac{1}{2}\right)^x$ is a reflection in the y-axis of $y = 2^x$.

A5 (a) If $x = 3$, then $y = 2^3 = 8$, so $(3, 8)$ is on the graph.

(b) $(3, 9)$

(c) The y-intercept is 2.

(d) $y = 2^x + 1$

A6 $y = 2^{x-3}$

A7 $y = 2^{x+1}$

A8 (a)

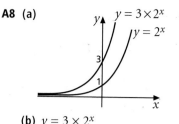

$y = 3 \times 2^x$
$y = 2^x$

(b) $y = 3 \times 2^x$

A9 $y = 2^{\frac{x}{3}}$

A10 (a) $y = 16 \times 2^x$

$= 2^4 \times 2^x$

$= 2^{x+4}$ as required

(b) $y = 2^{x+4}$ is a stretch of $y = 2^x$ by scale factor 16 in the direction of the y-axis.

$y = 2^{x+4}$ is a translation of $\begin{bmatrix} -4 \\ 0 \end{bmatrix}$ of $y = 2^x$.

A11 $y = 2^{x+5}$ is a stretch of $y = 2^x$ by scale factor 32 in the direction of the y-axis.

$y = 2^{x+5}$ is a translation of $\begin{bmatrix} -5 \\ 0 \end{bmatrix}$ of $y = 2^x$.

Exercise A (p 104)

1

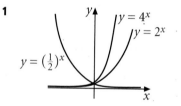

$y = 4^x$
$y = 2^x$
$y = (\frac{1}{2})^x$

2 (a) The graph of $y = 5^{x+1}$ is a translation of $\begin{bmatrix} -1 \\ 0 \end{bmatrix}$ of $y = 5^x$ or a stretch of $y = 5^x$ by scale factor 5 in the direction of the y-axis.

(b)

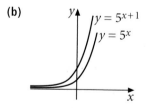

$y = 5^{x+1}$
$y = 5^x$

3 (a) $y = 6^{x-3}$ **(b)** $y = 6^x + 3$

4 (a) $f(x - 2) = 4^{x-2}$

(b) The graph of $y = f(x - 2)$ is a translation of $\begin{bmatrix} 2 \\ 0 \end{bmatrix}$ of $y = f(x)$.

5 (a) $g(3x) = 7^{3x}$

(b) The graph of $y = g(3x)$ is a stretch of $y = g(x)$ by scale factor $\frac{1}{3}$ in the direction of the x-axis.

6 (a) The graph of $y = 3^{-x}$ is a reflection in the y-axis of $y = 3^x$.

(b) The graph of $y = 3^x - 5$ is a translation of $\begin{bmatrix} 0 \\ -5 \end{bmatrix}$ of $y = 3x$.

(c) The graph of $y = 2 \times 3^x$ is a stretch of $y = 3^x$ by scale factor 2 in the direction of the y-axis.

(d) The graph of $y = 3^{x+4}$ is a translation of $\begin{bmatrix} -4 \\ 0 \end{bmatrix}$ of $y = 3^x$ or a stretch of $y = 3^x$ by scale factor 81 in the direction of the y-axis.

7 (a) $y = 16 \times 4^x$

$= 4^2 \times 4^x$

$= 4^{x+2}$ as required

(b) $y = 4^{x+2}$ is a stretch of $y = 4^x$ by scale factor 16 in the direction of the y-axis.

$y = 4^{x+2}$ is a translation of $\begin{bmatrix} -2 \\ 0 \end{bmatrix}$ of $y = 4^x$.

8 $y = 5^{x-1}$ is a stretch of $y = 5^x$ by scale factor $\frac{1}{5}$ in the direction of the y-axis.

$y = 5^{x-1}$ is a translation of $\begin{bmatrix} 1 \\ 0 \end{bmatrix}$ of $y = 5^x$.

B Logarithms (p 105)

B1 After 3.3 weeks the area covered is $10\,m^2$.

B2 (a) (i) $y = 4$ **(ii)** $y = 32$ **(iii)** $y = \frac{1}{2}$

(b) (i) $x = 0$ **(ii)** $x = 3$ **(iii)** $x = -2$

B3 (a) $\log_2 64 = 6$ **(b)** $2^7 = 128$

B4 (a) (i) $x = 1$ **(ii)** $x = 3$ **(iii)** $x = -1$

(b) (i) $x = 3$ **(ii)** $x = -2$ **(iii)** $x = -3$

B5 (a) $\log_5 625 = 4$ **(b)** $10^2 = 100$

B6 (a) $\log_3 81 = 4$ **(b)** $\log_7 343 = 3$

(c) $\log_8 0.125 = -1$

B7 (a) $3^2 = 9$ **(b)** $4^3 = 64$ **(c)** $9^{-1} = \frac{1}{9}$

B8 (a) $2^x = 2$ **(b)** $x = 1$

B9 (a) $2^x = 1$ **(b)** $x = 0$

B10 (a) $2^x = \frac{1}{2}$ **(b)** $x = -1$

B11 (a) $\log_a a = 1$ **(b)** $\log_a 1 = 0$

(c) $\log_a \left(\frac{1}{a}\right) = -1$

B12 (a) (i) $5^x = 5^2$ (ii) $x = 2$

   (b) $\log_3 3^4 = 4$

   (c) $\log_a a^x = x$

B13 (a) (i) $\log_2 x = \log_2 8$ (ii) $x = 8$

   (b) $3^{\log_3 9} = 9$

   (c) $a^{\log_a x} = x$

Exercise B (p 107)

1 (a) (i) $64 = 2^6$ (ii) $\sqrt{2} = 2^{\frac{1}{2}}$

     (iii) $\frac{1}{8} = 2^{-3}$ (iv) $0.25 = 2^{-2}$

     (v) $1 = 2^0$

   (b) (i) $\log_2 64 = 6$ (ii) $\log_2 \sqrt{2} = \frac{1}{2}$

     (iii) $\log_2 \frac{1}{8} = -3$ (iv) $\log_2 0.25 = -2$

     (v) $\log_2 1 = 0$

2 (a) $3^{-2} = \frac{1}{9}$ (b) $8^0 = 1$

   (c) $4^{2.5} = 32$ (d) $8^{\frac{2}{3}} = 4$

3 (a) $\log_6 216 = 3$ (b) $\log_3 243 = 5$

   (c) $\log_4 \left(\frac{1}{64}\right) = -3$ (d) $\log_{27} 9 = \frac{2}{3}$

4 (a) 2   (b) 3   (c) -2 (d) 0

   (e) $\frac{1}{4}$ (f) $\frac{1}{2}$ (g) 1   (h) -1

5 (a) 2   (b) -2 (c) $\frac{1}{2}$ (d) 7

6 $3^4 = p$ so $p = 81$

7 $t^{\frac{1}{2}} = 3$ so $t = 9$

8 (a) $x = 3$ (b) $x = 2$ (c) $x = 27$ (d) $x = 6$

   (e) $x = 5$ (f) $x = \frac{1}{2}$ (g) $x = -1$ (h) $x = \sqrt{3}$

9 (a)

x	0.25	0.5	1	2	4	8
$y = \log_2 x$	-2	-1	0	1	2	3

   (b)

   (c) The graph of $y = \log_2 x$ is a reflection in the line $y = x$ of the graph of $y = 2^x$.

C Laws of logarithms (p 108)

C1 (a) (i) $\log_2 8 = 3$ (ii) $\log_2 16 = 4$

     (iii) $\log_2 128 = 7$

   (b) $8 \times 16 = 128$ becomes $2^3 \times 2^4 = 2^7$, so $a = 3$, $b = 4$, $c = 7$ and $a + b = c$.

   (c) Since $a = \log_2 8$, $b = \log_2 16$, and $c = \log_2 128$, it follows that $\log_2 8 + \log_2 16 = \log_2 128$.

C2 As with C1, $2 + 3 = 5$, but $2 = \log_3 9$, $3 = \log_3 27$ and $5 = \log_3 243 = \log_3 (9 \times 27)$ so $\log_3 9 + \log_3 27 = \log_3 (9 \times 27)$.

C3 $\log_5 12 = \log_5 (3 \times 4) = \log_5 3 + \log_5 4$ so $\log_5 12 = 0.6826 + 0.8614 = 1.544$

C4 Let $x = \log_a m$ so $m = a^x$ and let $y = \log_a n$ so $n = a^y$.

$$\frac{m}{n} = \frac{a^x}{a^y} = a^{x-y}$$

so $x - y = \log_a \left(\frac{m}{n}\right)$

and $\log_a m - \log_a n = \log_a \left(\frac{m}{n}\right)$

C5 $\log_8 7 = \log_8 \left(\frac{21}{3}\right)$

         $= \log_8 21 - \log_8 3$

so $\log_8 7 = 1.4641 - 0.5283 = 0.9358$

C6 Let $x = \log_a m$ so $m = a^x$

$m^2 = (a^x)^2 = a^{2x}$

so $2x = \log_a m^2$

and $2\log_a m = \log_a m^2$

C7 Let $x = \log_a m$ so $m = a^x$

$m^k = (a^x)^k = a^{kx}$

so $kx = \log_a m^k$

and $k\log_a m = \log_a m^k$

C8 (a) $\log_3 4 = \log_3 2^2 = 2\log_3 2 = 1.2618$

   (b) $\log_3 16 = \log_3 2^4 = 4\log_3 2 = 2.5236$

   (c) $\log_3 \frac{1}{2} = \log_3 2^{-1} = -\log_3 2 = -0.6309$

   (d) $\log_3 \sqrt{2} = \log_3 2^{\frac{1}{2}} = \frac{1}{2}\log_3 2 = 0.3155$

C9 (a) $\log_{10} \frac{1}{2} = -\log_{10} 2 = -0.3010$

   (b) $\log_{10} 1.5 = \log_{10} 3 - \log_{10} 2 = 0.1761$

   (c) $\log_{10} 4 = 2\log_{10} 2 = 0.6020$

   (d) $\log_{10} 5 = \log_{10} 10 - \log_{10} 2 = 0.6990$

(e) $\log_{10}6 = \log_{10}3 + \log_{10}2 = 0.7781$

(f) $\log_{10}9 = 2\log_{10}3 = 0.9542$

(g) $\log_{10}16 = 4\log_{10}2 = 1.204$

(h) $\log_{10}20 = \log_{10}2 + \log_{10}10 = 1.3010$

Exercise C (p 110)

1 (a) $\log_a 10$ **(b)** $\log_a 4$ **(c)** $\log_a 9$

(d) $\log_a 8a$ **(e)** $\log_a 32$ **(f)** $\log_a 8$

2 (a) $\log_5 5 = 1$ **(b)** $\log_5 9 = 1.3652$

(c) $\log_5 \frac{1}{3} = -0.6826$ **(d)** $\log_5 \sqrt{3} = 0.3413$

(e) $\log_5 15 = 1.6826$ **(f)** $\log_5 25 = 2$

(g) $\log_5 0.6 = -0.3174$ **(h)** $\log_5 \frac{9}{25} = -0.6348$

3 (a) $\log_a \dfrac{x}{y} = \log_a x - \log_a y$

(b) $\log_a xy = \log_a x + \log_a y$

(c) $\log_a \dfrac{x^2}{y} = 2\log_a x - \log_a y$

(d) $\log_a \dfrac{\sqrt[a]{y}}{x} = \dfrac{1}{a}\log_a y - \log_a x$

4 $\log_5 5! = \log_5 (5 \times 4!) = 2.9746$

5 (a) $\log_a p^2 q$ **(b)** $\log_a ap^3$ **(c)** $\log_a \left(\dfrac{\sqrt{p}}{q^4}\right)$

6 (a) After t hours the size of the colony is multiplied by 2^t. If the population is 1000 times bigger then $2^t = 1000$.

(b) $\log_2 1000 = t$
$2^9 = 512$ and $2^{10} = 1024$, so $9 < t < 10$.

(c) $t = 9.97$

7 (a) $x = 4$ **(b)** $x = 4$ **(c)** $x = 9$

(d) $x = 11$ **(e)** $x = 2$ **(f)** $x = -2, 6$

D Equations of the form $a^x = b$ (p 111)

D1 Answers for C9 checked using calculator

D2 (a) $\log 2^t = t\log 2$

(b) $\log 2^t = \log 1000$
$t\log 2 = \log 1000$
$t = 9.97$ to 2 d.p.

D3 (a) 1% represents a monthly growth factor of 1.01. After m months the amount in the account will be 1000×1.01^m.
There will be £2000 in the account when $1000 \times 1.01^m = 2000$.
Dividing by 1000, $1.01^m = 2$

(b) $\log 1.01^m = \log 2$
$m\log 1.01 = \log 2$
$m = 69.66$
The amount will be a little over £2000 after 70 months.

D4 (a) A decrease of 5% represents a growth factor of 0.95.

(b) After t years the population has reduced to 0.95^t of its original value, so $0.95^t = \frac{3}{5}$, or $0.95^t = 0.6$.

(c) $\log 0.95^t = \log 0.6$
giving $t = 9.96$
After 10 years the population is just under $\frac{3}{5}$ of its original value.

Exercise D (p 113)

1 (a) $x = 5$ **(b)** $x = 2.5$ **(c)** $x = 2.67$

(d) $x = 2.10$ **(e)** $x = 1.38$ **(f)** $x = 2.71$

2 $n = 2.90$ years

3 $t = 5.0$ days

4 (a) $n = 250 \times 3.7^t$

(b) $t = 2.82$ hours $= 2$ hours 49 minutes

5 The time when there is $\frac{1}{5}$ of the original charge left is given by $0.9^t = 0.2$.
$t = 15.28$ seconds

6 $n\log 2 > 132\log 50$
$n > 744.99$
The smallest possible integer to satisfy $2^n > 50^{132}$ is $n = 745$.

7 (a) 1.06   **(b)** $P = 250\,000 \times 1.06^t$

(c) 8 years

8 (a) After t years the amount of isotope has reduced to 0.925^t of its original value. So if it is half of its original value then $0.5 = 0.925^t$.

(b) $t = 8.89$ years

9 The investment has increased by 25% after 7.0 years.

10 (a) $x = 2.465$ (b) $x = -0.0865$

     (c) $x = -0.8340$ (d) $x = 12.43$

     (e) $x = 0.1147$ (f) $x = 8.417$

11 (a) $a = 1.1270$

     (b) After 5 more years the population will have increased to 120.

12 (a) $y = 2, 3$

     (b) $2^x = 2$ giving $x = 1$ or $2^x = 3$ giving $x = 1.59$

13 (a) $3^x = 3$ giving $x = 1$ or $3^x = 1$ giving $x = 0$

     (b) $5^x = 4$ giving $x = 0.861$ or $5^x = 2$ giving $x = 0.431$

     (c) $2^x = -5$ which is not possible or $2^x = 2$ giving $x = 1$

14 (a) $1000 = 470 \times 1.029^t$

     $t = 26.4$

     so the population reaches one thousand million in 2006.

     (b) $t = \dfrac{\log 995 - \log 470}{\log 1.029 - \log 1.014}$

     $t = 51$

     The two populations will be equal after 51 years.

Test yourself (p 115)

1 (a) The graph of $y = 3^{x+2}$ is a translation of $\begin{bmatrix} -2 \\ 0 \end{bmatrix}$ of $y = 3^x$.

     (b) The graph of $y = 3^{-x}$ is a reflection in the y-axis of $y = 3^x$.

     (c) The graph of $y = 4 \times 3^x$ is a stretch of $y = 3^x$ by scale factor 4 in the direction of the y-axis.

     (d) The graph of $y = 3^x - 1$ is a translation of $\begin{bmatrix} 0 \\ 1 \end{bmatrix}$ of $y = 3^x$.

2 (a) $5^3 = 125$ so $\log_5 125 = 3$

     (b) (i) $\log_5 (125)^4 = 4\log_5 125 = 12$

        (ii) $\log_5 \left(\dfrac{1}{\sqrt{125}} \right) = \log_5 (125)^{-\frac{1}{2}} = -\frac{3}{2}$

3 (a) $y = 2^{x+3}$ is a translation of $\begin{bmatrix} -3 \\ 0 \end{bmatrix}$ of $y = 2^x$ or a stretch of $y = 2^x$ by scale factor 8 in the direction of the y-axis.

     (b) $p = 8$

4 (a) $\log_2 8 = 3$

     (b) $\log_2 9 = 2\log_2 3$

     (c) $\log_2 72 = \log_2 (8 \times 9)$

               $= 3 + 2\log_2 3$

5 (a) $\log_a x = \log_a 5 + 2\log_a 3$

           $= \log_a 5 + \log_a 3^2$

           $= \log_a (5 \times 3^2)$

           $= \log_a 45$

     so $x = 45$

     (b) (i) $\log_2 2 = 1$

        (ii) $\log_4 2 = \frac{1}{2}$

          $\log_2 y = \frac{1}{2}$

          so $y = \sqrt{2}$

6 $\log_a x = 2(\log_a k - \log_a 2)$

        $= 2\log_a \left(\dfrac{k}{2} \right)$

        $= \log_a \left(\dfrac{k}{2} \right)^2$

   so $x = \left(\dfrac{k}{2} \right)^2$ or $k^2 = 4x$

7 (a) $\dfrac{x^2 + 8x + 12}{x^2 + 2x} = \dfrac{x + 6}{x}$ (b) $x = 0.25$

8 (a) $x = 2.292$ (b) $x = 6.170$ (c) $x = 0.631$

9 The half-life is given by $0.88^t = 0.5$.

    $t = 5.42$

    The half-life is 5.42 years.

10 $(3^x - 4)(3^x - 1) = 0$

     $3^x = 1$ giving $x = 0$ or $3^x = 4$ giving $x = 1.262$

9 Differentiation and integration

A Differentiating x^n, where n is negative or a fraction

Exercise A (p 117)

1 (a) $-3x^{-4}$ (b) $-\dfrac{1}{x^2}$ (c) $\frac{1}{3}x^{-\frac{2}{3}}$

   (d) $\dfrac{1}{2\sqrt{x}}$ (e) $\frac{3}{4}x^{-\frac{1}{4}}$

2 (a) $\frac{3}{2}\sqrt{x}$ (b) $1 + \dfrac{1}{x^2}$ (c) $-\dfrac{6}{x^3}$

   (d) $-\frac{3}{4}x^{-4}$ (e) $-\frac{1}{3}x^{-\frac{3}{2}}$

3 (a) $5x + 5x\sqrt{x}$ (b) $5 + \frac{15}{2}\sqrt{x}$

4 (a) $\frac{3}{2}x^{-\frac{1}{2}} - \frac{5}{2}x^{\frac{3}{2}}$ (b) $2x + \frac{5}{2}x^{\frac{3}{2}}$

   (c) $6x - \frac{9}{2}x^{\frac{1}{2}}$ (d) $\frac{3}{2}x^{\frac{1}{2}} + \frac{3}{2}x^{-\frac{1}{2}} - 1$

5 (a) $-\dfrac{1}{x^2}$ (b) $1 + \dfrac{3}{x^2}$

   (c) $\frac{3}{2}x^{-\frac{1}{2}} - x^{-\frac{3}{2}}$ (d) $-2x^{-3} - \frac{3}{2}x^{-\frac{5}{2}} - x^{-2}$

6 (a) $x^{\frac{5}{2}}$ (b) 67.5

7 (a) $x + 2 + \dfrac{1}{x}$ (b) $1 - \dfrac{1}{x^2}$

8 (a) $\frac{1}{2}$ (b) $y = \frac{1}{2}x + \frac{9}{2}$

9 $y = \frac{1}{3}x + \frac{14}{3}$

10 (a) $1 - 8x^{-3}$

   (b) $(2, 3)$

   (c) When $x = 2$, $\dfrac{d^2y}{dx^2} = \frac{3}{2}$, which is positive; hence a minimum

11 Minimum at $x = \frac{1}{3}$, maximum at $x = -\frac{1}{3}$

12 (a) (i) $V = 2x^2h$ (ii) $A = 2x^2 + 6xh$

   (b) $A = 2x^2 + 6x\left(\dfrac{288}{2x^2}\right) = 2x^2 + \dfrac{864}{x}$

   (c) $\dfrac{dA}{dx} = 4x - \dfrac{864}{x^2}$, $\dfrac{d^2A}{dx^2} = 4 + \dfrac{1728}{x^3}$

    $\dfrac{dA}{dx} = 0$ when $x = 6$. For this value of x, $\dfrac{d^2A}{dx^2} > 0$.
Hence A is a minimum when $x = 6$.

B Integrating x^n, where n is negative or a fraction

Exercise B (p 119)

1 (a) $-\frac{1}{2}x^{-2} + c$ (b) $\frac{4}{7}x^{\frac{7}{4}} + c$

   (c) $\frac{2}{5}x^{\frac{5}{2}} + c$ (d) $4x^{\frac{1}{4}} + c$

   (e) $\frac{1}{2}x^2 + \frac{2}{5}x^{\frac{5}{2}} + c$ (f) $x + \dfrac{1}{x} + c$

   (g) $2x^{\frac{1}{2}} + x + c$ (h) $2x^{\frac{1}{2}} + \frac{2}{3}x^{\frac{3}{2}} + c$

   (i) $2x^{\frac{1}{2}} + \frac{2}{5}x^{\frac{5}{2}} + c$ (j) $x + \frac{4}{3}x^{\frac{3}{2}} + \frac{1}{2}x^2 + c$

2 (a) $x^{\frac{5}{2}}$ (b) $y = 2x^{\frac{7}{2}} - 1$

3 (a) $x^3 + x^{-2}$ (b) $4\frac{1}{4}$

4 (a) $\frac{4}{9} = 0.444$ (to 3 s.f.)   (b) $\frac{1}{10}$

   (c) 53.3

5 $-\frac{1}{3}$

6 $\frac{2}{9}$

C Numerical integration: the trapezium rule
(p 120)

C1 Too small, because the curve is above the line segments

C2 (a) 1   (b) 1.67, 1.92, 2.05; area = 6.64

C3 (a) 6.64

   (b) Make h smaller and increase the number of ordinates.

Exercise C (p 121)

1 (a) 5.79

   (b) Underestimate, because the curve is above the line segments

2 (a) 2.98   (b) 2.96

3 (a) 4.65   (b) $\frac{14}{3} = 4.666...$

4 (a)

x	2	2.2	2.4	2.6	2.8	3
y	1.58	1.63	1.68	1.73	1.78	1.83

   (b) 1.705

Mixed questions (p 122)

1 (a) $\frac{1}{3}x^{-\frac{2}{3}}$

(b) (i) $\frac{3}{4}x^{\frac{4}{3}} + c$ (ii) 12

2 $y = -\frac{6}{\sqrt{x}} + 9$ or $y = -6x^{-\frac{1}{2}} + 9$

3 (a)

(b) 4.41

(c) Greater, because the graph is below the line segments

4 (a) (i) $4\pi x - \dfrac{1000}{x^2}$

(ii) $\dfrac{dy}{dx} = 0 \Rightarrow 4\pi x - \dfrac{1000}{x^2} = 0 \Rightarrow 4\pi x^3 = 1000$
$\Rightarrow x^3 = \dfrac{250}{\pi}$

(iii) $\dfrac{d^2y}{dx^2} = 4\pi + \dfrac{2000}{x^3}$

(iv) When $x^3 = \dfrac{250}{\pi}$, $\dfrac{d^2y}{dx^2} = 4\pi + \dfrac{2000\pi}{250}$
$= 4\pi + 8\pi = 12\pi$

(v) $x = 4.3$, minimum

(b) $349\,\text{cm}^2$

5 (a) (i) $x^3 - \dfrac{64}{x^3}$

(ii) -63

(iii) $\dfrac{dy}{dx} = 0 \Rightarrow x^3 = \dfrac{64}{x^3} \Rightarrow x^6 = 64$

(iv) $x = 2$, $x = -2$

(b) (i) $\dfrac{x^5}{20} - \dfrac{32}{x} + c$ (ii) 17.55

6 (a) (i) Area of cross-section $= \frac{1}{2} \times 3x \times 4x = 6x^2$
Volume $V = 6x^2 h$

(ii) Total area of base and top $= 12x^2$
Area of sides $= 3xh + 4xh + 5xh = 12xh$
$\Rightarrow S = 12x^2 + 12xh$

(b) $S = 12x^2 + 12xh = 12x^2 + 12x$
$\left(\dfrac{100}{6x^2}\right) = 12x^2 + \dfrac{200}{x}$

(c) $\dfrac{dS}{dx} = 24x - \dfrac{200}{x^2}$; $\dfrac{d^2S}{dx^2} = 24 + \dfrac{400}{x^3}$

$\dfrac{dS}{dx} = 0$ when $24x^3 = 200 \Rightarrow x = 2.03$

When $x = 2.03$, $\dfrac{d^2S}{dx^2} > 0$; hence minimum S

7 (a) $-\frac{1}{2}$

(b) $\left(\frac{1}{4}, \frac{1}{4}\right)$

(c) $\dfrac{dy}{dx} = \dfrac{1}{2\sqrt{x}} - 1$

When $x > \frac{1}{4}$, $\sqrt{x} > \frac{1}{2} \Rightarrow \dfrac{1}{\sqrt{x}} < 2 \Rightarrow \dfrac{1}{2\sqrt{x}} - 1 < 0$

As $\dfrac{dy}{dx} < 0$, y is decreasing.

(d) $\frac{1}{6}$

8 (a) $x = \sqrt{3}$, $x = -\sqrt{3}$

(b) (i) $14 - x^2 - \dfrac{9}{x^2} = 4 \Rightarrow x^4 - 10x^2 + 9 = 0$
$\Rightarrow (x^2 - 9)(x^2 - 1) = 0$

(ii) $3, -3, 1, -1$

(iii) Area under curve $= \displaystyle\int_1^3 \left(14 - x^2 - 9x^{-2}\right) dx$
$= \left[14x - \frac{1}{3}x^3 + 9x^{-1}\right]_1^3 = 13\frac{1}{3}$

Area under line $y = 4$ is $2 \times 4 = 8$
Shaded area is $13\frac{1}{3} - 8 = 5\frac{1}{3}$

9 (a) $(2, 8)$

(b) (i) When $x = 1$, $x^2 + \dfrac{16}{x} = 17$

When $x = 4$, $x^2 + \dfrac{16}{x} = 17$

(ii) 18

(c) $f(4.2) = 18.55$; $2^{4.2} = 18.38$, so $f(4.2) > 2^{4.2}$
$f(4.3) = 19.36$; $2^{4.3} = 19.69$, so $f(4.3) < 2^{4.3}$
So $4.2 < \alpha < 4.3$

Test yourself (p 125)

1 (a) (i) $\frac{2}{5}x^{\frac{5}{2}} + c$ (ii) 12.8

(b) 3.2

2 (a) $\dfrac{256}{x^2}$

(b) $A = \text{'base'} + \text{'sides'} = x^2 + 4x\left(\dfrac{256}{x^2}\right)$
$= x^2 + \dfrac{1024}{x}$

(c) 8

3 (a) (i) $2 - \dfrac{54}{x^3}$ **(ii)** $x = 3$

(b) (i) $x^2 - \dfrac{27}{x} - 7x + c$ **(ii)** 9.5

4 (a) 2.23

(b) Overestimate

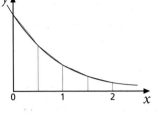

Index